THE DYNAMICS OF CHANGE

THE DYNAMICS OF CHANGE

Tavistock Approaches to Improving Social Systems

Mannie Sher

KARNAC

First published in 2013 by
Karnac Books Ltd
118 Finchley Road, London NW3 5HT

British Library Cataloguing in Publication Data

A C.I.P. for this book is available from the British Library

ISBN 978 1 78049 060 1

Edited, designed and produced by The Studio Publishing Services Ltd
www.publishingservicesuk.co.uk
e-mail: studio@publishingservicesuk.co.uk

Printed in Great Britain

www.karnacbooks.com

CONTENTS

ACKNOWLEDGEMENTS   vii

ABOUT THE AUTHOR   ix

INTRODUCTION   xi

PART I: PSYCHOTHERAPY IN THE PUBLIC SECTOR

CHAPTER ONE
Psychiatric social work and general practice   3

CHAPTER TWO
Counselling and psychotherapy in primary health care: 21
key professional issues

CHAPTER THREE
Ethical issues for psychotherapists working   39
in organisations

PART II: GROUP RELATIONS

CHAPTER FOUR
Splits, extrusion and integration: the impact of "potential space"
for group relations and sponsoring institutions   61

CHAPTER FIVE
Group relations conferences: reviewing and exploring   79
theory, design, role-taking, and application

CHAPTER SIX
From groups to group relations: Bion's contribution   91
to the Tavistock–"Leicester" conferences

PART III: ORGANISATIONAL DEVELOPMENT
AND CHANGE CONSULTANCY

CHAPTER SEVEN
In search of the "structure that reflects": promoting   123
organisational reflection practices in a UK health authority

CHAPTER EIGHT
Hopes, fears, and reality in a merger of two charities   153

PART IV: BOARDROOM EVALUATION

CHAPTER NINE
Corruption: aberration or an inevitable part of the   169
human condition? Insights from a "Tavistock" approach

CHAPTER TEN
Psychological and behavioural elements in board performance   183

CHAPTER ELEVEN
Inside the minds of the money minders: deciphering   195
reflections on money, behaviour, and leadership
in the financial crisis of 2007–2010

REFERENCES   215

BIBLIOGRAPHY   233

INDEX   237

ACKNOWLEDGEMENTS

It is a great pleasure to thank everyone who helped me in the preparation of this book. I owe sincere and earnest thanks to my two PhD supervisors, Trudy Klauber, Dean of Post-Graduate Studies at the Tavistock & Portman NHS Foundation Trust and Professor Michael Rustin, Professor of Sociology at the University of East London, who offered me his insight that I could be both dependent upon an institutional home and safely challenge it. Both provided the intellectual stimulation that led me to linking Herbert Rosenfeld's *destructive narcissism* and organisational corruption and Andrew Pickering's *symmetry principle of the sociology of scientific knowledge* to Trist's and Emery's *open socio-technical systems theory.* With their careful guidance, I grew to understand how the impact of work published in earlier decades could be tracked and its value appreciated. I thank Pauline Noble of the Department of Education and Training at the Trust for keeping me briefed on academic requirements and "next steps" along the way.

I gratefully acknowledge the many people who shared in joint consultative work and in research, academic, educational, and developmental activity. Many of them have been separately acknowledged at the end of each chapter. I am especially grateful for the institutional support of the members of Council of the Tavistock Institute of Human Relations; the personal support of Dr Eliat Aram, the Institute's CEO, and many Institute colleagues, past and present, whose commitment to the pursuit of knowledge in the social sciences and a critical attitude towards inquiry was a source of inspiration in the writing of this book.

I most want to thank my wife, Leonie, for her love, sacrifice, and kind indulgence, which she showed me as she herself fulfilled a demanding academic career of her own. I also credit our children, Shanan, Yoram, and Danny; daughters-in-law Sheera and Olee, and grandchildren Adeena, Nadav, and Hallel for challenging me to get on with the work and finish it on time. My thoughts turn at this time to the influence of my late parents, Hymie and Sarah Sher, to my sister Goldie, and the Altschuler family, in whose homes scholarship and further study always had pride of place.

ABOUT THE AUTHOR

Mannie Sher, PhD, TQAP, FBAP, is a Principal Social Scientist and Director of the Group Relations Programme at the Tavistock Institute of Human Relations, London. He manages organisational development and change projects and consults to top teams of organisations on the role of leadership in effecting strategic change. His research and consultancy work focuses on the impact of thought on the dialectic relationship between social constructivism, the unconscious and liberal democracy. He is a Fellow of the British Association of Psychotherapists (BAP) and a practising psychoanalytical psychotherapist. Mannie has published on subjects of consultancy, leadership, organisational development, ethics and corruption. He is a former member of the Board of the International Society for the Psychoanalytic Study of Organisations (ISPSO); and Member, the Israel Association for the Study of Group and Organisational Processes (OFEK).

Introduction

Introduction to the portfolio of published work

The contribution of this book is to offer:

- an account of theoretically and clinically informed practice;
- an account of the disciplines of that practice;
- an account of my personal contribution to that discipline as an innovator, an exemplar, and as a guardian.

This book includes eleven publications that cover my work over the past forty years. They describe and define my professional journey from social work to psychotherapy, to group relations, to organisational development consultancy, and, finally, to board evaluation. For most of that time I have worked at the Tavistock Clinic and the Tavistock Institute of Human Relations, and it would be natural, therefore, that my published work will mirror and add to the evolution of "Tavistock models" of theory and practice to understanding and working in the field of human endeavour.

This book includes descriptions of several major assignments in which my understanding of "Tavistock" systems psychodynamic models is applied. In short, these models can be described as *open socio-technical systems informed by psychoanalytical perspectives that illuminate unconscious processes in individuals, in the organisations with which they work, and in the physical and social environments in which these organisations are located.*

The book refers to the historical connections between the Tavistock Institute and social science pioneers such as Kurt Lewin, the founder of action research, who famously asserted that because systems have tendencies to move towards quasi-stationary equilibrium, the best way to understand systems is to change them. The book contains reflections of the most important theories and practices of the "Tavistock tradition" over the past eighty to ninety years: psychoanalysis (the role of thought); socio-technical systems (the interaction between people and technology in workplaces); theories of leadership, research, and evaluation methodologies; participant design; and greater democratisation of the workplace.

I offer an overview of the central feature of systems psychodynamics, the ubiquitous presence of anxieties and the mobilisation of institutional and social defense systems against them, a set of inspired ideas that have defined "Tavistock" social science research methodologies, organisational change initiatives, and executive coaching encounters for nearly a century.

This book aligns theory and practice. My publications describe examples of work explaining how systems psychodynamics concepts influence practice for the benefit of clients and the social good. In particular, I demonstrate how systems psychodynamic concepts enable understanding of beneath-the-surface forces in large systems that promote significant observable improvement in behaviour and performance.

The common theme in this book is the core challenge that is the hallmark of the Tavistock Institute—combining research in the social sciences with professional practice in organisational and social change. Central to this challenge is the use of open systems theory, which claims that organisms exist and survive only through continuous interaction with the environment. My publications clearly show that this idea cannot stand apart from the significance of boundaries and their management and the role of leadership as a boundary function, mediating between inside and outside. The book is a useful primer on the general Tavistock view that effective forms of work organisation actually combine two systems: the psycho-social and the technico-economic.

The second strand of my work is that the psychoanalytic contribution to work with organisations and society rests on the theories of infant development and its influence on adult relationships, especially the Kleinian views that the infant instinctively seeks pleasure and comfort and avoids pain, and polarises its world accordingly. For the infant, discovering that the "good" and the "bad" are manifestations of the same person is a source of anxiety that is defended against and remains a permanent part of psychic life alongside emergent feelings of guilt, reparation, and love.

Arising out of these ideas, my book takes a hard look at organisations as serving a function that defends against unconscious anxieties of their members, and reminds readers that groupings and relationships designed for work not only carry a social component, but are also channels for psychic projections. Actual ways of working might not just be used, but might be distorted, by defensive needs.

I also follow in the tradition of Bion's theories of basic assumptions that every group operates at two levels simultaneously: a work group engaged rationally in pursuit of a task; a basic assumption group in pursuit of one of three primitive basic assumptions: dependency, fight/flight, or pairing. These theories are clearly explicated in work with a health authority and banks and show how these states are products of the inherent "groupishness" of human behaviour and, therefore, become a vehicle for primitive instinctive drives for survival—pleasure-seeking and pain-avoidance.

I show how basic assumptions get in the way of effectiveness and that awareness of unconscious processes helps our understanding of resistance to change. Because uncertainty and ambiguity of the work task makes groups vulnerable to basic assumption disturbance, the definition of the primary task is critical to organisational design.

The theme of this book argues that whether in group relations, research and evaluation, or organisational consultancy, the work is an ongoing collaboration in which the researcher/consultant and client work together in gaining a deeper understanding of the system and generating possible courses of action. As some of the papers demonstrate, an action research approach implies that the decision to act (or not) rests with the client; both jointly review the outcomes and move to a next phase.

Other important concepts which I describe in this book are transference, where the consultant becomes a screen on to which the client projects underlying and unconscious feelings towards key figures in the client's earlier life, and countertransference, where the consultant is put into a role and has the experience of becoming the fantasised character in the client's internal drama. The book covers ideas like Winnicott's "holding environment", which serves as a safe container that can accept and survive the anxieties and hostile projections coming from the client system.

The book is practical in orientation and emphasises "application" in answering the "how to" question, stressing outcome (the task for which the consultant has been hired), implementation (often at variance with the way organisational managers have determined the planned route), and recognises organisational obstacles (resistance to change). The book shows how consultant and client system are partners in the process of organisational analysis and design, and how the two together generate a culture of an ongoing learning organisation.

The book pays tribute to Pierre Turquet, Robert Gosling, and Mary Barker at the Tavistock Clinic, and Eric Miller, Isobel Menzies Lyth, and Gordon Lawrence at the Institute, who inspired the author and who were influential in generating and shaping systems psychodynamics thinking: the confluence of dominant framing perspectives of organisational and social systems thinking and psychoanalytic perspectives on individual mental processes and group and social dynamics. It also salutes the many others in the international group relations and organisational development networks who are tested daily in their work by the hidden unconscious processes of their client systems.

I begin this introduction by providing an outline of my personal and career development and then go on to describe the main fields of my research and publications and their development. Separate sections that follow introduce each of these specific fields of work and summarise the publications I have included for each of them.

Interdependence and collaborative teamwork, communication and uncertainty, lie at the heart of the Tavistock enterprise, (Higgins & Jessop, 1965). The general context of my work has been in applied change consultancy with communities and organisations, which has proceeded alongside my academic activity. Over the years, there have been cycles of influence of the work of the Tavistock: pioneers like Emery and Trist (1960, 1965) had a wide audience in the academy, followed by a period when "human relations" fell out of sight and re-emerged later in scholar–practitioner organisations such as the International Society for the Psychoanalytic Study of Organisations (ISPSO), the Organisation for the Promotion of Understanding of Society (OPUS), the A. K. Rice Institute in the USA, the Israel Association for Group and Organisational Processes (OFEK), and the Belgirate Conferences on Group Relations. I am a member of, and have lectured or taught courses in, these institutions.

Eleven publications have been selected that most highlight my thinking and my contributions to the theory of Tavistock systems psychodynamics and its application to work in community and organisational development and related fields. Organisational development consultancy is a developing profession, advancing rapidly and finding a new role for itself as a result of the influence of new technologies and the ways that organisations are being redefined (Cacioppe & Edwards, 2005). Organisations are not clearly bounded entities with more or less clear goals and fixed tasks. This notion of the bounded organisation has been undermined by rapid advances in technologies and greater stakeholder interest and involvement (Rowley & Moldoveanu, 2003). The pace of change introduced by digital computerisation has revolutionised work with parallel changes in the social contract between the workforce and employers. The chapters in this book have been selected for their contributions to Tavistock Institute ideas about organisations and their changing roles in society, with an emphasis on the integration of socio-technical systems theory (Emery, 1959; Emery & Trist, 1960, 1965; Trist, 1981; Trist & Bamforth, 1951; Trist, Higgin, Murray, & Pollock, 1963) and later perspectives in the Tavistock Anthologies (Trist & Murray, 1990, 1993a,b), and psychoanalytic theory and the role of unconscious processes in individual, group, and social behaviour.

An over-arching influence in the book is the Tavistock Institute's commitment to producing new knowledge in the social sciences and the application of knowledge for improving the clarity of objectives and the nature of interactions, relationships, and negotiations at work and in communal life. An example of this would be the Quality of Working Life movement developed by Westley (1979), who analysed four types of problems generated by the factory system: political (insecurity), economic (inequity), psychological (alienation), and sociological (anomie), and examined individual remedies such as worker directors, profit sharing, job enrichment, and socio-technical design for their capacity to solve these problems. The history of the Tavistock Institute as a not-for-profit organisation means that new knowledge generated by the Institute is available for all. The Articles of Association of the Institute (1946, revised 2010) state that

> The objects for which the Association is established are specifically restricted to advance the study of the psycho-sociology of relations (in the widest possible sense of the word) between human beings and groups or classes or categories of human beings, and of the influence of environment in all its aspects on the formation or development of human character or capacity, to conduct research and experiment for this purpose, and to publish the results of such study research and experiment for this purpose, and to train students in or for any branches of the said study.

Intellectually, the Tavistock's integrated psychoanalytic (Bion, 1970) and general systems theories (Lewin, 1943, 1946, 1947, 1950; von Bertalanffy, 1950a,b, 1951) have had a huge impact on the Institute and the Clinic and on the work of many other organisations and individual practitioners in social science research and consultancy. I have attempted to bring coherence to knowledge of unconscious dynamics and cognitive and intellectual capability in order to raise human potential for creative collective endeavour. The chapters focus on efforts to achieve specific organisational goals as much as they do on resistance to learning and change. They also offer explanations for these very human polarities (Hinshelwood & Skogstad, 2000; Huffington, Armstrong, Halton, Hoyle, & Pooley, 2004).

Personal and career development

As a young person growing up in post-Second World War South Africa, I witnessed the country's social and political upheavals as different racial, religious, and cultural groups asserted themselves (Carter, 1977). I remember the fear among family and friends following the formation of the new South African Nationalist government in 1948 that the anti-Semitism and race legislation of Germany, which the Nationalists had supported in 1939, would recur in South Africa.

Most people learnt to live in the narrow space between criticism and acceptance of the new order of formalised racial segregation (Weisbord, 1967). Few understood that repression of one section of society meant the repression of all sections, that freedom was indivisible. Suppression of knowledge formed part of the general climate of repression. Social science knowledge was regarded as belonging to the "left" and was viewed as subversive by the authorities. For the Nationalists, threats were perceived everywhere and dealt with harshly. Reason was abandoned and prejudice was officially sanctioned through race legislation that was designed to support the dominance of the white group over black groups. This was considered a God-given right, enshrined biblically, and was meant to last forever. Scientific experimentation, evidence, and knowledge were regarded as useful mainly to explain how objects moved, not what moved people. In this environment, where great natural beauty and vast mineral wealth co-existed with large swathes of poverty and injustice, the University of the Witwatersrand in Johannesburg was an oasis of liberal thought (Murray, 1982). I studied the social sciences there between 1961 and 1964, and the rigid social stratifications I had grown up with suddenly looked nakedly ridiculous. The traditions of academic freedom and knowledge seemed to offer a new and fairer order and a possible answer to my quest for another way of understanding (Shear, 1996).

I arrived in London in 1967 to study for the diploma in psychiatric social work at the London School of Economics, and I was exhilarated and anxious about finding a place and assimilating new ideas. I started my personal psychoanalysis, where I learnt that despite attempts to think freely and liberally, prejudices persisted. The powers of the transference and striving to hold on to discredited roles were painful but exciting discoveries. I realised that irrational anxiety and fear of relinquishing out-of-date ideas and relationships and forging ones based on new learning lay at the root of a natural conservatism that interfered with development. At the LSE, I had the privilege of attending Donald Winnicott's lectures and seminars (Rodman, 2003; Winnicott, 1965), and I attended the Winter Porchester Lectures (Gosling, 1968; Joffe, 1968; S. Klein, 1969; Sutherland, 1968) organised by the Institute of Psychoanalysis, which were important in expanding my rudimentary understanding of mind, attitude, and behaviour and raising my enthusiasm to pursue a career in psychoanalysis and its applications. Mindful of the general resistances to awareness of unconscious processes, I believed that with the right professional tools, it should be possible to develop insight and awareness of dynamics in ways that would enhance people's work and improve organisational effectiveness.

Writing and research work

In 1971, I joined the Adult Department of the Tavistock Clinic to pursue the four-year training in psychoanalytic psychotherapy. This training allowed me to obtain professional membership of the British Association of Psychotherapists (BAP) in 1977, and for the next twenty years I was an active member of the Association as Chair of its Council (1986–1989) and Chair of its Ethics Committee (1989–1996). I was attracted to the Kleinian school of psychoanalysis, and with it I found a home in the strongly "Kleinian" Adult Department of the Tavistock Clinic. The approach there combined thorough investigation of the influences of early infantile experiences: for example, the factors that affect attachments between the individual infant and mother, parents, siblings, etc., on later adult life (Klein, 1959), and the application of this knowledge to social phenomena. Contributions to professional dilemmas and social processes made by the mostly Kleinian senior staff members of the Department in joint work with public service organisations such as hospitals, primary healthcare, social services, probation service, and education services, fitted well with my professional social worker identity that was embedded in theories and values of the interdependence between individual personality development and social and cultural dynamics (Fairbairn, 1952; Grotstein & Rinsley, 1994; Hornby, 1993; Kelley & Thibaut, 1978; Scharff & Birtles, 1994). Understanding one had to include understanding the other. I recall during my induction week at the Tavistock Clinic in October 1971, Dr Gosling, Chair of the Professional Committee, addressing the newcomers to the effect that an example of a Tavistock approach would be that if one wished to understand the dynamics of the hermit on a mountain, one could not avoid studying the society from which he had chosen to withdraw himself (Gosling, 1973; Gosling, Miller, Turquet, & Woodhouse, 1967).

The psychotherapy training included modules for applying psychotherapeutic skills in primary healthcare settings that allowed more people to access a mental health practitioner without going through the complicated and time-consuming process of referral to specialist psychotherapy clinics. This is described in Part I of the book.

Attendance at group relations conferences was an essential part of the training. The shared Kleinian orientation between the Adult Department and the Group Relations Training Programme of the Tavistock Institute, directed by Eric Miller, made the Programme a logical place to experience group relations (see Part II).

Part III of the book describes organisational development and change consultancy. I was attracted to the challenges of integrating psychoanalytic thinking and general systems theory, involving the role of transference and countertransference, projection, and projective identification and how these constructs could assist in socio-technical systems analysis as methods for successful strategic planning. I believed in participative design principles for introducing democratic forms in workplaces and educational and social institutions, based on a trend toward participative democracy that encouraged managerial and employee involvement in thinking strategically (Emery, 1989). The chapters in this section all typically address organisational change methods in which top management retain a steering role while representatives of middle management, technical specialists, and employee groups take up leadership roles on multiple groups looking at planning and implementation in specific areas. These ideas, stemming from integrated systems and psychoanalytic thinking, have constituted the core of my work with the construction and finance industries, public protection agencies, social care enterprise, and vehicle manufacture.

Finally, the role of boards is producing fresh interest because of the relatively unrestricted way they had hitherto been established, led, and regulated. Their tasks and boundaries are often difficult to define, yet boards are meant to play significant roles in the system of balances and checks in maintaining financial probity, sound governance, and high integrity. As a result of work I did following the financial crisis of 2007–2009, I have taken up new roles as adviser to financial authorities and evaluator of boards of companies and institutions. The government's "Big Society" agenda emphasises the devolution of leadership to local communities, who will be expected to take more responsibility through board membership for work with their local organisations. Knowledge of the role and functioning of boards and training for skilled board membership is increasingly becoming a focus of social science research (Part IV).

I have developed a career that integrates research and evaluation, organisational development consultation, group relations conference work, role consultation, and writing and publishing. I feel privileged to be part of a community of practice that is committed to helping others through research and consultation development work and through the dissemination of new knowledge and ideas that derive from that practice.

Part I: Psychotherapy in the public sector

The chapters in this section consider the relationship between clinical practice and its organisational, professional, and social contexts. This relationship is often overlooked by training organisations that focus specifically on the therapist–patient relationship. Psychotherapy should be concerned with integrating the psychological needs of individuals with ethical and organisational frameworks in which those needs are clinically attended to.

Dr Pierre Turquet was a towering figure in the development of adult psychotherapy training at the Tavistock Clinic. He was passionate about revolutionising NHS-based psychoanalytical psychotherapy. His vision for this publicly sponsored venture stated that the training would (i) be fully multidisciplinary; (ii) lead to the establishment of a new profession of adult psychotherapist; (iii) encompass all psychotherapy modalities (diagnostic assessment, individual, couple, family, and group treatments; short- and long-term; in-patient, day-care, and out-patient), plus organisational development and group relations consultancy; (iv) be outward-looking and community-based (Turquet & Boreham, 1976).

Trainees on the psychotherapy programme were schooled in negotiating the boundaries between the "inner world" of unconscious fantasy, emotion, and feeling and the "outer world" of family, school, community, work, and public care organisations (Shapiro, 1997; Shapiro & Carr, 1991). Trainees worked in community services and intervened early in the growth of individual and family pathology. Trainees, attached to general medical practices for half a day per week, pioneered a unique model of community mental health consultation

(Brook, 1967; Brook & Temperley, 1976; Sher, 2010). The project extended psychodynamic knowledge to front-line professionals who daily worked with patients with difficult psychological problems, and who did not have the background or the time to address their emotional lives or psychiatric disturbances. This work led to decreased pressure on specialist services (in value-for-money terms, this approach had a beneficial impact on all participants), the GP and patient, the surgery and clinic, the sponsoring health and social care authorities, and the professions (Blount et al., 2007). From a 1970s experimental project in North London, thirty years later it was estimated that more than half the practices in Britain had counsellors as members of the primary care team who treat emotional, psychological, and social issues that influence a person's well-being (Mellor-Clark, Simms-Ellis, & Burton, 2001).

Chapter One outlines the need for the primary care professions to work together by sharing the despair, hopelessness, anxiety, and anger that often accompany their work. We make the case of added value that comes from joint work in the prevention of mental health problems before they grow into major pathology and more extensive treatment is needed (Brook & Temperley, 1976; Johnson, 1976).

This chapter describes the challenges and benefits of extending the role of the psychodynamically trained worker to understanding and managing the boundaries between the "inner world" of patients' unconscious fantasies, emotions, and feelings in relation to their illnesses and their relationships with their doctors. During their half-day attachments at the surgery, Tavistock psychotherapists assessed the psychological needs of two or three patients and then discussed these with the referring GP. Thereafter, in a proportion of cases, the GPs themselves would manage their patients' emotional and psychological needs within the surgery. The psychotherapists would see other patients for up to four interviews; a concise description of their mental states would be formulated and shared with the patient and the GP, and psychological support would be continued by the GP. Only in about 10–15% of cases were patients referred to specialist psychotherapy centres.

The authors describe the impact of their joint work on each of them and on their patients. Central to this is the containment of feelings that are aroused in the professionals that could interfere with the doctors" normal decision-making capabilities and their capacities to help their patients. Casement (1985) offers a useful definition of "containment":

> . . . what is needed is a form of holding, such as a mother gives to her distressed child. There are various ways in which one adult can offer to another this holding (or containment). And it can be crucial for a patient to be thus held in order to recover, or to discover maybe for the first time, a capacity for managing life and life's difficulties without continued avoidance or suppression.

The effect of joint consultations leads to clearer perspectives of the doctor–patient relationship, and deeper understanding and greater ability to manage the emotional needs of patients and the disturbing feelings that patients sometimes arouse. Knowledge of the emotions of patients and their families and the dynamics of their relationships with their doctors improve the psychological work of doctors. By understanding the nature of anxiety that patients project into their doctors, the psychotherapists help to contain it, leading to increased tolerance by patients of their problems—their self-esteem, tendencies towards addictions, and issues of control. The results are improved levels of mental health, especially for patients' children. GPs in the study made two-thirds fewer referrals to psychiatric hospitals. More psychiatrically disturbed patients and their families were contained in the surgery. We were pioneering new models of intervention and demonstrating that working psychodynamically and holistically did not mean long-term therapy for only a limited number of individuals. Significant, life-changing interventions could be made in four sessions or less. Medically unexplained symptoms (MUS) could be explained by using psychological models of the mind. In this way, we demonstrated the value of integrated medico-psycho-social models of work.

Chapter Two describes the social and environmental circumstances that impinged on key professional issues in the changing professional culture of primary care in the mid-1990s. Issues of confidentiality, communication, and employment of psychotherapists and counsellors, redefinition of patients' expectations, and the roles and responsibilities of doctors and therapists are described. The dynamics of teamwork are an essential part of a practice's pool of skills (Pritchard, Pritchard, & Pritchard, 1992; Clements, Dault, & Priest, 2007). Supervision and consultation in general practice have become the norm and are vital in dealing with problems that potentially impede effective work, as well as improving the professional effectiveness of the doctor and the medical team. In an increasingly litigious work environment, which has seen medicine redefined as a business labouring under financial pressures, problems have worsened through playing off the practice, health authority, and social care services against one another by desperate patients who rely on splitting for survival.

In the 1990s, assumptions about universal care from "cradle to grave" were changing and the dependency culture of the post-war decades was being swept aside. People were being urged to take greater responsibility for their health through exercise, diet, and lifestyle and to prepare themselves financially for their old age. GPs became fund-holders and they had to reassess their allocation of funds. Who gets what and how much—"the politics of choice"—was delegated to the local level so that decision making in health care could be more community and patient responsive. But public expectations had risen sharply and waiting rooms were still rife with stress, confusion, and unhappiness; GP stress was continually compounded (Obholzer & Roberts, 1994). They were confused as to whether their patients' problems were medical *or* social, or medical *and* social. For cases that were not strictly medical, fund-holding GPs introduced ancillary services, including counselling.

The main impact of teamwork in primary care with attached psychodynamically trained psychotherapists is the sharing of psychodynamic perspectives of patients and their relationships with their doctors. These dynamics invariably centre on issues of power and control, rivalry and competition. Issues of effectiveness, standards of practice, and theoretical approaches dominated debates at that time, and there were the inevitable territorial disputes, the most notable of which was the one led by Dr Graham Curtis Jenkins of the Counselling in Primary Health Care Trust, who argued for a strictly applied six-session model with a clear single focus (Jenkins, 2002; Jenkins, Barkham, Mellor-Clark, Rain, & Fitzgerald, 2010). This model was lifeless, doctrinaire, and devoid of understanding or elaboration of the transference or unconscious dynamics that underpins the psychodynamic approach to change. A battle ensued between the merits of the Jenkins and Graham Sher models. The psychodynamic approach was criticised as unfocused and unscientific. The historical influences of present-day counselling, notably Michael Balint, who trained GPs to counsel their patients within the time-frame of a normal medical consultation—six minutes—were ignored (Balint, 1957; Balint & Balint, 1961; Balint, Balint, Gosling, & Hildebrand, 1966; Balint, Joyce, Marinker, & Woodcock, 1970; Main, 1978). Psychodynamic counselling, Jenkins claimed, was psychoanalysis done in the surgery, when patently it was not. The free association method of the psychoanalytic couch, when translated into therapeutic work in the surgery, was as sharply focused and time-limited as that proposed by Jenkins.

This chapter addresses the key ethical issues for psychotherapists working in organisations that provide psychotherapy services: how psychotherapy practice is affected by the aims of the larger employing organisation. Psychotherapists are faced with having to balance key organisational issues, such as employer liability, allocation of resources, accountability, and authority and the ethical demands imposed on them by the psychotherapy profession in relation to confidentiality, research and publication, disclosure, access to records, and use of information technology. The relationship between psychotherapist and employing organisation often turns out to be one of conflict of interests, rather than a forum where different interests, practices, and values may be debated and reconciled by mutual agreement. There are different ethical requirements and codes of practice in different organisations, but the ethical issues are identical for psychotherapy practised in them: confidentiality is a core issue which forms a central pillar in the psychotherapist's duty of care towards the patient; responsibility towards children at risk overrides all other considerations, and no psychotherapist, medical or non-medical, can claim protection under the principle of *privileged communication* (Lasky & Riva, 2006; Slovenko, 1998).

In the 1980s, "ethics" was considered to apply mainly to strictures against breaches of confidentiality and sexual and financial exploitation of patients. In the 1990s, with the formation of the UK Council for Psychotherapy, "ethics", alongside "training", became the major arena for determining standards of professionalism in psychotherapy. The Ethics Committee of the BAP, which I chaired from 1989 to 1996, developed a new Code of Ethics and a formal framework for assessing and judging breaches of the Code. These codes and procedures were subsequently incorporated by the UK Council for Psychotherapy and its constituent member organisations. Psychotherapists working in organisations with other primary purposes—the health service, the prison service, social services, and voluntary organisations—were frequently confronted with ethical conundrums. Finding a place for the practice of psychotherapy in these organisations was a continuing challenge. Because of the not-so-visible and non-technological nature of psychotherapy practice, ethics and training came to be the main defining parameters of the profession and formed the basis of psychotherapists' contributions to multi-disciplinary professional teams.

This examination of the ethical conundrums of psychotherapists working in the public services has had an impact on the colleague professions of medicine, nursing, social work, and psychology. This chapter widened the debate about the potential conflict between the needs of the individual and the ethical and organisational framework in which those needs are clinically attended to. It also promoted deeper understanding of the nature of patients' transference relationships to the institution. The debate on ethics has huge relevance to psychotherapy practice in institutions. Clinics, hospitals, prisons, etc., provide treatment for patients whose disturbance is usually enacted through violence, paedophilia, and other borderline personality manifestations, where the issue of detention and withdrawal of human rights, the necessity to work within multi-disciplinary and multi-agency arrangements, produces significant ethical questions. But irrespective of context, the main ethical issues have been shown to be the same: duty of care towards the patient, confidentiality, protection of minors, and prevention of crime. This duty includes keeping patients' information confidential, exercising care in the matter of communications between professionals, record-keeping and protection of records, and consultation with patients on all matters concerning their treatment.

Part II: group relations

By the mid-1960s the basic design of the Tavistock group relations conferences had been established by the early pioneers: Ken Rice (1958, 1963, 1965, 1969), Harold Bridger (Bridger & Higgins, 1964), Pierre Turquet (1975, 1985), Eric Miller (1990a,b), and later workers such as Gordon Lawrence (1993, 2000), Robert Gosling (1979, 1981), David Armstrong (1992, 1997), and Larry Gould and colleagues

(Gould, Stapley, & Stein, 2001, 2004). Despite numerous adaptations and innovations to group relations conference design, the Tavistock Institute's group relations programme continued to be criticised for being intellectual, authoritarian, and anachronistic—a reference to the Northfields military setting in which Bion's and Bridger's work originated (Harrison & Clarke, 1992). Nevertheless, group relations conference work has continued to provide opportunities for learning about the dynamics of roles, groups, leadership, and organisations. The role of Director of the Group Relations Programme is variously described as "preserving the tradition" and "innovating for change". Despite regular changes in conference theme and design, the perception remained of a Tavistock fixed in old paradigms (Wasdell, 1997). The persistence of this projection was explained by Tim Dartington, in a personal communication, that the next generation of group relations practitioners seems to need to retain an image of an "old Tavistock" so that their own innovations and efforts at growth can be progressed without experiencing the feelings of guilt that often accompany altering or abandoning a tradition. Therefore, the Tavistock's vigorous engagement in continuing leadership in the field (Brunner, Perini, & Vera, 2009; de Jager & Sher, 2009; Hupkens, 2006; Lahav, 2009; Litvin & Bonwitt, 2006; Nutkevitch & Triest, 2009; Viswanath, 2009), its vitality and innovation in group relations conference work, has to be denied. Chapters in this section demonstrate the relevance of the role of the Group Relations Programme in role clarification, leadership development, organisational and environmental transformation, and its impact on social issues.

Chapter Four discusses the particular dynamics of four types of "sponsoring" institutions that provide group relations conferences as part of their broader functions: (i) research and evaluation; (ii) clinical; (iii) educational and professional development; (iv) spiritual, how each uniquely influences the theory and practice of group relations, and why "group relations" is both an object and a source of ambivalence in the politics of each.

An analysis of the group relations field reveals the presence of several different forms of organisational support for group relations work, each with specific bearing on the viability of group relations conferences. Despite the establishment of new group relations institutions, a number had ceased to exist, and this has led to an investigation of the attitudes and relationships between group relations programmes and the organisations in which they are embedded. This chapter is concerned with the institutional "spaces" in which group relations either flourishes or withers. Group relations conferences around the world naturally have altered, reshaped, and developed over time. The dynamics evident in conferences depend on where in the world the conference is located (www.grouprelations.com). Whatever is current in the organisational, social, and political contexts comes into the conference and the conference, therefore, informs about the state of the members' own institutions and society and their particular preoccupations (Coleman & Bexton, 1975; Coleman & Geller, 1985; Cytrynbaum & Noumair, 2004). In addition to the contributions made by the early pioneers, there have been quieter, but significant, influences on the development of group relations as a method of investigation that come from the purposes, cultures, and values of the four types of institutions described as "sponsors" of group relations work.

Group relations—the experiential study of group and organisational processes—has influenced social science research. It offers additional ways of collecting and analysing data and knowledge creation and dissemination. Especially relevant is group relations' understanding and working with unconscious processes, for example, Menzies (1959), Menzies Lyth (1988, 1989) and Jaques' (1951, 1955) conceptualisation of social defences against anxiety. "Learning from experience" methods are now applied to many forms of social science investigative processes (Abraham, 2011; Child, 2009, Hills & Child, 2000). This chapter considers the impact of group relations when it is introduced to other organisations, such as universities, clinics, institutes, and membership organisations and the mutual influences that are exerted. In some cases, these institutions, by sponsoring group relations conferences, somewhat ambitiously hope group relations conferences would help to reshape them and their societies—politically, culturally, economically, and socially. Group relations as a force for change requires more published critical research. Group relations as a movement, as it has often been termed, tends to be self-authorising, and it has a poor record of critiqued analysis. Group relations rests on sound investigative traditions, but it is criticised for its attempts to bring different worlds together—the mystical and the organisational (Tarnas, 1991). Consequently, conversations in the group relations network often sound like people talking to themselves, perhaps as a reaction to the general suspiciousness towards it by traditional research investigators.

Chapter Five and the book in which it was later published describe the conference on group relations conferences that was held in Belgirate, Italy in 2003. The conference was organised by Avi Nutkevitch of OFEK, a group relations organisation in Israel, and myself representing the Tavistock Institute. The primary task of this conference was to review and explore the theory and design, taking up roles in group relations conferences and the application of learning derived therefrom. The Belgirate conference, as it came to be known, was intended to be a "space" that is not normally available during group relations conferences themselves—to review and explore dilemmas and questions that lie at the heart of group relations work.

The absence of sufficient opportunities to explore these questions during actual group relations conferences is a constant source of frustration. The chapter underscores the principle in group relations conferences that staff should work on their own particular conceptual and relationship issues in the same way that conference members are invited to. This principle stands in the service of the undertaking by staff to do everything possible that promotes the conference's primary task of furthering the learning of the dynamic relatedness between the different parts of the conference and between the conference and society. The Belgirate conference was, therefore, designed as a particular structured opportunity for reviewing, exploring, and learning about the different aspects of group relations conference design. The conference was conceptualised as a "transitional space" that would contain traditional scientific modes of learning, such as lectures and discussions, and an experiential "here and now" mode of learning. The chapter describes the difficulties and the opportunities for creative learning and exploration presented by this blend of modes. The Belgirate conference was open to anyone who had previously taken up a conference staff role as administrator, consultant, or director, and where the conferences they had attended were based on the Tavistock–Leicester model. These two elements had political and conceptual meanings. It established the Tavistock–Leicester model of group relations conferences as the prototype group relations conference. This forced individuals and group relations organisations around the globe to face questions of identity, as well as allegiance to the Tavistock–Leicester group relations conference model. These two conditions of membership made explicit the boundary of inclusion and exclusion of the Belgirate conference, which helped preserve the primary task of the conference, which was not learning *about* group relations conferences, but, rather, reviewing and exploring the theory and practice of group relations conferences from within a boundary, termed the "group relations network".

This chapter was later published as a chapter in a book (Brunner, Nutkevitch, & Sher, 2006). Volume I was followed by Volume II (Aram, Baxter, & Nutkevitch, 2009) and Volume III (Aram, Baxter, & Nutkevitch, 2012). The Belgirate conferences attest to the vibrancy of group relations conference work around the world. The question of how this conference came into being reverberated throughout the first conference. It was understood that the organisers of the Belgirate conference took their own authority and made the conference self-authorising, signalling that the authority to act in the arena of world group relations would no longer come from the Tavistock "above", but, henceforth, would lie within the "network".

In Chapter Six, I explore Bion's interest in pushing further "into the primitive" of the group, which was extended by his colleagues at the Tavistock Institute, working in particular on the challenge to memory and desire, to the very human wish that everything should revert to the *status quo ante* (Bion, 1961). Elaborating and working through the obstacles to group and organisational learning, formed the basis of much of the work of the Tavistock Institute (Miller, 1959, 1976, 1993a, 1995, 1997; Miller & Rice, 1967; Rice, 1958, 1963, 1965, 1969). The purpose of this chapter is to rediscover Bion's thinking in relation to the life of contemporary institutions and specifically the impact of Bion's ideas on Tavistock group relations conferences.

Soon after returning from my first "Leicester" conference in 1974, the supervisor of my group psychotherapy practice at the Tavistock Clinic, Robert Gosling, who had been a close colleague of Wilfred Bion, recognising my dilemmas about group relations and group psychotherapy, said that he supposed my way of thinking about my group of patients would have been changed forever by my "Leicester" experience. I began to look for ways of bridging competing models of work that were predicated, in the one case, by individual pathology and the paired relationship of patient and therapist and, in the other, attending to individual pathology within group-as-a-whole dynamics. Chapter Seven is a reflection on my first experience of directing the

"Leicester" conference in 2000. Dr Gosling encouraged me to be as open as possible about the swirling dynamics of the conference and to use my feelings stirred up by the chaos to deepen my understanding of those dynamics and to find ways of sharing that understanding with the staff group. The chapter, therefore, includes parts of a daily diary that I kept during the conference, which reveals the power of projections that the membership and staff have to grapple with, how these get "sent" upwards in the hope that they will be "dealt with" or resolved "up there".

On account of this chapter, my colleagues have suggested that guardianship of Tavistock Bion–Kleinian orientations in group relations, once held by Rice, Miller, and Lawrence, is now held by me, especially because of my interest and work with the constructs of transference, countertransference, splitting, projection, and projective identification, the group unconscious, Oedipal conflicts, leadership, and authority. I realise the significance of this view when I observe the potentially destabilising unconscious dynamics in intragroup and intergroup relations, where group members' feelings and emotions are sometimes overwhelmed in relation to both the group's task and the individual's desire for security and safety. Group relations conference design provides a robust framework for experiential learning and studying the behaviour of groups in the "here-and-now". Group relations conference thinking can be useful also in working with groups outside conference work, where Bion's constructs of the work group and basic assumption group apply to the interplay between conscious and unconscious dynamics in organisations. This chapter describes the struggle of directors and staff to achieve understanding of intragroup here-and-now experience and intergroup interactions between sub-systems and authority issues of the individual and the group (Lawrence, Bain, & Gould, 1996).

Part III: organisational development and change consultancy

In 1976, I participated in a research project on rising unemployment under the direction of John Hill of the Centre for Social and Industrial Research at the TIHR (Hill, 1977). The psychodynamic component of research and consultancy was the link to clinical practice. "Tavistock" approaches to research interviewing were based on encouraging interviewees to reflect on and describe their emotional experiences of unemployment. We learnt that, despite seeing interviewees for only one interview, by adopting a non-intrusive, empathic stance, it was possible to rely on the use of countertransference feelings to shift the interview to deeper layers of awareness and work with unconscious fantasy in the research enterprise. Interpretative empathic statements, which are the currency of clinical work, had dramatic impact on the research interview, opening up a fuller narrative of the interviewee's family work history as these impacted upon the interviewee's identity formation, levels of confidence as a worker, attitudes towards authority, and their role as a citizen. This approach to interviewing offered interviewees a psychodynamic formulation of their experiences of their situation in ways that were helpful to them despite their pain and despair. In exchange for participating in the research project, the interviewee gained a useful idea, a changed perception and even a sense of increased confidence. This approach to research was based on "Tavistock" action research principles—a series of two-way transactions leading to an altered state. Change-orientated action research and consultancy are at the centre of the Tavistock Institute's work and psychoanalysis plays a special role in this (Trist, 1981, 1990). Rustin (2001) argues the justification and legitimacy of psychoanalytic knowledge and its relevance to political and social questions. He relates the British psychoanalytic tradition to recent developments in the sociological understanding of the sciences. Psychoanalysis is a late form of "modernism", Rustin argues, that provides coherence of thinking about the needs of society, making public policy more effective if based on a psychoanalytically informed understanding of relational needs and unconscious anxieties. From my appointment to the Tavistock Institute in 1997, my organisational development and change consultancy extended to the construction, health, public protection, vehicle manufacture, banking, social care enterprise, arts, and faith sectors. This work was reinforced by my associations with the Organisational Change and Technological Innovation Unit (Cummings & Huse, 1989; Holti, 1997; Miller, 1997; Neumann, Miller, & Holti, 1999) and the Evaluation, Development and Review Unit (Stern, 2005) at the Institute. From my participation in these units, I learnt the importance of the role of technology as a critical determinant influencing the nature of political and psychological relationships in organisations and the need to engage in constant evaluation of permanently changing technological processes (Mumford, 1997).

My work portfolio at the Tavistock Institute is a combination of researcher and consultancy work that continues despite difficult market conditions, as social and organisational leaders anticipate and prepare for a different future. All so-called "new" knowledge appears to confirm the basic knowledge of the unconscious. No matter what attacks are made on established knowledge (Cooper, 1988), our experience confirms the unconscious as a powerful force that makes leaders and managers aware that they are not in control. Tavistock Institute clients and prospective clients see knowledge of the unconscious as a strength. Evidence for this is demonstrated by the use of the defence mechanism test (DMT), developed by Kragh (1955) for the selection of pilots of the Swedish Air Force (and air forces worldwide). It is available under licence to two associates of the Tavistock Institute—Ralph Woolf and Olya Khaleelee (Khaleelee, 2007). The DMT tests defence mechanisms that prevent pilots from assessing acute stressful situations realistically with high levels of validity and reliability, that is, the DMT measures what it purports to measure—psychological defence mechanisms (Ekehammar, Zuber, & Konstenius, 2005).

Chapter Seven identifies how learning in modern organisations feed and sustain learning at individual, group, and organisational levels (Argyris, 1999). The chapter also notes that current accounts on "reflection" in organisational and management studies have two main limits (Reynolds, 1999): (i) they often do not address how "reflection" can be put to work in practice; (ii) reflection often occurs at the individual level rather than at the organisational level. The meaning of "reflection" is often restricted by a perspective of individual problem-solving activity, whereas in reality, in most situations, the individual alone cannot address or solve meta-organisational problems. This chapter discusses how these issues were addressed in the context of a far-reaching three-year project aimed at introducing reflection as a legitimated and stable practice among a group of middle managers of a health authority in the National Health Service, in a programme that combined elements of the organisational development and the critical action learning traditions. We discuss how combining several action learning sets into a structure that connected them into a larger and more powerful whole rendered the learning "organisational".

This chapter proposes that reflection works both at individual and organisational levels, when it is public, participative, and authorised. Despite the size of the NHS, the conflicting interests that are its main characteristic features, and the massive changes in the shift to primary care trusts (PCTs), the programme provided the managers with new skills and tools for working with the realities of a fragmented and politicised organisation. This was achieved by devising a model of reflection that emphasised the importance of learning from real life issues. We describe working with a steering committee to form an internal referent group that created the necessary leverage to support organisation-wide change.

Chapter Eight presents the situation in which a decision to merge two organisations, however much determined by economic factors, contains the hope that the new organisation would combine the strengths and overcome the weaknesses of the old ones. Managers, preoccupied with planning the shape of the new organisation, fail to take sufficiently into account the anxieties that are aroused. These are concerned with threats at various levels: actual job loss, old relationships, and the implications of changing organisational identity and values. Senior managers are prey to the same anxieties and might well focus their energies on omnipotent fantasies of "getting it right", as if, thus, all pain could be avoided, rather than on containing anxiety and working through the inevitable difficulties.

The chapter describes working with two merged charities serving the elderly. Their boards had believed that merging would give both organisations, serving the same population of elderly and mentally and physically disabled clients, a better chance of survival. Unit costs in the 1980s rose alarmingly, which, together with a diminishing sponsorship population to support their work, compelled the leadership of both charities to search for solutions. Job security was a major concern for the management groups of both charities: savings, it was said, would be made through natural wastage, and a "no redundancy" policy was adopted, which later turned out to be impossible to support. Like most mergers, implementation was rushed when caution would have been better advised.

At the time, mergers and acquisitions were considered instruments of growth and survival. Critical reviews of this process (Krug, 2008) point to the mainly financial aspects of proposals, with scant attention to the behavioural and intergroup and interpersonal dynamics involved. The drive towards mergers often ignores the coming power struggles that staff in both organisations would have to endure as two or more sitting role-holders applied for the one available job. After two years, few felt that the new merged organisation's performance had changed for the better, especially in respect of the "no redundancy" policy. Deeper motivations behind the merger had not been considered, such as over-confidence about expected benefits from the merger and the wish to manage a larger institution and gather more power.

The chapter describes the impact of the merger on the consultant and the fusion of his roles. When a merger is proposed, profound anxieties are inevitably evoked. There is a genuine threat of loss of identity. The organisation with which one identifies will no longer be the same organisation. There might be direct threats—one's job might no longer exist, or it might be given to someone else from the twin organisation. The "no redundancy" policy was an omnipotent denial of the reality of the merger. Leadership reneged on taking responsibility for unpopular decisions, passing them down into the organisation unprocessed. The planners wanted harmony—a single merged organisation in which differences would be swallowed up. The chapter describes the consultant's experience, feeling drawn into a mad world, where unacknowledged difference was equated with harmony. Harmony felt like an omnipotent wish for differences to disappear. The chapter describes the pressures on the consultant to be drawn into splitting processes (people *vs.* population, procedure *vs.* personal experience) or homogeny (living in happy harmony), rather than the more difficult position that there will always be a disruptive influence from somewhere. A description is offered of moving from the depressing "one never gets it right" to the socially depressive "one can never get it right" and preparing to work through the difficulties.

Part IV: boardroom evaluation

The Walker Review (2009a) referred to the phenomenon of "group-think" (Janis, 1972) in some boards of banks that disabled them and prevented anticipation of difficulties ahead. Walker was disinclined to change or add to existing legislation as a means of changing this tendency. He called for "behavioural change" in the boardroom and he consulted on the latest thinking and practice on the psychology and dynamic behaviour of groups. His statement that "principal deficiencies in boards relate much more to patterns of behaviour than to organisation" led to regulators relying on experts in psychology, human behaviour, and group, organisational, and ecological dynamics. Corruption—the conscious and deliberate attempts to pervert probity and unconscious degeneration that results in an internal breakdown of standards of ethics and behaviour—suddenly gripped the imagination of the media, politics, and the public. The chapters in this section are attempts to probe the dynamics of the boardroom on the grounds that, like all groups, boards, too, are subject to bouts of irrationality that need careful attention (Long, 2008).

Chapter Nine describes the interconnectedness of corruption at three levels: the intrapsychic, the relational, and the societal, that is, developing ideas of corruptibility in the individual, in the family, and in the organisation and society. This thesis is built on the notion of human development that moves from states of undifferentiated fusion between self and object (Winnicott, 1958), in which high levels of persecutory anxiety are experienced, to states of thoughtfulness and consideration of others and a sense of being in touch with reality, to states of being urged back to phantasies of possession of unlimited wealth through a corrupted sense of entitlement. The role of leadership in corruption is described in the evolution of processes of moving away from caution and valuing others, towards the excitement of narcissistic and omnipotent gratification.

Business leaders are often driven to present their image of success, their capability to influence people and events around them; they are also prone to creating and sustaining impregnable defensive barriers around themselves. Our research with bankers and regulators suggests that many start with positive intent, but, over time, as success is achieved and a corresponding fear of failure and loss grows, their commitment to original organisational aims weakens. During the crisis that nearly destroyed Western economic systems (Cohan, 2010; Greenspan, 1996; Hare & Babiak, 2006; Lanchester, 2010; Mackay, 1841; Rustin, 2008; Shiller, 2005), leaders and organisations failed to understand the extent to which they were caught in the grip of a group process where thought had collapsed (Bohm, 1994; Goldsmith, 2008). The dynamics of "corruption" were reflected in the Milgram experiments (Milgram, 1974), which show how the influence of "authority" makes people give up discretion and independence of thought. Few in the finance industry dared to re-examine the primary aims and tasks (Lawrence & Miller, 1976). People were persuaded to preserve the status quo even if that went against the public good and, ultimately, their individual interest. Self-preservation and the maintenance of power, it seemed, took over as the new unconscious primary task.

In this chapter, I offer the view that "corruption"—a tendency for human relationships to become distorted and perverted—has a basis in our biological and social inheritance. This idea of corruption as presented here is different to that of actual wrong-doing and refers more to the sense of internal moral degeneration and flight from reality. This chapter helps to explain the differences between conscious criminal behaviour and unconscious internal disintegration, but it also has practical impact, stimulating the debate on the causes of corruption and turning public expressions of righteous indignation into learning. The proposition is put that corruption is inherently part of all living systems that should lead everyone to reflect on their own inclinations towards self-deception and tendencies towards "turning a blind eye" (Steiner, 1985, 2006) and avoiding recognising that all parts of the ecology/system are connected to one another. This chapter offers an approach to the universal human defensive response to evidence that undermines perceptions when we are wrong, or where self-interest is at stake (Jensen, 1998; Schulz, 2010). Self-interest is at the heart of corruption—leadership of the financial sector used its authority to say that the system would fail if changes were introduced. That fear led to collusion and paralysis in those who could have introduced thoughtfulness and change (Bollas, 1989; Maris, 1984). The primary task of leadership is to examine whether there are better ways of doing things. When leaders' self-interest predominates and principles and values change, destructive narcissism (Rosenfeld, 1987) leads to temptations of short-term benefits. That is the bait that is presented by the "gang" (Steiner, 1993). People are blinded by leadership's omnipotence and self-delusion and tend to lose their capacities to think (Klauber, 2004). Klauber writes on working with autistic children whose reactions and behaviour, especially their deep sense of isolation and feelings of difference, are difficult to manage and to understand. Klauber's application of psychoanalytic understanding to this condition helps to illuminate the tendency among many people at the top of financial institutions to retreat into a rigid form of isolationism that limits communications and the development of real-istic appraisals of the world around them, paralleling Steiner's (1993) notion of "psychic retreats". Fears about survival or being left out take over as the strongest force. People are persuaded that values instead of work practices have to change, whereas good leadership, based on the life instinct, normally weighs the balance in ways of working, not values.

Chapter Ten suggests that board behaviour cannot be regulated or managed through organisational structures and controls alone; that behaviour develops both as a result of existing and anticipated situations and is prey to unconscious dynamic forces. The dynamic nature of behaviour means that Chairs have responsibility to ensure that their boards take time to purposefully evaluate the assumptions on which their behaviour rests and the implications of these for effective functioning of their boards. This chapter is a pragmatic piece that arose out of the confusion of the financial crisis and the questions that were being asked about the failed leadership of many boards (Tett, 2009). The chapter has sections that cover the behaviour of Chairs of boards, selection and training of board members, optimum size of boards, and relationships between boards and sub-committees. The chapter emphasises the importance of regular assessments of board behaviour, and this was written into the Financial Services Authority's new UK Code on Corporate Governance (2010), which ruled that the boards of companies in the FTSE 350 index should be evaluated for effectiveness every three years by external independent evaluators.

Annex 4 (see Appendix, below) was well-received in the national press and it led to invitations by the Financial Reporting Council and the Financial Services Authority to contribute to the then forthcoming UK Corporate Governance Code. These developments led Sir David Walker to urge the TIHR and others to form an independent body that would evaluate board effectiveness in the hope of avoiding a repetition of the crisis of 2008. Walker felt that extending the statutes and over-regulating the financial system would be counterproductive. He was persuaded that the heart of the problem lay in culture, attitude, and behaviour—the "dynamics", as he and others termed it. The Tavistock Institute created a board evaluation and development team that is based on a research approach. It contributes to the work of legislators, regulators, Chairs of boards, senior independent directors, non-executives, and executives, and helps to better understand the cultural, attitudinal, and behavioural influences on boards. Bvalco researches and publishes on topics such as financial leadership, board effectiveness, the psychology of risk, "challenge" and the board, the board and strategy, role of remuneration, and nomination committees and succession planning.

Chapter Eleven investigates why senior, intelligent, and respected leaders of the finance industry failed to prevent a crisis that had been predicted. It explores the dynamic influences—personal and global—on the thinking of industry leaders. "Thinking" is considered alongside "not thinking", the "inability to think", and "hatred of thinking". The chapter hypothesises that money, finance, and capital serve as "containers" for hidden individual and social meaning. The dynamics and operating paradigms of banks and other financial institutions are examined for the ways they contributed to the financial crisis. By relying on free associations and uncensored thoughts, we were able to access below-the-surface dynamics of leadership of financial institutions and the financial industry as a whole.

Money and its unconscious meanings forms the focus in this chapter through an examination of relationships between bankers, regulators, civil servants, and other professionals in relation to money. Our methodology, rooted in the theory of the interplay between conscious and unconscious, helped us to gather data about "beneath-the-surface" dynamic phenomena of the finance industry that would otherwise be inaccessible, and helped us to formulate working hypotheses about the functioning of the finance industry. We were concerned that any anxiety and guilt that leadership might have felt about their roles in the financial crisis would evaporate soon after the crisis passed. We were concerned, too, that the expectation of a "bail-out", the complacent "too-big-to-fail" idea, and the role of government as lender of last resort would lead to a business-as-usual attitude and the opportunities for learning from the crisis would be lost.

This chapter casts a light on the thinking, attitudes, and beliefs of those charged with regulating the economy and influencing markets. The research demonstrates that bankers, regulators, shareholders, politicians, and civil servants have a reasonable grasp of issues that influenced behaviour in the financial crisis. They were able to differentiate between fraudulent behaviour and the invisible dynamic forces that drove particular types of behaviour. Competition, rivalry, and aggression were posited as positive forces, yet the "masters of the universe" found it hard to believe that there are forces having an impact on them over which they have little or no knowledge or control. They could not see how they contributed to the general culture of high risk and high leverage and high debt. The differences between individual and systemic accountability were not truly understood. Judgement was displaced, guilt and anger objectified, and projected into "the market". Respondents were appalled at their collusion and self-justifying rationalisations that led to their participation in "sinful practices" (Sir David Walker, unpublished speech, 2009b). All were "unnerved" and sought reassurance that things would right themselves again naturally. The balance between the positive forces of optimism, humanitarianism, and hope and the negative forces of competition, rivalry, envy, narcissism, and greed were distorted and could not be discerned. Little regard was given to how language and reality had been distorted and perverted. This chapter describes how the financial crisis had forced a paradigm shift in an understanding of interconnectedness and how it played out between retail and investment banking; between governments globally; between government and the financial sector, between financial services and the media and between lender and borrower.

Further developments

For most of my consulting career, I have worked with top teams—CEOs, executive teams, managing directors. More recently, I have worked as an evaluator of board performance, paying attention to the nature of boardroom dynamics and the impact of their morale and functioning on the behaviour of executive teams and so on further into the organisation, that is, the board reflecting the organisation and the organisation reflecting the board in a dynamic reflexive loop. Jaques (1976, 1997) calls boards, executives, managers, and the organisation "accountability hierarchies" (AcH), and in order to create one, there first has to be an association (board). AcH come into being when the governing body of an association decides to get its work done by employing people. My exposure to the cultures and functioning of boards has led me to the view that, although boards are themselves part of accountable hierarchies, they often behave as if they are either

quite separate from, or unhelpfully compounded with, the organisation. It is important to distinguish shareholders (or stakeholders) from
employees; proprietor–entrepreneurs from employed entrepreneurs,
and political appointees from career civil servants. Because of tendencies towards either fusion or remoteness, the structures and
dynamic relationships within boards and between boards, their stakeholders and the organisation, the board, boardroom dynamics, and
boardroom behaviour becomes a significant area for research. Jaques
(1997) claims that despite efforts by social scientists to systematise
knowledge of the "association", organisation, and management, "we
are only at the beginning of our understanding of them, usually
due to the use of vague and ill-defined terms that impede thinking, the testing of propositions and talking to one another with understanding".

Gosling (2004) takes a similar view in arguing for clarity in the
definitions of the objectives of leadership ("direction setting"), sometimes involving the arts of persuasion and intuition as much as
sciences of analysis, synthesis, and design. The problem with defining
leadership as "direction setting", he claims, is like the problem of
defining strategy as competitive positioning—it becomes too cerebral,
theoretical, and may be little more than wishful thinking. Leadership
must take into account problems of facilitating emergent strategies
and human and group dynamics associated with the processes of
change and organisation and must go beyond the intellectual activity
of setting directions to the pragmatics of getting things done. Like
Clarke and Hoggett (2009), Gosling is critical of the split between
psychological and sociological definitions and he believes that the
study of the distribution and exercise of institutionalised power is due
for a comeback to compensate for the domination by psychological
approaches that often reduce leadership to so-called "people skills"
(Huys, Sels, van Hootegem, Bundervoet, & Henderickx, 1999).

Geert van Hootegem, Professor of Sociology of Work and Organisation, Catholic University of Leuven (Belgium), is part of an active
network of organisations and people in the Low Countries that are
committed to socio-technical theories of Emery and Trist, including
Eijnatten (1993). A link was also made to the Tavistock's role in the
Quality of Working Life movement. As in the UK, socio-technical
systems was dominant in the Low Countries during the 1980s–1990s,
and was then by-passed by the structural–functionalist approaches of

Merton and Parsons. A balance with socio-technical systems is being re-established as the pressure to keep more people at work longer grows in Europe.

Roethlisberger (Roethlisberger & Dickson, 1939) was a key member of the team that studied employee relations at the Western Electric Company Hawthorne Plant in Hawthorne, Illinois. The Hawthorne Studies had started in 1924 under the supervision of MIT's Dugald C. Jackson. Western Electric brought Elton Mayo and the Harvard Business School Industrial Research Group into the studies in 1927. Professor Roethlisberger worked on the studies actively from 1927 to 1936, first as Mayo's assistant, and later as his collaborator. The aim of the studies was to explore the relationships between physical working conditions (e.g., lighting levels), worker morale, and industrial output. Answers to questions about such relationships proved to be elusive in the early years of the project. Roethlisberger regularly expanded the boundaries of the investigation while searching for deeper insights into the behaviour of employees. Approximately 20,000 employees were interviewed and many others were observed at their jobs under laboratory conditions measuring productivity, individual physiology, and changes in physical working conditions. The studies became a milestone in the development of the Human Relations School of Industrial Management. Roethlisberger and fellow researcher William Dickson summarised the results of the studies in 1939 in the classic book, *Management and the Worker* (Mayo, 1933; Roethlisberger & Dickson, 1939).

Pickering (2001), Elias (1987), and Sofer (1961) were concerned with what was termed the "civilising process" through which individuals absorb and internalise social rules, thus enabling an understanding of social life. Pickering describes a post-humanistic sociology of people and things, a reference to the exploration of the inner human experience of technology—"industrialised consciousness". Pickering recounts that after the Second World War, a post-humanist philosophy developed in operational research, systems dynamics, systems theory, ergonomics, cybernetics, quality of working life, participative design, and collaborative work movements that addressed specifically the realm of production. "All of these are linked to the human and the nonhuman, the interactive tuning between subjects and objects." Pickering describes his sense of *déjà vu* when he discovered that, as far back as the 1950s, the Tavistock

Institute of Human Relations—the home of the Quality of Working Life movement—were thinking seriously about the open-ended practice of cultural transformation, a topic he worked on in the late 1980s. He discovered that the phrase "socio-technical systems" was coined at the Tavistock (Miller & Rose, 2008; Rose, 1998), leaving him with "a reaction of distaste" in discovering that his own interpretative scheme was actually articulated by others before him. He consoles himself with "the symmetry principle of the sociology of scientific knowledge".

Flowing from this, understandings that derive from Tavistock socio-technical systems thinking, theory and practice of group relations, and psychoanalysis offer the promise of further developments in the study of organisations, social policy, and international conflict. Future challenges centre on extending these bodies of knowledge into practical means of moving beyond conference work and organisation-centred consultancy into the realm of uncontained, and sometimes uncontainable, dynamics and forces in society. These challenges will include engaging political institutions and academia in partnership to participate in further research assignments. Group relations institutions are currently being developed in Argentina, Brazil, China, and Lithuania. Work is progressing well in Lithuania in establishing a Lithuanian group relations institution based at the University of the Vilnius. The Lithuanian organisers see the development of a group relations institution as necessary for local and national leaders to address problems of national identity within a democratic framework which they are struggling to maintain after twenty years of independence from totalitarian rule by the former Soviet Union. Despite achieving national independence, the authorities wish to change the common mindset of apathy and suspicion towards authority and reluctance by people to step forward for leadership roles. Tavistock thinking in group relations conference work is seen by them as a useful means of illuminating the hopes, fears, and realities of people towards social and organisational leadership (Lawrence, 1977, 1979). The hope is that Tavistock group relations conferences and other research interventions will help clarify blocks and resistances to authority that would make these relationships less toxic than they were in the past. People's greater natural affinities with families and friends have translated into nepotism and sinecures in organisations as a way of dealing with fears. "Keeping your head down" and "keeping it in the family" are accepted as the behavioural norm today, just as it had been under the former Communist regime.

Further developments are likely to include work in international conflict—for example, Eastern Nigeria, the Middle East, and Northern Ireland. In these arenas group relations modelling would underpin interventions and studies of wider political and social phenomena where the core intergroup dynamic is conflict, not collaboration (Lawrence, 1982). Tavistock approaches are adaptable. New intervention designs are planned to address these conflict situations that will enable skilled social and group relations consultants who have been schooled in the Tavistock tradition to address, study, and consult on the destructive dynamics within cultural, tribal, religious, and political contexts.

Work on the role and function of boards is likely to increase in the future as they come to play a bigger part in the government's current "Big Society" agenda. This would necessitate the development of a conceptual framework to guide people on the size and complexity of interlocking global systems and the greater possibilities for things going wrong. Mega-project theory emerges from extremely large-scale investment projects, typically defined as costing more than US$1 billion and attracting a lot of public attention because of substantial impacts on communities, environment, and budgets. The paradox of mega-projects consists in the fact that more and bigger mega-projects are being planned and built despite their poor performance record in terms of cost overruns, schedule delays, and benefit shortfalls (Flyvbjerg, Bruzelius, & Rothengatter, 2003). Mega-project theory could be aligned with socio-technical systems theory and participative design (Asaro, 2000), methodology and psychoanalytic theory, and be applied to large complex social and technical systems (Lawrence, 1986). Participatory design typically actively involves all stakeholders (e.g., employees, partners, customers, citizens, end users) in the design process to ensure that the product designed meets needs and is usable. The term is used in a variety of fields, for example, software design, urban design, product design, sustainability, planning, and medicine as a way of creating environments that are more responsive and appropriate to their inhabitants' and users' cultural, emotional, spiritual, and practical needs. Participatory design has a political dimension of user empowerment and democratisation. In Scandinavian countries of the 1960s and 1970s, it was rooted in work with trade unions; its ancestry also includes action research and socio-technical design.

Further research development work is planned to establish why certain banks did not get into difficulties during the financial crisis. Regulators, politicians, academics, and bankers themselves are interested in knowing more about what kind of banking milieu existed and what kind of mindset people relied on that led them to remain prudent, cautious, and solvent. Surviving shock will, in future, depend on a number and type of interdependent variables that many in the field would like to know and be able to discern. Tuckett and Taffler (2008), and Tuckett (2011) claim that the financial crisis of 2008 clarified that emotions really matter. They argue that economists' explanations for what happened in the financial crisis miss the essence because they ignore deep flaws in the organisation of financial markets, which have ignored critical components of human psychology. Tuckett suggests that emotion can be systematically incorporated into theories about financial markets and their understanding can be used to create policies to make them safer. His argument, based on research interviewers with money managers, is that the crisis resulted from failures to understand and organise markets so that they control the human behaviour they unleash. Financial assets have an intrinsically uncertain value, and so a particular ability to provoke exciting and then frightening stories and to create what the author terms "divided" mental states and "groupfeel", not unlike Janis's "groupthink". Supporting his ideas with interdisciplinary evidence, Tuckett constructs a framework for a new economic theory of financial markets.

These aspirations for the future work would be consistent with Clarke and Hoggett's (2009) critique of the changes in the social sciences with reference to the place of emotion and affect, and the familiar, but unhelpful, split between "individual" and "society", psychology and sociology. They suggest that in seeking to overcome such splits, psychoanalysis increasingly illuminates core issues within the social sciences, for example, role of loss and mourning, nature of identity, experiences of rapid social change, and negotiation of ethical dilemmas.

Appendix A: media response to Annex 4 of The Walker Review

Financial Times 27 November 2009

Walker report fans the wind of change, by Kate Burgess and Brooke Masters

Mannie Sher from the Tavistock Institute of Human Relations says the Walker requirements for training directors, for example, can be applied broadly although he points out that a straight translation of the Walker proposals may clash with some sector-specific regulations.

The Guardian 26 November 2009

Susceptibility to social influence: 'groupthink'

What is the point of non-executive directors if they will not ask difficult questions? Like most of us, they suffer from the age-old phenomenon of not wanting to stick their heads above the parapet, or, as it has become known, "groupthink". It has been pointed to during the credit crunch many times.

Writing about the behaviour of boards for the Walker report, Mannie Sher, a consultant at the Tavistock Institute of Human Relations, argues that susceptibility to social influence is "not a trait of those who lack willpower; it is hard-wired into all of us". Groupthink, says Sher, relates to the group unconscious. "In boards that are dysfunctional, we find there is a tendency . . . not to put your head above the parapet", says Sher, whose Institute co-wrote a section of the Walker report with consultants Crelos. "Non-executives come in with a bit of diffidence about not making waves and they stay like that . . . If you don't ask questions early . . . then you are never going to".

Chartered Institute of Management Accountants (CIMA)

"Walker" and behaviour, posted by Gillian Lees of CIMA on 07 December 2009

I'd certainly agree that the banking industry needs a fresh look at and it would have been good if they could have got a newcomer – I'm thinking a respected business voice who is not heavily involved in banking. But Sir David Walker is what you'd call a City grandee – former director at the Bank of England and other City experience. But having said that, I think Sir David is absolutely right to focus on behaviour and I'm glad he resisted the temptation to change structures wholesale. *In terms of groundbreaking material on behaviours, Annex 4 of the Walker Report is something I never thought I'd see in a HM Treasury sponsored report – it looks at the psychological and behavioural elements in board performance.* There's hope for us yet!

Financial Services Authority

Annex 4 was thoroughly reviewed and critiqued by Sir David's advisers. The following is a statement attesting to that fact from Galina Carroll, Internal Audit, Financial Services Authority.

The issue with the Annex was not the content or approach – Sir David was convinced of that from his meeting with you – but more one of editing and language. Comments on your annex after the review was published I recall were mainly positive. With regard to advisers advising Sir David, and Sir David himself – his gut instinct that you and Ali had a unique insight proved correct. After the meeting, I recall support (from Sir David, me and James Templeton – his other chief of staff/adviser) for your insights and the inclusion of your Annex.

PART I

PSYCHOTHERAPY IN THE PUBLIC SECTOR

Psychiatric social work and general practice*

Introduction

I n the field of psychiatric social work (PSW) and general practice (GP) collaboration, conflict of roles, different functions, lines of accountability, and distributing scarce resources are key issues. If the two professions are to work comfortably together, then both also need to share the despair, hopelessness, anxiety, and anger that are the occupational hazards of each. We suggest new ways for GPs and PSWs to look at the pain their patients are suffering for the benefit of the patient and the professionals' own working relationships. We present our view of a psychodynamically orientated PSW attachment to a large London group medical practice. The attachment forms part of a larger research project initiated by the Community Unit of the Adult Department of the Tavistock Clinic in 1972.

---

*This chapter is based on: H. Graham and M. Sher (1976) Social work and general medical practice: personal accounts of a three-year attachment. *British Journal of Social Work*, 6(2): 233–249. Also: *Journal of Royal College of GPs*, 26(163): 95–105, 1976. © Material reprinted with permission.

The project

Brook and Temperley (1976) describe the aim of the project "to study the contribution that can be made to group medical practices by the presence in the surgery of a professional worker with specialised training in a psychotherapeutic approach" (p. 86). By close co-operation and mutual education, they hope to increase the psychotherapeutic resources of the practice. As part of the project, several Tavistock Clinic workers, drawn from the disciplines of psychiatry, psychology, and psychiatric social work, but all having training in psychotherapy, are attached for one session a week to group practices in the vicinity for a period of two years.

Brook and Temperley describe the type of referrals made to the attached workers in the project. Because of the workers' psychotherapeutic bias, many referrals focus on psychological and relationship difficulties, especially in younger patients, who are more likely to be at stages of life when relationships are in states of change: for example, marriage, parenthood, divorce, or death. As the attachment developed, more referrals involving physical illness and disability are being referred to the PSW. We note that there is a tendency to select those cases for referral where the GPs "know" they need support; where the task is of such a dimension that one person working alone cannot be expected to listen, understand, treat, and manage the patients' clinical problems. Such referrals, for example, marital problems particularly, make use of the PSW resource to diminish the confusion and wastage through a meagre understanding of the meaning of the presenting problem: for example depression, anxiety, or psychosomatic symptoms. Working together makes it easier for the GP and PSW to recognise the locus of the problem and to avoid potentially being misled by the patient's perception of the problem.

The practice

The practice described in this chapter (one of four in the project) has 17,500 patients, six partners, two assistant general practitioners, one trainee general practitioner, twelve reception and administration staff (many part-time), and two health visitors (liaised). It is a large

practice and is administered like a health centre. This provides opportunities to explore and understand the complexities of liaison, referral, and shared care of patients. It is common, for instance, for case
conferences to take place in the practice, attended by local authority
social workers, educational psychologists, psychiatrists, and teachers,
thus adding weight to the philosophy of whole-person medicine with
the local general practice serving as a central base for patient care and
decision making.

The attachment

The PSW attends the surgery for half a day a week, when one new
referral and one or two old cases are seen for about an hour each. The
remaining time is spent in consultation with the referring general
practitioner, who retains medical responsibility for the patient. The
attachment confirms the view "of the crucial importance of giving
time and thought to advance planning" (Brook & Temperley, 1976).
The PSW and referring GPs have agreed to discuss all cases before
taking any action. These discussions help us to determine how to
proceed: either for the PSW to see the patient, the patient to be seen
jointly by GP and PSW, to include other members of the patient's
family, or, where the GP feels, after discussion, that he understands
something additional about the patient, to continue independently,
secure in the knowledge that support is available. In addition to these
discussions, an alternative way of communicating is through regular
practice meetings, partly to discuss cases and partly to monitor the
experience of the attachment.

With heavy pressures on both PSWs' and GPs' time and emotional
resources, the need for careful exploration of the patient's presenting
problem and environment, before acting, is even more important.
Precipitate action, before the problem is fully understood, we know,
often leads to the rejection by the patient of the help offered. GPs and
PSWs can easily feel themselves to be acting out of role because they
have unrealistic expectations of each other, and the patient often has
unrealistic expectations of both. This can confuse them and the
patient, resulting in everyone feeling frustrated and angry and unable
to collaborate profitably.

Sharing work

In this section, we illustrate a variety of planned interventions and how we work together with patients in different ways.

Patient 1

Miss K, a young single librarian, tells her GP about her depression due to a lack of feminine sexual characteristics, viz. flat chest and a masculine-type physique. She cannot maintain stable relationships with men. The GP feels unable to like this angry young woman, but she reveals intriguing insights into her relationships with men, and, in particular, with her father. The GP believes that further exploration of the relationship with her father is appropriate, but he is unable to take up these issues directly with her, because he fears that to do so would interfere with a well-entrenched neurotic relationship with her father and would probably invite an angry response towards himself.

The GP and PSW discuss the matter and decide that the PSW will see the patient in order to better understand the relationship with her father. She is seen alone by the PSW for five sessions, during which it emerges that she is drawn to men who are inferior to her and have serious emotional problems themselves, and even though she is aware of this tendency, she cannot desist. She feels she has to "make the going" in all her relationships, because if men show any interest in her she is convinced there is something unstable about them. Unwittingly, she chooses men she knows will not gain the approval of her parents, who would be hurt by her choice. Miss K feels that she is just getting over her irrational need to hurt her parents, but she fears that, at thirty, she might have left it too late to sort out her conflicts. She sees herself heading for a long and bitter spinsterhood. Miss K describes her mother as weak, ailing, and demanding, holding on to her husband through illness. Their marriage, she claims, is empty and they stay together for the children. She expresses warm and protective feelings towards her father, whom she feels she needs to save from a sterile marriage. The close relationship with her father and the disparagement of her mother might, in fact, be a denial of the anger she feels because her parents are more important to each other than she is to either of them, and, in addition, a denial that the original longing may have been for her mother. The first indication of these angry feelings is the subjective experience of "unlikeability" felt by the GP that leads to the referral.

She returns later to her GP with more physical complaints and she tells him she is angry with the PSW for unreasonably concentrating on her relationship with her father. Nevertheless, when more openly challenged, this time by her GP, she acknowledges that she is less depressed and has been able to limit the extent to which her alcoholic boyfriend sponges on her, without feeling guilty. She is able to question the belief in her parents' lack of sexual relationship, which makes her feel unrealistically responsible for her father. She sees that maintaining this position during adolescence had prevented her from seeking and receiving adequate help from her parents when, because of her masculine sexual characteristics, she felt so desperate and lonely. She would call attention to her psychological needs by being aggressive and demanding, which alienated her family. Over the five sessions with the PSW, Miss K is gradually able to disengage herself from her parents as well as her current boyfriend, and, after some months, she returns to her GP asking for referral for psychotherapeutic help.

Discussion

The GP refers this case to the PSW because of troubled feelings about his patient's anger towards him. This stirs his own anger, which threatens to interfere with his capacity to continue working with her. Discussion of these feelings with the PSW frees the doctor–patient relationship of some of its hostility, which, in turn, allows the patient to express her anger and to ask for help.

Patient 2

Mrs N, a mother with three children, presents herself as a physically diseased, depressed alcoholic with murderous feelings towards her children, husband, parents, and parents-in-law. The GP is concerned for the safety of the children, but he has been cautioned by a psychiatrist, who previously had seen Mrs N, not to accede to her request for psychotherapy since she is thought to have minimal defences to cope with the horrors and her huge childhood deprivation that included rape by her alcoholic father. For these reasons, it is suggested that Mrs N and her husband should attend a joint consultation with a view to providing support through her family. The contrast in their appearance is startling—Mr N is well-dressed in jacket and tie and has a neatly trimmed beard; Mrs N arrives late with many apologies, dressed in dirty jeans, broken sandals, and with uncombed hair. The workers are struck by Mrs N's need to cling to the depressive aspects of her past and present life and by her fascination with destructive aspects of society, for example, racial tensions and nuclear annihilation, probably standing for the state of her inner feelings, whereas Mr N, with ample reason to be depressed, as he, too, comes from a disturbed family background, with early separation from his parents, maintains a detached, almost carefree attitude. It seems to us that Mr N's feelings of anger and depression are off-loaded on to his wife, who is left unsupported in her misery and chaos. This process of getting rid of painful feelings leaves Mr N free to indulge in his pleasurable pastimes away from home without feeling too guilty.

Behind Mrs N's near-madness lies a desperately sane plea for a need to be separate from her husband and in-laws and not exploited in her vulnerable state. To this end, the workers support Mrs N's desire for greater separateness coupled with practical support from the health visitor, PSW, and GP, and strongly discourage further invasions of her feelings through psychotherapy, which Mrs N is requesting and Mr N pushing her towards. Mr N appears unable to face his own depressed feelings and does not attend further meetings. Mrs N is supported in her role as a woman and mother. A year later, with the help of occasional fairly calm contacts with her GP, Mrs N is still working as an art teacher and caring adequately for her family, but without her husband, who has left.

Discussion

This case illustrates the difficult dilemma often facing GPs and PSWs, which is to resist pressures from the families of patients, and even from patients themselves, to regard them as mentally ill, requiring immediate treatment or hospital care. Resisting the pressure and adopting a different treatment plan for the patient can infuriate other members and even lead to the break-up of the family, as happened in the case of Mr and Mrs N. Should the GP collude with the diagnosis of "mental illness" in Mrs N, admit her to hospital, separating mother from children? Or should he act independently on his judgement and provide enough environmental support for a vulnerable and deprived woman so that she can cope a little better and risk the husband leaving? Either way, the decision is difficult, since other people, often vulnerable children, are affected. This kind of situation impinges upon GPs philosophies about mental illness, families staying together, and mothers remaining with children. These issues are discussed and the GP is helped to face the guilt and anxiety arising from whichever decision he takes.

Patient 3

This case describes the experiences of a GP who feels crushed by the tragedy of a very promising ballerina of twenty-three, Miss D, who became permanently tetraplegic, as a result of breaking her neck in a dancing accident on stage.

The GP is much involved in the management of the physical aspects of the patient's care: for example, electronic aids, chairs, lifts, retraining. He realises, after a light-hearted reference to suicide by Miss D, that he is ignoring the full extent of her despair and hopelessness, which is overtaking him, too. He asks for consultation with the PSW, who like himself, feels the horror of the tragedy and also experiences a wish to "do" things, whether or not they are realistic. Both realise that it is necessary to discuss the implications of a bleak and depressing future openly and honestly with Miss D. This decision is given added weight because the GP has responsibility for her general medical care and the patient turns to him in despair when she realises how vain her hopes are of ever walking again. It is agreed that the PSW should act as a consultant to the GP, so that he can understand his sense of inadequacy stirred by her tragic situation. The PSW would be available for certain crucial joint interviews, in order to monitor and regulate the pace with which Miss D is confronted with her feelings of depression and despair. One particular joint interview is arranged to coincide with the first anniversary of the accident, a time especially painful for the patient, since there has been no apparent improvement in her condition.

Both GP and PSW soon discover, when they nearly drop Miss D trying to carry her upstairs, how easy it is to be blind to the limitations which her disability imposes. Miss D values these interviews, which extend over three months, in which her feelings of rage, resentment, and despair are understood and accepted, rather than denied, as they tend to be by others around her. Later, having acknowledged the unlikelihood of walking again, Miss D successfully applies to study art. She still retains an interest in the world of ballet in the different, but more appropriate, area of set design and promoting safety standards for ballet dancers.

Discussion

This case illustrates how a tragedy can overwhelm a GP and lead to denying the truth of a dreadful disablement. Sharing these feelings through discussion with a colleague enables the GP to spot and check his impulse to take flight. The case also underlines the GP's continuity of care and responsibility for the patient, which extends beyond the merely physical aspects of the condition, important though these are. Care professionals are in their roles to give comfort and put things right. Tragically, some conditions cannot be put right, and when this is discovered there is a danger of the patient being abandoned. The PSW's presence in a number of crucial interviews helps bring into the open some of the harrowing feelings overlooked by both the patient and GP; it also strengthens the practitioner's ability to grasp and talk honestly about the very disturbing emotions aroused by the permanently crippled life of a young person.

Summary

These three brief examples give some idea not only of the variety of problems presented in general practice, but also different styles of collaboration between the professionals concerned. The common factor in all the cases is in the GP identifying feelings that are bewildering and threatening to his normal decision-making abilities and capacity to offer help. The consultations release the GP from a frustrated position and help him regain a clearer perspective of the doctor–patient relationship. The nature of this relationship is different in each case. In the first case, the GP feels uneasy on account of his anger towards a difficult young woman. He hands the case to the PSW, who deals directly with her angry feelings and this removes some of the hostility from the doctor–patient relationship. In the second case, involving joint marital interviews, the GP is shocked by the violence of the material. Through joint interviews, a more practical appraisal of the GP's contribution becomes possible. Care is exercised not to be over-enthusiastic, or to dwell upon morbid and destructive thoughts and ideas.

In the third case, both GP and PSW share the horror and despair of a young person whose hopes and ideals are suddenly dashed. The GP is nearly submerged by the patient's enormous despair when the realities of her future dawn upon both. Working together helps contain the threat to the GP's integrity, and provides the patient with opportunities to face her dreadful situation honestly with people who understand and accept her position, in ways that others do not.

The help given in all the examples consists of increasing the GPs capacity to listen and be responsive to the patient's mode of communicating, thereby helping patients take stock of themselves and think seriously about their lives, problems, and attitudes.

Experiences of working together

We have indicated how the attachment of a PSW provides the practice staff and the patients with an additional resource for dealing with psychological problems. It is common for general practitioners to offer help to patients with emotional and relationship difficulties. Through this attachment, they are themselves helped to recognise the danger of persisting on their own for too long and possibly getting out of their depth with the patient. Equally, the GPs are, in many instances, encouraged to support patients further, rather than refer them to specialist agencies in the belief that specialists could offer something more masterful.

In considering the nature of the attachment and what it offers to the professional workers, we need to look at what we started with: a doctor, primarily trained in the physical aspects of medical care, and a PSW with psychotherapeutic skills and an understanding of relationships. The workers had different philosophies about human behaviour, different methods of care, attitudes to use of time, and the giving of advice.

Ratoff, Rose, and Smith (1974) draw attention to the inevitable feelings of dependency aroused by the fact that everyone since childhood has had direct experience of doctors as patients. In addition, there is the complex relationship between GP and PSW of rivalry and envy: the PSW's envy of the GP's capacity to make quick decisions, their higher status, and apparent ability to make patients "better". To the GP, the PSW's seeming detachment, ability to work with patients in painful and disturbing areas, the different usage of time, and the ability to check the need for "quick cures" seems cold and unfamiliar.

We are describing our subjective experiences in a situation that is new to us, that is, sharing in the care of patients and their families, bearing in mind the traditional possessiveness of the helping professions, the competition to be the one who is seen to be doing the best for the patient, the irrational hurt we feel when patients reveal intimate information to one professional and not the other, the anxiety caused when one's method and techniques of working are scrutinised by the other, or simply when one wants to be rid of a problem—the pressure we exert on others to take the problem away.

What are the difficulties and rewards for GPs and PSWs of working together?

For the general practitioner

- Professional gains
- Novelty and challenge.

For the GP, the attachment provides an almost infectious excitement, as well as an extension of interest and understanding—a chance to view patients' problems from a perspective that was negligibly dealt with during medical training. The desire to know more about the patient's psychological composition can lead into complex and threatening areas. It can also sharpen one's powers of observation and deepen the understanding of the doctor–patient relationship. Collaboration and consultation with a worker skilled in psychodynamics can be taxing, but it can also strengthen the general practitioner to be sensitive to, but not overwhelmed by, the patient's emotional difficulties.

Close working with a colleague allows for a greater "reality testing". The danger of crossing personal boundaries can be appreciated, and this awareness often leads to setting appropriate limits against intrusion by patients on their GPs and *vice versa*. This point is particularly relevant where GPs live in the same locality as their patients and are likely to be related to them in other ways, for example, where their children attend the same school, where the doctor is the patient's shop customer or friend.

The mixing of social and professional contacts can prevent the GP setting reasonable limits. For example, the GP, without the help of the PSW present, feels unable to tell a married patient, known to him socially, and on first name terms, that by insisting on having extra-marital relationships he is acting irresponsibly and sadistically towards his depressed wife, even if, for her own reasons, she is allowing him to do so.

Use of time

This type of attachment obviously demands time, rather differently from the shorter interactive interviews of general practice (Balint & Norell, 1973). Spending 45–60 minutes with a patient, couple, or family and then a further 15–30 minutes in discussion afterwards means considerable changes occurring elsewhere in the practice. This might lead to other partners carrying a larger workload, or the receptionist holding all but the most urgent calls. The resentments created among the rest of the staff by this deployment of time have to be faced. There are feelings of unease among other staff when doctors have "special" patients, particularly when that means extra duties for others. Where joint work is undertaken, the time is well spent. We find that the PSW's support has a ripple effect, enabling the GP to help other patients with similar difficulties at earlier stages and working independently. A common example could be an unresolved grief reaction after bereavement where a patient might, without some psychotherapeutic understanding, continue in a state of minor ill-health for months or even years.

Pressures on the doctor

Often the doctor tries to give the patient the experience of being understood, and then, without fully realising it, gets taken up by the patient's account of the story, and subsequently has difficulty resisting the pressure to *do* something. "Doing something" might mean writing out a prescription, referring another member of the family to a specialist, or simply offering the patient further unnecessary interviews. Attempts by GPs "to do something" could mask a degree of uncertainty, a lack of understanding of the problem, or a sense of helplessness. On the other hand, GPs might become excited about, and get caught up in, the psychodynamics of the patient, particularly when they seem clear to him. In such instances, sharing care with the PSW can be a useful way of re-establishing distinct professional roles, as opposed to personal ones, that should make future help to the patient possible, since GPs also take care of the intimate physical aspects of patients.

There are subtle defences used by many doctors to resist pressures that might also prevent a full understanding of their patients, and, instead, keep them at a distance. These defences can aggravate a stressful situation even further. These might be expressions of phoney cheeriness or the offering of placebos, given unknowingly by the doctors for themselves as much as for the patient, or premature advice, or an attempt to unload the whole unmanageable problem on to someone else.

When this happens, patients might feel they cannot talk honestly to their doctors, feel rejected and unaccepted, that their problems are too great, or too messy, or even too lurid to handle. Prior discussions with the PSW about the effect patients have on the GP's own feelings are useful. When anxieties can openly be admitted and discussed, they are much less likely to interfere with the GP's capacity to cope and they can make greater use of their resources.

Difficulties in learning and sharing (interprofessional problems)

Close attachments of this kind are certainly not without their difficulties and, indeed, might be too threatening for some GPs and care professionals. The difficulties described are probably those that would emerge in any relationship of shared responsibility, that is, feelings of rivalry and competition, doubt about one's own as well as the other's competence, anger aroused by disagreements or different points of view.

The GPs, for instance, often want to protect their patients from what is perceived as the cruelty of the psychodynamically orientated PSW. We find our working relationship bedevilled by all these emotions and more. However, working on the principle that what we are experiencing inwardly might, in part, be the result of what the patient is unconsciously trying to make us feel, we are able, with considerable gratification, to gain a clearer picture and understanding of many additional aspects of doctor–patient relationships.

Thus, it is not uncommon for pressure to be placed on the PSW to see patients, a request which arises from the patient's pressure on their GP to be active. Sometimes, the PSW considers the referral is inappropriate and, as an alternative, offers comments on what might be happening between patient and GP. The GP sometimes feels this approach is unhelpful and disappointing and is saddled with a restless patient, with whom the GP alone has to cope. The referral might be made, not because the patient requests it or even needs it, but because the GP might be unclear about the nature of the problem, or how to proceed, or anxious about veiled threats of suicide, or fears of patients' children coming to harm; the GP might feel at a loss dealing with patients' apparently unreasonable fears, or how to explain repeated headaches or other physical symptoms for which no abnormality can be detected.

In these situations, it is fruitful to consider our own fears, anxieties, and sense of helplessness. An understanding of these feelings in ourselves is often more effective in helping patients than an outright referral. This, however, can strain the relationship between PSW and GP because of feelings aroused when the GP's initial request is questioned. It makes GPs feel foolish asking for the referral in the first place and forces them to think carefully about subsequent referrals. Furthermore, as so often happens, referral poses more problems than it solves. It is often seen as opening a Pandora's Box, with more difficult problems being exposed, but doing so makes the task more gratifying in so far as one is dealing with the whole person and not one isolated aspect of the patient's life. The GPs gain a better understanding of the meaning of referral, both for themselves and their patients. They are better equipped to decide whether to leave the problem well alone, to explore a little further on their own, or to refer the patient directly to a psychotherapist.

For the PSW

A new learning situation

For the PSW member of this attachment, the exercise provides an opportunity to work in consultation with colleagues of different disciplines in a new setting. New skills and techniques of working are being developed, since the pressures and demands are different from those in a setting of specialist psychotherapy setting. In addition, a broader range of patients are seen at earlier stages of their problems, thus allowing short-term interventions of up to six sessions in which some therapeutic clarification is achieved without extensive costly psychotherapeutic strategies.

The attachment provides opportunities to explore relationships between members of different disciplines—nurses, doctors, health visitors, and social workers. The attachment generates anxiety in the PSW over fear of failure or raising excessive expectations. Prior discussion between the surgery members and the attached PSW, we believe, is essential in determining ways of future working together, particularly to clarify what the PSW can or cannot do. Nevertheless, there will remain a sense of discomfort because of the untried and new situation, mixed with feelings of uncertainty, self-doubt, and magical notions of being able to solve everything.

The PSW comes with the authority of psychodynamic skills plus the authority of the Tavistock Clinic, but there is still a nagging fear that he might be called upon to do the impossible—to cure long-standing psychiatric problems, mend marriages instantly, etc. These fears contrast with a wish to show the practice that he, too, has tangible resources to offer.

One of the complications in the practice is the antipathy towards the Tavistock Clinic for the very high degree of selectivity used in accepting referrals. It is easy to veer between being "too smart" and a sense of being lost in the world of general practice, coupled with a sense of envy of the GP: their quick-thinking, ability to make snap decisions, the huge responsibilities they carry on behalf of their patients, the visible, tangible repertoire of helpful techniques at their disposal. One worries about being able to give the expected help and, when the PSW is unable to help, to explain it in a way that is not rejecting, but leaves the door open to alternatives. On the other hand, in those situations where one can help, there was a fear of being "sucked dry" by desperate professionals whose behaviour might have the unconscious design of making the PSW feel what it is like to be on call twenty-four hours a day. While, on the one hand, it might be gratifying to be needed by important people, on another level, one fears appearing incompetent by not being able to "deliver".

Management of the task and its emotional aspects

Because the demands of a large group practice are unlikely to be met in an attachment of one session per week, a system of allocation is necessary, with the consequent rivalry and competition for the PSW's time and skill. Setting limits on the number of referrals accepted evokes feelings of guilt, especially as the GPs cannot do the same with their patients. However, we all feel that working through these problems of time allocation has beneficial effects in facing patients with their demands on GPs for more than they realistically can offer. For example, the repeated introduction of a child in the mother's appointment time shows itself to be, in a joint family interview, a disguised demand by the father to cope with the sleeping problems of his daughter and her intrusion into the marital bed. To regard the child as the patient could be an easy way out, but not necessarily the most honest or effective. We feel that facing our limitations on what we offer each other helps to diminish our sense of guilt when doing the same with our patients.

Behind the guilt there is a degree of mutual envy between the PSW and the partners, a familiar aspect of any new situation. This is often masked by overt expressions of admiration and gratitude, followed by the referral of an almost impossible case, as if conveying a feeling of "if you're so marvellous, try solving this one". First referrals are often of the "testing out" type and constitute the difficult patient who is continually pestering the surgery. Even though we have previously discussed the type of referrals most likely to benefit from a psychotherapeutic assessment, an explanation of referring the "difficult patient" might be an underlying wish to force the PSW to witness and even experience the never-ending care of the most intractable patients which is the doctor's lot. The PSW can feel that he is being got at, even disliked, for working within well-stated boundaries, using different time scales in the work, and acknowledging limitations. Doing so runs the risk of being accused of being cold-blooded, heartless, aloof, or uncaring.

Conclusions

The benefits of collaboration far exceed the price we pay for it. We are developing new ways in which the psychodynamically trained PSW can work in general practice. This requires modification of therapeutic skills that are more appropriate to the setting of a specialist clinic. With gratification, we witness one another's adaptation to these skills, and, provided we can withstand unrealistic expectations, external and internal, to produce magical cures, we also observe patients' responses to their doctors with enhanced psychodynamic understanding of their situations.

By establishing close working relationships, in which experiences are shared and feelings freely expressed, we believe we manage to avoid the traditional split functions of the interdisciplinary medico–psycho–social team, where each member of the team has a rather limited view of patients and their families. We believe that we have a more balanced effect on one another, that our respective roles are reinforced, rather than undermined. In actively working together in this way, we present to patients a model of a successfully integrated medico–psycho–social system that offers better therapeutic opportunities than when parts of the system operate separately.

1. This chapter only touches on the broader aspects of social work attachment to general medical practice (Goldberg & Neill, 1972; Ratoff, Rose, & Smith, 1974). We have attempted to examine more deeply the nature of the experiences of the members of two, sometimes three (nursing), different disciplines working together.

2. Patients are able to bring and explore their emotional problems in the relatively non-threatening setting of their local general practice. We find that attending to what lies behind patients' symptoms often results in a reduction of the number of their attendances at the surgery. If this is done early enough, formal referral out is often unnecessary.

3. The attachment provides opportunities for lively discussion of case material that are crucial to the establishment of agreed goals of treatment.

4. The development of relationships between the caring professionals in general practice allows them jointly to share and begin to understand the anger, despair, uncertainties, and psychic pain experienced by patients and by themselves. The setting of general practice allows confused or fearful patients to return with reduced apprehension at a time of their own choosing.

5. The attachment of psychodynamically trained workers to general practice should be officially recognised through the employment of mental health workers in general practice because it strengthens and enhances services for patients. We also recognise that not all doctors or all social workers would find sharing professional care an easy experience. (Note: Twenty years later, it is estimated that 50% of all general practices in the UK have psychodynamic workers attached (Mellor-Clark, Simms-Ellis, & Burton, 2001).)

6. Although it might appear that time spent in discussion between the care-givers is time lost, our evidence suggests otherwise. Misuse of practice services by patients is substantially reduced and experiences gained by GPs are more widely used.

Acknowledgements

We wish to thank the joint Chairs of the Community Unit Project at the Tavistock Clinic, Alexis Brook and Jane Temperley, supervisors, colleagues, and secretarial staff for all their help and support throughout the attachment, as well as the partners and staff of the group practice in Highgate, London, whose forbearance and assistance is much appreciated.

CHAPTER TWO

Counselling and psychotherapy in primary healthcare: key professional issues*

The changing professional culture of primary care

A wind of change is sweeping through the health service and its repercussions are being felt at the grass-roots level in primary care. Inevitably this is affecting patient care. Doctors' and counsellors' expectations, their roles and their relationships are being redefined. Patients are now expected to be more responsible for their own health. Exercise, diet, and a healthy lifestyle are a few examples of this. Old assumptions about universal care "from cradle to grave" are changing and now that the dependency culture of the post-war decades is being swept aside, governments are urging us to invest in pensions to see us through our old age. The same applies to primary care and the rise of fund-holding practices. Doctors have had to reassess their allocation of funds. Who gets what and how much has been delegated to the local level, which means that decision making in healthcare is community and patient responsive. Choice has been

*This chapter is based on: J. Wiener and M. Sher (1998), Key professional issues. In: *Counselling and Psychotherapy in Primary Health Care* (pp. 127–142. © Macmillan, London, UK. Material reprinted with permission.

the political justification for many of the changes, but few believe that there has been an equitable distribution of resources geographically and generationally, and even across gender and illness lines. While fund-holding practices have broken new ground by providing on-site counselling services for their patients, this might be financially moti-vated: counselling is cheaper than psychiatry. There are cases where counselling is beneficial, provided it is underpinned by adequate resources and is part of a larger network of caring that can be called on to assist with troublesome cases. There is evidence to suggest that this is not happening. Without recourse to broader networks, includ-ing health visitors, social workers, and psychotherapists, counselling in primary care cannot succeed.

Interprofessional relationships

The changes referred to above highlight the need for healthcare pro-fessionals to co-operate with one another in the interests of improved patient care. Relationships with other professional groups have been a running theme of the BMA's ethical guidance. The BMA recognises other professional groups once they have acquired statutory status, and relies on their codes of ethics to govern professional behaviour and maintain high standards of practice. The GMC (1993, p. 17, pars 42–43) has consistently welcomed "the growing contributions made to healthcare by persons who have been trained to perform specialised functions". Doctors recognise that other disciplines can offer their skills independently, outside their sphere of responsibility, so that independent professionals assume responsibility for their own actions.

In recent decades, there has been a shift in healthcare policy away from institutions towards the community, where emphasis is placed on a multi-disciplinary approach to health management. Medicine has also witnessed a decline in its traditional monopoly on health matters in favour of interdisciplinary or team approaches, and a consumer-led interest in the potential of other therapies. The inde-pendence of other health professionals has become increasingly recog-nised and respected. This movement takes us into an arena where key professional dilemmas for GPs and counsellors will become apparent.

Liaison with other disciplines

It is estimated that about sixty-five per cent of UK patients use non-conventional methods of treatment as a supplement to orthodox medicine (Thomas, Carr, Westlake, & Williams, 1991). Many doctors employ professionals from other disciplines and GPs have been encouraged to do this since 1990 by government-led contractual changes. The GMC (1993, pars 42–43) makes it clear that "a doctor who delegates treatment of other procedures must be satisfied that the person to whom they are delegating is competent to carry them out".

For professionals who are accountable to a recognised registering and disciplinary body, this poses few problems. The British Association of Counselling (BAC) is the professional umbrella association for most counsellors. The BAC sets the standards for counselling training, and can be consulted when a doctor seeks to validate a counsellor's credentials. The Counselling in General Practice Working Party of the Royal College of General Practitioners (RCGP) adopted the use of the term "counselling" to refer to trained counsellors undertaking counselling as defined by the BAC, with its distinctive ethic and philosophy, and specifically referred to the patients' capacity for self-determination:

> Counselling is the skilled and principled use of relationships which develop self-knowledge, emotional acceptance and growth, and personal resources. The overall aim is to live more fully and satisfyingly.

> Counselling may be concerned with addressing and resolving specific problems, making decisions, coping with crises, working through feelings and inner-conflict, or improving relationships with others. The counsellor's role is to facilitate the client's work in ways that respect the client's values, personal resources, and capacity for self-determination. (quoted in Bond, 1995, p. 5)

The growing inclination to supplement orthodox medicine, together with the burden of fund management, have forced GPs to rely on ancillary disciplines to ease their load. Delayed feedback, longer lines of communication, and the freer availability of restricted information can all strain the boundaries of confidentiality. This leads us to a key professional issue.

Confidentiality

Confidentiality is a traditional professional principle and a practical requirement shared by doctors, counsellors, and their patients.

Privacy

Privacy is a fundamental right that allows individuals to decide the manner and extent to which information about themselves is shared with others. Self-determination in this respect is also central to preservation of the dignity and integrity of the individual. According to the BMA (1993), on occasion public interest may override the primacy of individual privacy, but in such instances the facts must be examined closely to determine whether there is a genuine necessity for disclosure.

Secrecy

Confidentiality is not the same as secrecy. Confusion between the two terms arises when patients expect all revelations within the doctor's surgery to remain veiled in secrecy. There are, however, many occasions when doctors believe it necessary to make the contents of such conversations available to others. Although this is not the secrecy the patient might have sought, the doctor's actions remain within the bounds of confidentiality; external and internal referrals, statutory requirements to report notifiable diseases, and certain criminal activities must be reported by law.

The ethos of confidentiality

Long before the contemporary emphasis on privacy, the principle of confidentiality was germane to the ethics of medical practice. It is also an overriding professional principle in psychotherapy and counselling. The function of the confidentiality principle is to protect the doctor–patient and counsellor–patient relationship, although at the present time neither doctors nor counsellors are shielded by legal privilege, unlike communications between lawyers and their clients. The concept goes back to the time of Hippocrates and is restated in the International Code of Medical Ethics, which says that "a doctor must preserve absolute confidentiality on all he knows about his patient, even after the patient's death".

However, issues of confidentiality are beset with contradictions. Professional bodies recognise that new pressures, largely outside the control of the professionals, are being brought to bear on the confidentiality rule. These come from changing patterns of healthcare delivery, the increasing emphasis on healthcare promotion and preventive measures, and the commercial demand for health-related information. Many find it hard to believe that apparently small compromises in confidentiality, made in the name of efficiency or convenience, erode patients' rights.

Information has always been given to doctors and counsellors with the intention of providing a sound basis for appropriate care. Increasingly, details about life-style and family history are being sought as part of health promotion and research, but personal, health, and family data can also be used for a wide range of other purposes, such as insurance policies, housing applications or referrals to specialists. Health records have an increasingly important social function and doctors and counsellors frequently complain that, instead of preserving the secrecy of medical and personal family data, they expend much effort on circulating it to different recipients who sometimes share ill-defined obligations regarding its confidentiality.

Sharing information

Doctors and counsellors have a duty to preserve the bounds of confidentiality. To reveal information there must be adequate grounds, and it usually requires the patient's consent. One criterion governing confidential disclosures is that the receiving health professional has a demonstrable "need to know" that particular piece of information in the interests of patient care. Increasingly, care is provided by multidisciplinary teams and agencies collaborating with each other in difficult cases, such as those where the welfare of children is at stake, and it is important that patients are aware of this and explicitly agree to information being passed on to those who need to know. Passing on information cannot be justified for any other reason. The right to privacy is considered an essential element of human rights, but it is not absolute.

Models of confidentiality

Confidentiality is fundamental to both doctors and counsellors individually and as partners in a multi-disciplinary team. In such a new and uncertain environment, counsellors seem to rely on one of two broad models:

- some believe that all exchanges between patient and counsellor are absolutely confidential and that GPs need know nothing about them;
- some believe that as members of a multi-disciplinary team, joint confidentiality applies to the team as a whole.

The second model acknowledges that it is in the patient's best interest to pool some knowledge among appropriate members of the team, particularly the GP, so that information is shared on a "need-to-know" basis. This approach is a pragmatic one from the standpoint of counsellors, as they acquire a great deal of background information that the GP does not need in the general management of patient care. It is rare for GPs to need more than basic information about patients' counselling sessions. Most of the subtleties of the counselling session are of interest only to the counsellor and the patient.

Staff meetings

Confidentiality in primary care has more than one dimension. There are times when conversations about patients are held in order to help members of the team increase their psychological understanding of patients generally. For these conversations to be effective, there needs to be a "space for thinking", a protected time for staff members to meet. These meetings, like counselling sessions, have a defined membership, start and end punctually, and should not be interrupted. Telephones should not be answered and the doors should be kept closed with the "engaged" sign on. These meetings have a clear purpose and everyone bears responsibility for ensuring that the professional nature of the discussions is maintained. The counselling model of paying attention to the details of time, space, and boundaries can serve as a model for responsible interdisciplinary work for the members of the primary care team. Boundaries are often lax. Staff might talk about patients aloud and patient information might be visible from the reception area. The message should be clear: privacy and respect for the patient have been thought about and implemented. The meetings should be conducted confidentially and professionally in the interests of mutual learning. When meeting with professional colleagues, the principles of confidentiality might have to be adapted, but the core element of respect for the patient must never be lost.

Whether counsellors are working directly with patients or meeting with colleagues to discuss their patients, or even communicating with outside agencies about patients, say in preparing a referral, any information that needs to be passed on must be handled sensitively and with the patient's consent.

Written notes and use of computers

Confidentiality in counselling cannot be addressed without stating what should be put into the medical notes. There are cases where note taking is an extremely delicate issue when dealing with health centre staff. In such cases, notes may not be taken at all. This issue is complicated by the widespread use of computers, which allow quick and easy retrieval of information by a whole variety of personnel who have access to the health centre's computer system. While computers allow urgent information to be communicated quickly, technology has increased the danger of patient information falling into the wrong hands. Some counsellors prefer to store their notes at home, perhaps hoping to ensure greater confidentiality that way, but they should be aware that the Data Protection Act applies to them, too, and even privately held notes can be subpoenaed. Patients' statutory right to access to their own records also needs to be considered, as this is bound to influence the kind of information counsellors record. Whether counsellors keep handwritten notes or use computers, many compile brief "thumb-nail" summaries of interviews for their records. Counsellors might want to keep separate detailed notes on those patients they discuss with their supervisors. One of our colleagues offered us the following piece of sensible guidance on note taking: "they should contain only what you would not mind appending to the tree on the village green". Patients are anxious about the safety of having their personal details stored in a computer. Computers offer built-in protection in the form of passwords and other security

arrangements, but even with the most sophisticated safeguards, counsellors should be cautious and reassure themselves that all aspects of
confidentiality are being observed.

The new recording methods employed in primary care have implications for everyone. Computerisation is here to stay and, if used
wisely, it can bring enormous benefits. It is easy to claim that "security breaches never happen here", or to take the view that occasional
lapses are the price to be paid for a streamlined system and improved
efficiency. Patients' feelings and fantasies surrounding the location of
their notes and how they are handled should be respected and every
safeguard employed. We should bear in mind that communications
flow around the practice setting fairly freely:

- when patients arrive for their appointments, their medical folders are stacked on the receptionist's counter, to be collected by the
  doctor when he or she calls the patient from the waiting room.
  These folders and their contents can sometimes be seen by other
  patients;
- professional staff might loiter in the reception area and discuss
  their patients aloud;
- active computer screens might still display information about a
  previous patient.

Funding psychological services

Since its inception in 1948, the pride of the British NHS has been that
medical services are free at the point of delivery. The patient does not
pay for treatment and healthcare professionals expect to be able to
deliver the best care possible within the constraints of supply and
demand. However, over the years, public expectations of doctors and
healthcare services have risen sharply. Doctors are rushed off their
feet, waiting rooms are rife with stress, confusion, and unhappiness.
The faster the patient load is mopped up, the faster the waiting rooms
refill, so that GP stress is continuously compounded. Are the problems they see medical *or* social? Or medical *and* social?

Clearly, a significant proportion of cases presenting in primary care
are not strictly medical and are not treatable by traditional medical
methods. In response, GPs have begun to introduce a whole range of

ancillary services. These might include visits by hospital consultants with various specialities, or other services such as a practice nurse, a baby clinic, well-women and well-men clinics, homoeopathy, chiropody, osteopathy, physiotherapy, dietetics, counselling, and so on. The result of local arrangements of this breadth is that the patient load of doctors is reduced, but they remain at the hub of their patients' treatment plans and retain overall control of their patients' care.

Patients presenting with psychological problems in a primary care setting can be attended to quickly and cheaply. GPs assess their patients' overall medical, social, family, and psychological condition and decide which problems are within the competence of the psychological specialists on hand. It is said that eighty per cent of doctors' time is taken up by twenty per cent of patients whose needs might not be purely medical. Many of these people are drawn to their doctors for reasons of dependency, loneliness, fear, isolation, or apathy, and although they might not overtly reveal the underlying problem, it can be recognised and brought to the attention of a counsellor, who might be able to shed light on the patients' use of illnesses to communicate inner psychological needs.

In the past five years, however, government funding to set up specialist clinics has been reduced, because the health authorities consider that some services are not strictly medical, but rather expensive ways of ridding GPs of their neurotic and demanding patients. The result has been a more disciplined consideration of referrals to all ancillary services in the practice, including counselling. Critical studies have been undertaken recently to assess the contribution counsellors have made to patient health. As a consequence of this research, counselling has had to redefine itself more precisely and make a case for itself as a vital adjunct to medical services in the relief of pain, stress, and a variety of physical symptoms. Psychological needs alone are no longer considered sufficiently pressing to justify the allocation of resources. Grants for new specialist clinics within primary care are drying up. After a decade of expanding services, we can now expect that some will be withdrawn or centralised once more. Many GPs now protest that it is impossible to cover everything, and, given the choice, they would prefer to attend to problems that are strictly medical. Others insist on having a counselling service in their surgeries, validating their commitment to a holistic approach to patient care. The fragile political and economic climate means that the future of counselling in primary care is a key professional issue and might depend on its ability to demonstrate its worth.

Communication

Current changes in primary care demand wide consultation and communication between professions at both national and local level. Although research has highlighted the need for counselling to hone its methods and increase its effectiveness, GPs seem satisfied with the status quo, especially where "heart-sink" patients are concerned. The following example shows what can be achieved by sensitive and honest discussion about a difficult case. Here communication facilitated a radical shift in established patterns of relating to difficult patients.

Case example: dynamics of practice meetings

At a practice meeting attended by two GP partners, a trainee GP, and three counsellors, a GP and the trainee agree to present one of their "heart-sink" cases for discussion: two children aged five and seven have presented with their parents at the surgery on numerous occasions with dyslexia, compounded by a range of behavioural problems, such as uncontrollable temper tantrums, excessive clinging to the mother, battering and stabbing each other. Strangely, the children are regarded as well behaved at school and get on with their work. The father has been seen once by the counsellor, to whom he spoke about the difficulty of controlling his two children. He said his wife had left the family on several occasions, giving no indication of when she might return, if at all. During these absences, she stayed with her mother, who suffers from Huntington's disease and dementia. The trainee GP explains to the meeting that Huntington's is a genetic disease: females have a fifty per cent chance of developing the disease if their mothers have had it. The onset occurs in middle age, and once it establishes itself the victim dies within ten to twenty years. There is no medical cure. The view among the GPs is that Huntington's disease and its associated dementia are difficult and intractable and best "exported" from the surgery as soon as possible.

An awkward silence follows and one of the counsellors then suggests that a review of models of work might be necessary and that the counsellors in the practice might contribute to this review. Current models of work seem to be based on the principle of extrusion rather than containment, especially in the case of patients whose problems do not fit neat medical categories. One GP partner is excited by the possibility of extending medical care by developing new ways of looking at patients. Much to everyone's surprise, this GP says that her association with the counsellors in the practice over the previous six years has radically altered her way of thinking about medicine: "Life has never been the same since the counsellor discussed case X with me." She recalls that during the early years of her medical practice, she had been fired with enthusiasm to treat and cure patients. Seven years later, she had become disillusioned and pessimistic with many of the medical aspects of her practice, but, over the past few years, she has recovered her sense of mission, acquired greater wisdom and patience, and realises that patients will not always recover their health as a result of her interventions.

The meeting discusses the idea of containment and the important role it can play in primary care, since patients such as the family described will always return to the surgery. It is noted that the family has not kept its appointments at the family therapy clinic. Parallels are drawn with other "heart-sink" families, for whom strenuous efforts have been made to obtain specialist help, all of which have come to nothing because the families have sabotaged the arrangements. The patients appear to be saying that they perceive the surgery as their main source of help, and they want their doctors to be available to talk to them about incurable, life-threatening problems.

All present are buoyed up by this meeting and agree to have regular discussions about individual patients and families, as well as to address a variety of other specific problems, such as alcoholism among women patients, of whom the practice has a large number.

This staff meeting felt like a turning point in the life of the practice. It provided an opportunity for the team to discuss a difficult problem. Attitudes towards patient care and staff relationships seemed to be changing. In spite of the everyday pressures of general practice, there was a real willingness to rethink some of the traditional and stereotypical ways of relating to patients. The idea gaining ground was that teamwork could actually be a valuable adjunct to traditional ways of working with patients. Those with seemingly impossible problems would no longer need to be kept at arm's length. The GPs would be more aware of the true nature of their patients' anxieties and could provide emotional help at source. They need not feel trapped by the purely scientific limitations of their role. Instead, it would be possible to extend the range of personal skills in the surgery by reassessing the nature of illness and understanding the hidden communications that pass between patients and their helpers. Where problems were potentially overwhelming, greater consideration would be given to the way in which responsibilities were shared among doctors and counsellors. The team, rather than the individual doctor, would temporarily share the responsibility, delegating one or two of its members to assess a family and report back to the group with their findings. Releasing the GP from the full weight of decision making and solution finding would have enormous benefits for patients and staff alike.

One result of this meeting was that the doctors and counsellors came to view each other with respect. This led to a reappraisal of the services offered by the surgery, without major resource implications. GP job satisfaction would be likely to improve under these conditions and cost savings would follow as an indirect result of patients feeling better understood. Unnecessary referrals to specialists, so common with multi-problem families, could be avoided.

Employment and accountability

The changing culture of primary care and increasing specialisation at local health centres has had an impact on patterns of employment. Three main methods of employment are as follows:

- direct employment by fund-holding GPs;
- secondment from the local NHS Trust, usually from departments of psychology or psychiatry, in which lines of accountability can run two ways:
  - to the GP for the standard of service they provide;
  - to their own managers back at the hospital, who aim to provide the highest standard of psychological services to the community;
- semi-private practice, where counsellors are employed partly by the practice, but spend time after hours in the surgery seeing surgery patients in a private capacity, usually for a reduced fee.

In all cases, responsibility for patient care lies with the doctor and, therefore, accountability should be to the doctor. Whatever the employment arrangements are, it is important to establish lines of accountability so that it is clear who is responsible for what if things go wrong. Professional accountability also lies with the counsellor's profession, which is responsible for ensuring the ongoing professional development of its members and has established procedures for handling ethical problems. The patient, the practitioner, and the employer expect the counselling on offer to be based on the secure foundations of rigorous training and high standards. The counsellor in primary care might be part of an integrated mental health team, but in the primary care setting it is the GP who bears clinical and legal responsibility for every aspect of patient care taking place in health centre premises. It is the GP who is answerable to any charge of mal-practice or other complaints, since the GP is the purchaser of the coun-sellor's services, not the patient. Assessing, selecting, and referring, monitoring and, in particular, evaluating effectiveness all fall within the GP's orbit. Employment contracts have a direct influence on the professional relationship between doctor and counsellor and, unless both sides are clear about the nature of their professional objectives, each is likely to construe the other's tasks differently. To complicate matters further, as soon as a patient enters the picture, a three-way relationship emerges, bringing with it all the inherent complications of triangular relationships. These need to be considered very carefully and require ongoing discussion and consultation in order that the professionals involved remain on-task in the care of their patients.

Group dynamics

Teamwork and the dynamics of teamwork constitute two overlapping key factors in primary care. Counsellors have a psychodynamic pers-pective of their patients, and, in order to work effectively as team members, they also need to bear in mind that groups and teams have dynamics operating within and between them. Counsellors and GPs bring different characteristics to the workplace and these affect the dynamics that develop in the primary care team. Group dynamics invariably centre on issues of power and control, rivalry and compe-tition, who has more and who has less. Possessiveness of the patient could play a part, no matter how committed teams might be in theory to joint working arrangements. These feelings can seriously undermine the efficiency of all groups, not least the primary care team. The corrosive influence of these dynamics can be averted through open and frank team discussions, and by the presence of strong leaders whose clear vision of the purpose of the team can inspire others. In reality, this ideal is seldom met. GPs and counsellors like to get on with their work unimpeded by extraneous considerations. Administration, management, and leadership roles, therefore, might be regarded as limiting their direct care of patients. Consequently, one dynamic affecting the primary care team is avoidance of leadership and management by doctors and counsellors alike. These roles are given to others, for example, practice managers, who could lack the authority to fulfil their roles adequately. In group practices, doctors cannot avoid the issue of leadership. One of them will have to be appointed senior partner, even if on a rotating basis, to oversee the policies and practices of the surgery as a whole, including the integration of counselling into the general provision of services for patients.

Gender

It is more common for GPs to be male and for counsellors to be female. In the main, this alliance can be described as a kind of "marriage" that finds its reflection in the dominant male–submissive female stereotype. Primary care structures and the nature of the employment relationship lend themselves to this kind of male–female split, but might not always bring with it all the negative associations that this division implies. It might well be necessary for the GP to process the patient rather more quickly than the counsellor, who works gradually and developmentally. This division generally works successfully for all three parties involved. However, it is open to that stereotypical pitfall of the controlling male doctor and the accommodating female counsellor. Some responsibility for establishing and sustaining these polarities must lie with socialisation processes inherent in their respective professional training backgrounds.

Training

Doctors are graduates with at least six years of undergraduate clinical, hospital-based training. Counsellors might emerge after far shorter training programmes. They come from a variety of professional back-grounds, and, for many, counselling is their second or third career. Their training is heavily theory-based, with the clinical component rarely extending beyond six hours per week. Unlike doctors, whose medical training emphasises diagnosis, rapid decision-making, responsibility for decisions, and active behaviour in the treatment process, counsellors wait for their patients to reach decisions at their own pace. They are less concerned with diagnosis and more interested in process and the evolution of the patient and the patient–counsellor relationship. Such differences in approach and attitude, learnt during training, have a significant influence on team dynamics.

Time

It is not uncommon to hear doctors and counsellors complaining about each other's use of time. Doctors can become exasperated at ways counsellors apply time. They fail to comprehend why such long lead times for patient appointments are necessary, or to see the point of repeated visits. Doctors often regard this as indulgence. They might not understand why counsellors insist on their appointments lasting fifty minutes when theirs last, on average, less than ten.

Split transference

Transference is rife in primary care settings, and GPs and counsellors can be attributed the roles of "good carer" and "bad carer". Patients might play one off against the other to allay feelings of intolerable ambivalence towards their doctors; or they might lay all negative feelings at the feet of their counsellors and discuss them critically behind their backs. Counsellors would prefer their patients to talk to *them* about any feelings they might have regarding the counsel-ling or the counsellor, and they do not understand why patients might prefer to talk instead to their doctors. Counsellors need to understand the "split transference" that goes on in general practice and the primitive parental transferences that patients have with their doctors.

External referrals

Counsellors have different arrangements for referring patients to outside sources of help. In some cases, they make all the necessary arrangements; in others, GPs prefer to make the decisions. Where this happens, counsellors might feel marginalised, because the GPs retain a deciding role and their decisions might be based on financial or other grounds. Counsellors' sense of identity and professional worth can be safeguarded and strengthened by having discussions and reaching an agreement on the parameters of authority for decision making.

Leadership and authority

The GP

GPs exercise leadership by drafting clear guidelines, job descriptions, and personal specifications for the counsellors, and by becoming directly involved in the employment selection procedures. The fact that they have the right to hire and fire presupposes that GPs are moderately familiar with professional training of counsellors, ongoing supervision of its practitioners, BAC qualification requirements, codes of practice, codes of ethics, and the machinery to deal with breach of ethics.

The counsellor

Counsellors also need to assume appropriate leadership responsibility. They are able to draw on their professional identity acquired during training and on their status as members of a professional body, reinforced by their employment or secondment contracts. Counsellors usually exercise authority by attending to their patients' emotional and psychological needs, whatever obstacles there might be. In terms of practical hurdles, funding appropriate treatment for patients might require assertive advocacy by the counsellor. It is worth remembering that an important facet of counsellors' professional discipline is the understanding and clinical usage of their own emotions and feelings.

Case example: coping with anger

A GP has taken much trouble to arrange an appointment for a patient at a specialist clinic. The GP is annoyed by the patient's failure to keep that appointment and she is reluctant to make another referral. The counsellor argues that because a child is involved, one more referral should be attempted. The GP is relieved that her irritation with the patient has abated and she makes a second referral.

Counsellors' authority as professionals means that they are answerable for their actions and omissions. Although overall legal responsibility for patient care rests with the employing GP, professional responsibility cannot ever be abdicated. Counsellors are expected to share fully in the deliberations and decisions of their teams, and to be responsible for the contributions they make to the team and for their work with patients. As responsible professionals, they monitor and evaluate their work with a view to improving standards and effectiveness. Authority and accountability are two key issues for counsellors. They are accountable to doctors in the same way that any service provider is to a purchaser, but they are also accountable to their own sense of professionalism, to their profession of counselling, and they must be dedicated to upholding standards and improving performance.

Summary

Several key professional issues have emerged out of the changing professional culture of primary care in the mid 1990s. Issues of confidentiality, communication, and employment characterise the main aspects of the GP–counsellor relationship. Group dynamics, or the dynamics of teamwork, are an essential part of the practice's pool of skills. Supervision/consultation is vital in dealing with problems that can potentially impede effective work. In this litigious age, which has seen medicine redefined as business labouring under financial pressures, group dynamics have become more complicated than ever. These problems are often exacerbated when a GP does not work well with the newly affiliated disciplines in his or her practice, or when professional relationships between the practice, the health authority, or other professional associations become fraught with tension.

CHAPTER THREE

Ethical issues for psychotherapists working in organisations*

Introduction

This chapter addresses the key ethical issues for psychotherapists who are employed by, and work in, organisations that provide psychotherapy services.

Working in organisations raises issues of how psychotherapy practitioners relate to the objectives, goals, and methods of the departments, sections, or units in which they work, and, beyond that, with the broad aims of the larger employing organisation. This chapter makes the assumption that psychotherapists will inevitably be faced with the need to balance the key organisational issues such as employer liability, allocation of resources, accountability, and authority, and the ethical demands imposed on them by the psychotherapy profession in areas such as confidentiality, research and publication, disclosure, access to records, and information technology. It is often said that the relationship between psychotherapist and organisation is

*This chapter is based on: M. Sher (2003), Ethical issues for psychotherapists working in organisations. In: H. Solomon & M. Twyman (Eds.), *Ethics in Contemporary Psychotherapy Practice* (pp. 137–151): © Free Association Books, London. Material reprinted with permission.

defined as one of a conflict of interests, rather than a forum in which a number of different interests, values, and practices may be debated and reconciled by mutual agreement. Such agreements as emerge out of these debates are likely to stand a better chance of working in the interests of everyone involved—patients,[1] professionals, and organisations—because the agreements will be supported by systems with converging interests.

It is not an uncommon view that the practice of psychotherapy in organisations and in the private sector is so different in character as to make them unrecognisable from one another. The research that went into the writing of this chapter reveals a different picture in terms of ethical requirements and codes of practice. Surprisingly, the ethical issues, debates, and final agreements are identical for psychotherapy practised in organisations and in private practice.

Naturally, there are differences in context, method, and task of psychotherapy practice, but all the essentials of the ethical position are the same: confidentiality is a core issue, which forms a central pillar in the psychotherapist's duty of care towards the patient, responsibility towards children at risk override all other considerations, and no psychotherapist, medical or non-medical, can claim protection in a Court of Law under the principle of privileged communication.

Ethical frameworks

It is a truism that all professional relationships are predicated upon differential power positions between the professional and the user. Moreover, this applies to the relationship between user and the organisation through which the service is provided and is complicated by the fact of there being three parties to the transaction. However, that is also the case in private practice, where the practitioner's professional organisation/association is never far from both parties' minds. The way the power relationships are played out lies in the tension between the patient's need for help and care and the need for both of them for a form of protection against exploitation. The patient approaches, or is referred to, the professional or the professional's organisation in order to seek the benefits of specialist knowledge and skills in a particular area of human functioning in which the patient believes themselves to be deficient. The patient hopes that, as a consequence of the intervention by the professional, their situation will improve. A partic-ular characterisation of the professional, acquired through their social-isation as they pass through training programmes over many years, is that they will develop solid commitments to work for the benefit of their patients and that they will not abuse the power that their greater knowledge and skill bestows upon them. Differentials of power in the psychotherapy situation are self-evident in so far as patients appearing before psychotherapists are usually very troubled, fearful, vulnerable, and dependent. They are likely to have experienced rejection, abuse, and victimisation. Psychotherapists will be committed to an ethical framework that holds the interests of the patient paramount, that patients will not be exploited, financially or sexually, that psycho-therapists will observe the principles of confidentiality, will act com-petently, and ensure the maintenance of their competence through continued professional development.

But how do these ethical principles stand up in practice when there is a tension between professional practitioners and their employ-ing organisations? In cases where there is a conflict of interest, how does it affect the psychotherapist's commitment towards the individ-ual patient? Where the psychotherapist is not engaged directly by the patient, for example, when the psychotherapist is employed by an organisation such as the health service, the prison service, education department of local government, or voluntary organisation, the psychotherapist's duty of care would normally be orientated towards both the patient and towards the employer, but their ethical duties would be more strongly biased towards the patient. Where psycho-therapists work for an organisation, it is incumbent upon them to explain very carefully to the patient the nature of the three-way rela-tionship between patient, psychotherapist, and organisation.

Psychotherapists working in organisations are likely to be subject to the demands and constraints of a number of codes of ethics. The first is the ethical framework of their psychotherapy training organi-sations. The second is the framework of their core profession. The third is the framework of their employing organisation, which is usually within the public sector but could also be in the voluntary sector. In certain situations, there could be a degree of conflict between these different ethical frameworks. It is the purpose of this chapter to outline these possible conflicts of interests and to describe how psychotherapists and organisations alike deal with them.

Psychotherapists working in hospitals will have a duty to the Chief Executive of the Trust to ensure the best and most effective use of public resources. However, as psychotherapists, they will have an ethical duty to care for their patients: for example, to seek investigations and services provided by other specialists and organisations if considered necessary. At what point does the psychotherapist make a decision between a duty of care to the patient and duty not to expend resources unnecessarily? A psychotherapist has a duty of confidentiality to the patient regarding the material that emerges during the psychotherapy work, but others in the Trust might have other duties in respect of the patient, for example, to prevent the spread of infectious diseases, protect children, or increase the clean-up rate of crimes. These issues raise ethical controversies between different care organisations and between different disciplines practising psychotherapy, for example, social workers, psychologists, prison officers, nurses, and doctors.

Confidentiality

From their first days as psychotherapy trainees, psychotherapists are educated to the strong injunctions regarding confidentiality. This part of the ethical code is drummed into trainees as the most important ethical foundation of the psychotherapy enterprise. On the other hand, psychotherapists, but especially trainees, need to talk to others (supervisors, colleagues and other professionals), all for good professional reasons. Supervision is an elemental part of training and development; others might simply need to talk about what is bothering them after a difficult session. Psychotherapists will tell their patients at the beginning of psychotherapy what the limits of confidentiality are. The statement will include that the work is confidential to the organisation. It will be explained that confidentiality is not absolute and there might be times and situations where others might have a right to know what happens in the psychotherapy treatment. For example, letters might need to be written to patients' GPs or psychiatrists informing them if a crisis is looming.

Patients might be under the care of other services, in particular, the primary care services and possibly psychiatric services. Patients would be asked for permission to contact these if necessary. In all these eventualities, the important principle on confidentiality requires patients to be told about these links and their contents and for patients to provide written permission for when and if communication with these services becomes necessary.

Psychotherapists might be asked by patients or by others to provide letters in cases involving insurance claims, divorce, or custody of children. In general, psychotherapists will avoid writing letters. Instead, they will try to understand with the patient why they are being drawn into the patient's life in this way.

There are pressures on the concept of confidentiality that arise from working in organisations and in working with specific age groups, such as adolescents and children. Even in organisations that do not provide psychotherapy directly to children, there will be obligations on psychotherapists if there are risks of harm to minors. This situation may conflict with the psychotherapist's duty of care to patients. For example, if a paedophile tells his therapist about abusing a child who is not located in the psychotherapy system, the therapist would have a duty to inform someone. That duty may be viewed differently by the different disciplines. The Children's Act of 1989 states that everybody has a duty of care to children and this duty of care overrides their duty of care to their patients. This principle operates in any setting where the psychotherapy takes place, even if the minor might not be located there. This is a serious issue in working with paedophiles, because they could be reluctant to talk in their therapy if they believe that the therapist's overriding duty of care to children might make them have to act. The psychotherapist working with paedophiles has a conflict regarding their individual patient as a perpetrator of terrible things, and regarding the same individual as a victim of terrible things. The way this is understood leads to a swing between a collusive empathy, which can obscure the individual patient, on the one hand, and a sadistic countertransference, on the other. The hope is that by exploring the patient's past experiences as a victim, it might enable him to be aware of the damage that he had done to his victim. So, in the way that patients were damaged as victims, by getting an emotional grasp of the effect their victimhood had on them, they might have some emotional grasp of the effects that they have had on their own victims. The obligation to act on hearing of abuse to minors might prevent this important working through of these dynamics. The aim of psychotherapy is, after all, to engage with the patient's internal conflicts in order to prevent future acting out.

Containing the conflicts of ethics that the duty of care to minors at risk imposes upon the psychotherapist working with a paedophile adds to the burden of the therapeutic task. But the very containing of conflicts might actually constitute the psychotherapy task.

Working in a "safe" environment is a *sine qua non* for psychotherapy practice, safe, here, meaning to have as few impingements from the outside world as possible, including freedom from anxiety of infringing both the law and the psychotherapist's ethical codes. Sadistic countertransference enactments that involve telling how horrible the patient's crimes are and how dangerous they are themselves are unethical and represent a recapitulation of the abuse that the patient had experienced in his earlier life. On the other hand, it is equally unethical to collude with paedophiles who are in the process of trying to seduce the psychotherapist. The contract between patient and psychotherapist is that they are engaged in a process based on the understanding of the meaning of seduction and punishment through the use of interpretation. The expectation is that others are not to be involved.

There are debates within organisations providing psychotherapy about the nature of interactions between patient and psychotherapist. Organisations might have anxieties about the psychotherapy community within it. For example, some might want to see the gradual dismantlement of confidentiality within the psychotherapy setting in the organisation. The Human Rights Act (1998) has drafted into it the notion of the statutory requirement to disclose risk, rather than a statutory requirement to consider whether risk should be disclosed, so that it would be a breach of the law not to disclose any risks. The difference between a general organisational psychotherapy provision and the psychotherapy encounter itself is that what is said in an organisation is a matter of public record, because it is legally defined as a public place, so, by this definition, psychotherapy records are public documents. Disclosures made in organisations are available to others, and there is no boundary, as there is in a psychotherapist–patient relationship. In the work with paedophiles, this principle can be circumvented by telling the patient to be vague about "time, place, or person" in relation to previous crimes on the grounds that the police are not interested in pursuing investigations where they do not have specific information on "time, place, or person". Psychotherapy, therefore, whether in private practice or in organisations, provides a transitional space in which people can talk about current or previous offences that have not been cleared up or they have not been prosecuted for. If patients talk about such cases, but do not mention "time, place, or person", the matter need not be pursued. If patients do mention "time, person and place", psychotherapists should encourage them to disclose this to the authorities and so wipe the slate clean. The hope is that, as a result of the therapeutic work, the patient would come to a position where they themselves would want to wipe the slate clean.

In many organisations providing psychotherapy services, the members of staff are drawn from different disciplines while still retaining some of the statutory responsibilities of those disciplines. This could mean that social workers, nurses, or prison officers acting as psychotherapists might be obliged to disclose to the police things that they hear, but others, such as doctors or psychotherapists, are not obliged. This points to differences in ethical codes between the disciplines and organisations.

The basic ethical implication is that organisations are responsible for setting up the psychotherapeutic settings, where people are meant to feel free and be encouraged to disclose their free associations. In the process of these associations, they could disclose things that are not in their interest to disclose. But, with some types of patient, crimes might have been committed, a body might be buried somewhere, and there is no closure for grieving relatives. There is a difference in magnitude in terms of the severity of undisclosed risk and the crime clean-up rate.

Organisations create structures for therapeutic work to take place in the safest possible way. Inevitably, questions about boundaries and ethical issues have to be resolved, especially in relation to records and confidentiality, and the relationship between the statutory responsibilities of different disciplines. Different disciplines might be bound by different ethical codes and the organisation would somehow have to work towards resolving them, although, in some situations, the different professional ethical codes might have advantages. Since achieving one fully integrated ethical system is difficult, managers and professional staff of psychotherapy services have to work at these issues all the time, in order to minimise conflicts and tensions. Resolution of those issues emerges through multi-disciplinary and multi-agency debate, and, in a broader context, in the debate with government, leading to a consensus view as to what is needed in terms of ethical codes. However, sharp differences of opinion on confidentiality are emerging. The UK government has foreseen the possibility that the confidentiality issue, as it pertains in the criminal justice system, might be extended across the National Health Service and other care professions (Royal College of Psychiatrists, 2000; Scoggins, Litton, & Palmer, 1998). The professions object to this, and the government is currently rethinking the situation, but the new Mental Health Act might, nevertheless, contain the provision of statutory disclosure that pertains at the present time. Psychotherapists operate in a statutory disclosure environment because policymakers believe that there is a need in the public domain for care professions to have a statutory duty to disclose risk. The point that psychotherapists are seeking to impress upon policymakers is that confidentiality is absolutely essential in order to facilitate free association disclosures, even if they reveal things that people have not been committed for, for example, an unsolved crime. Because the therapeutic discourse takes place in an organisation that might be bound to disclose, the issue of confidentiality affects the work considerably.

Although confidentiality forms an important basis of professional psychotherapy practice, it is not absolute, because everyone is subject to the law. The law requires all professions to release information in certain circumstances. Psychotherapists need to recognise that they are never going to get full protection for psychotherapy information. We can argue that we do not need that protection. But psychotherapists need to make sure that psychotherapy information is recognised by government departments as something to which they do not have a right of access. It is important that policy and lawmakers understand that if they undermine the principle of psychotherapy confidentiality, the result will be a destruction of healthcare generally. Psychotherapists have a duty, not only to their patients directly, but in the institutional setting within which they are working, to look at the way information is handled. This could be the way physical records are held and computers are organised, but also the way in which the organisations, whether hospitals, prisons, or voluntary organisations, respond to queries and check their methods and systems to make sure that there is no unnecessary sharing of information.

Psychotherapists must be pragmatic. Current thinking is that patients and their carers and helpers should be the ones who decide who else should share their information. There needs to be a partnership between patients and psychotherapists regarding decisions on patient care. The view of psychotherapists has always been that there should be full and frank discussions on every aspect of disclosure when other parties have requested information, for whatever reason.

Supervision

All organisations have systems of supervision in place for psychotherapists. Reasons for supervision often emphasise the deepening of the supervisee's insight and awareness of the therapeutic process. But the management aspects of supervision of psychotherapists in both statutory and voluntary organisations are often overlooked. Supervisors are entrusted with the dual task of promoting the individual development of the psychotherapy trainee and ensuring that policies, ethical standards, values, and practices of the organisation are being followed. Supervisors might carry development roles, but they also work within certain authority structures.

Supervision in organisations has a different definition attaching to it than the kind of supervision that is normally part of psychotherapy training and development. In organisations, supervision is normally associated with seniority and management control over juniors. Distinctions are also made between supervision and consultation that is based on peer and collegial relationships.

In training organisations and private practice, supervision is regarded as absolutely essential. These organisations will consider the continuation of supervision as part of professional development and, therefore, an important ethical principle. These organisations will require weekly supervision for all their trainees and less frequent supervision for qualified psychotherapists. Psychotherapy trainees seeing training patients might have two separate individual supervisors weekly. Supervision is regarded as a discipline in its own right, and these organisations will have training for supervisors, not something that any psychotherapist can do. Supervisors are expected to take responsibility for the conduct and management of the cases they are supervising as well as developing the thinking part of psychotherapy theory and practice. Supervision has a firm authority base in training, seniority, skill, wisdom, and managerial responsibility. If necessary, supervisors can instruct trainees and can make recommendations to pass or fail them. In this way, they play a part in the management of the training organisation. The supervisors are accountable to management of the organisation and are expected to voice their concerns, if they have any, about trainee psychotherapists.

In psychotherapy carried out in organisations, the nature of supervision carries two frames. One is supervision in order to help the practitioner do better clinical practice, and the other is to ensure that junior personnel are held within a framework of quality control. Senior psychotherapists within a clear hierarchical structure will do the supervising of junior personnel. Case discussion among psychotherapists of equal seniority would be called consultation, because they would be peers and one would not have authority over the other.

Codes of practice for different disciplines

Codes of practice or codes of conduct are elaborations on codes of ethics. These are discussed in the context of working in organisations where conflicts or differences in codes of practice for psychotherapists might be present. Psychotherapists diagnosing and/or treating patients do so on the understanding that they are acting on behalf of the organisation providing the service. Consequently, they are bound by the codes of ethics and practices of the organisation on whose behalf they are working with their patients. In some organisations, notably voluntary psychotherapy organisations, distinctions between the disciplines are removed or regarded as irrelevant, and they work under the broad heading of psychotherapist. They do not perform any disciplinary function and, as such, they would all be bound by an organisation's unitary code of ethics. In others, different disciplines might have different duties of care, as between, say, those that exist for forensic psychologists and psychotherapists. These two disciplines contain the kernel of the whole debate between the interests of the individual and the interests of third parties. In some cases, the organisation might work under civil service ethical codes and codes of conduct. These codes of conduct could conflict with the psychotherapy codes of conduct that demand free speech. Free speech is a *sine qua non* of psychotherapy. Psychotherapists attempt to speak the truth and the truth of what is in mind at a particular time. However, in some organisational contexts, it might be prudent not to say what is in mind if it leads to an official complaint. In organisations where psychotherapists in training are drawn from different disciplines, there could be conflict between a psychotherapist's discipline of origin role and their psychotherapist role. If, for example, psychotherapists or patients express strong feelings in what is considered to be discriminatory, offensive, or abusive language, they could be exposed to investigation and admonishment for allowing things to take place that are psychotherapeutically normal practice. There is potential confusion for registrars, nurses, social workers, and prison officers (the latter being trained in methods of control), who, as a result of working psychotherapeutically, incorporate new attitudes and practices. But the strength of therapeutic work derives from the different codes being debated and coming together in the best interests of the patient as part of a multi-disciplinary process. For example, psychotherapeutic work in personality disorders units in high-secure healthcare settings involves people whose core profession is health—doctors, nurses, psychologists—and prison officers who are primarily concerned with custody. These professions work in new clinical situations where personality disordered people are able to manipulate them. Looking at it positively, these professionals can make a contribution from a very structured custodial point of view. They are actually able to maintain the boundaries very effectively and keep clear perspectives of the boundaries.

Authority and accountability

Authority structures and dynamics are always present in organisations, and members of organisations are obliged to resolve them in order to produce appropriate working conditions. Psychotherapists, too, have to address the ubiquitous tension in authority relationships that occur between the employer's legal liability and the psychotherapist's professional ethical requirements.

Some organisations, especially voluntary ones, attempt to deal with the therapeutic and authority functions by separating supervision and management roles, believing that in this way they can avoid confusion. The supervisor has a separate role, which, in theory, frees them to concentrate on dynamic clinical issues alone. From the perspective of this role, supervisors avoid potential conflict between the trainee's training requirement and what might be in the patient's best interests. Some voluntary organisations might depend in part upon fees paid by patients. Indeed, their charitable status requires them to offer treatment in return for low fees. But, as they struggle to meet their financial obligations, organisations might ponder how long they should go on treating someone who is paying a very low fee. Can the organisation afford to let the patient stay in treatment for years, which might be what the psychotherapist says they need? The length and frequency of treatment is left to the professional judgement of the supervisor and trainee psychotherapist, but there is a question as to whether the organisation can support their decision. There is usually tension over whether training requirements and clinical needs will dovetail sufficiently. The organisation's ethical obligation is not to take on more patients than it can deal with, but it often does so if patients are willing to remain as long-term treatment cases for its trainees.

Statutory organisations

The issue of legal liability arises because statutory organisations are part of the systems that are legally defined and determined. In some psychotherapy services, the doctors might be employed by a Trust, the psychologist by another authority, and the social workers or probation officer by yet another. All of them might provide services to the one patient and each claims the right to make decisions. Other organisations might be structured differently, where, for instance, the staff are all employed by the same service. In such cases, there would be a unified structure in the management line, which might, nevertheless, provide a diversity of conduct and codes. In the case of a medical psychotherapist employed in a non-medical setting, or in a medical, but non-psychotherapy setting, the clinical governance of the doctors would need validation by a doctor who might not be available within that structure. There could be a problem in operating with diverse ethical codes that would not be reflected in the different accountability structures. Medical psychotherapists in those cases would be accountable to their chief executives and also be accountable to other senior doctors in another service who are not psychotherapists who have to validate the work of a medical psychotherapist. This leads to a complicated picture of organisational authority and accountability.

Ethical implications of research and publication in organisations

Organisations have a duty to evaluate performance and to seek more effective methods of delivering goods and services. Evaluation involves researching the efficacy of treatments, which, in turn, involves patients directly or indirectly. Patients' records and other methods might be used. All evaluation methods involve sensitive matters around consent, confidentiality, and the potential for identification, archiving, and publication. In most psychotherapy training organisations, evaluation of the performance of individual therapists is made through supervision reports, and evaluation of the organisation as a whole is by means of auditing every few years.

There are three areas of research: audit, empirical research, and descriptive research. Descriptive research relies on the use of clinical material. This normally requires the written permission of the patient, who should be shown the written material and give a signed release that he is in agreement with it. It is the duty of all organisations that undertake research to ensure that patients fully understand what is being done.

Empirical research is governed by hospital ethics committees, which are locally structured committees protecting patient rights. The ethical standards for research and consent are set out by hospital ethical committees.

Audit activities do not give rise to major ethical issues. The variety of different audit structures ensures anonymity. Gathering pre- and post-treatment data on a variety of psychological diseases based on large numbers of cases is not regarded as having ethical dimensions because it relies on pooled, collective data and is not individual data. The ethical implication of audit within the public services generally has not been raised.

Disclosure and "psychotherapist privilege"

There is an overlap between the issues of disclosure, "privileged" communication, and confidentiality. Disclosure and psychotherapists' "privilege" are important issues for psychotherapists working in organisations, especially in their dealings with other statutory bodies, such as the courts, social services departments, the National Health

Service, education departments, etc. The extent and limits of "privilege" are different for different organisations and professions.

Legally, psychotherapists do not enjoy "privileged" communication. Psychotherapists may be approached by patients' solicitors seeking reports and asking for letters and clinical notes. Psychotherapists should not write anything to anybody without first seeking permission from the patient. Sometimes, the patient might want the psychotherapist to write a report and this might cause difficulties to arise. Even when the patient asks the psychotherapist to write, minimal information should be given. Psychotherapists know, of course, that if they refuse to disclose they can be subpoenaed, and would be subject to the same penalties as anybody else. Bollas and Sundelson (1995) are worried that psychotherapists might be obliged to report on all manner of clinical details that would gradually and ultimately erode the principle of confidentiality on which all psychotherapy work is based.

"Privilege" for all psychotherapists might be deemed desirable, but it could also backfire. The patient, knowing that the psychotherapist would not disclose, could talk endlessly about a deviant situation, and continue acting out sadistic fantasies, say, towards a minor, behaving similarly in the transference towards the therapist, and never feeling inclined to stop. In such a situation, the psychotherapist and patient, instead of existing in a safe environment, could become tied up in a merciless trap without end. "Privilege" and trust could be seen as two sides of the same coin. Therefore, issues like "privilege" and confidentiality always have to be qualified; neither is absolute. Psychotherapists, like all other professionals, except legal representatives, do not have "privilege". However, health information in the UK is regarded as being "special", not "ordinary". Courts do not generally regard health information as being privileged, but it is set aside as "special" because of its sensitivity. All health information is regarded as having special status, but certain categories are particularly sensitive: for example, mental health. Courts will be sympathetic towards psychotherapists who seek private audience with a judge to explain the sensitive nature of psychotherapy material and are willing to divulge it privately to a judge (Supreme Court of the United States, 1996; The British Psychological Society, 1993; The Master of the Rolls, 1996).

Access to records

There is often uncertainty regarding the ownership of psychotherapy notes. These are generally regarded as the property of the employing authority. The conditions of their storage, protection, and use will have implications for psychotherapists. There is the question of what notes: the brief notes that are placed in the formal file? Detailed notes of each session that are usually used for supervision purposes? Or *aides-de-memoir* that psychotherapists sometimes rely on to refresh their memories of the immediate past sessions and which are not usually kept in the formal case note files? In the current position where patients have rights of access to their records, which notes would they have access to? All categories of notes? Or only the formal records?

Organisations (and private practitioners, too) have strict rules about the storage and protection of records, how they may be used, where they may be taken, and who may access them. These rules are firmly laid down. Patients are recognised as having the right of access to their records. But if patients want to see their records, it is expected that the therapist will discuss the reasons widely with the patient and explore with them what it is they want to achieve by seeing their records.

Organisations might have two or three sets of files. First, there might be a kind of "everything" file, which has everything in it concerning the individual's crossing-into-the-institution process. A second file might contain only treatment details. Normally, there is a very tight confidentiality barrier between the two sets of records and the rest of the organisation. Bizarre situations can emerge to the detriment of the individual's overall care if certain information is not allowed to be shared, just as there might be serious infringements of rights if certain information is shared. The arrangement of multiple files is a way of dealing with splits in organisations. Some information can be shared with others on a need-to-know basis, and some not. In some cases, a third record might be kept, which is a therapy record that is for the private use of the psychotherapist. But the different levels of confidentiality and access should be made explicit—what the contents of the files are, their use, and who can access them. The "everything" file is a public record that other professions can access. The treatment file would be accessible by members of the multi-disciplinary team only. Patients would have access to all records. Ownership of the records is usually in the hands of the organisation, and, therefore, the organisation and the individual psychotherapists have individual and collective responsibility to ensure their safekeeping under lock and key.

In the past, the argument ran that patient's records were owned by the Secretary of State. It is now agreed that ownership of the paper is irrelevant, but what matters is who controls them on a daily basis. Records departments or administrators and receptionists are the agents, but it is effectively the psychotherapist and patient who are the people who should control the records. Release of information from the notes should only be done with the patient's consent, except on rare occasions where the law requires the release. Patients should have access to their records, within the one caveat that they do not have rights to information concerning other patients that might be in their notes. Requesting to see a patient's notes is usually a matter of helping the patient to understand what is in the notes.

Consent and coercion in psychotherapy treatment

A chapter on psychotherapy and organisations needs to include situations where patients do not enter treatment voluntarily, but where the psychotherapy treatment is part of a court order or prison sentence. Patients never receive treatment involuntarily. They might be imprisoned involuntarily, but their treatment is entirely voluntary and they can discharge themselves from treatment at any stage. The only compulsory treatment that might be considered is when an individual has a psychotic breakdown and is in need of psychiatric treatment. If they wish to carry on psychotherapy treatment, but are judged too ill to continue with the treatment, they will be compulsorily discharged and moved to another place where they can receive the appropriate psychiatric treatment. Patients may be discharged from psychotherapy treatment compulsorily for a transgression of the law, but usually patients have two or three chances before being discharged.

Where psychotherapy treatment facilities exist within a framework of compulsory detention as, say, in a goal, there will inevitably be a debate about whether patients should ever be compulsorily discharged from treatment. Some will want a policy that will be part of the constitution and others will want each situation to be regarded as different and be judged on its own merits (Hale, Minne, & Zachary, 2000). There is a dialectic between an aggressive wish to have a set of rules that will follow in certain circumstances, for example, compulsory discharge if found positive for drugs. On the other hand, there is a case for flexibility and clinical application: for example, when someone who takes drugs acknowledges this, as they are demonstrating that they are working on the issue. But where someone is caught several times in possession of drugs, they would be much more likely to be compulsorily discharged.

The Mental Health Act has very limited authorisations, but more important is the issue with children who refuse treatment and/or are incompetent and where the court orders treatment or where the parents authorise it. In cases where children are given treatment without consent, there are grave concerns that their right to refuse treatment is being overridden. On the other hand, it is argued that the child's competence and ability to understand, and, therefore, to give consent, might be limited.

Patients might talk to their psychotherapists about their wish to die, their fears of dying, the pain, leaving their loved ones, etc. Only two medical societies at the World Medical Association are in favour of recognising that occasionally suicide could be a sane act and that suicide is not something that one should always stop. By being open and by talking through the issues helps patients. The psychotherapeutic principle is that by talking through a fear, patients might get to feel better. The psychotherapist is on the side of the patient's survival, attempting to understand with the patient those aspects of his current feelings that impel towards self-destructive acts, with the intention that this would make such enactments less likely.

The psychotherapist has to decide whether it is best to listen and explore the issues. If the psychotherapist has doubts about the patient's competence, if he is acutely depressed or chronically ill, he could consider intervening under the Mental Health Act. When someone is sane and competent and not depressed, the psychotherapist might take a different view and talk to the patient, exploring the issues around living and dying before choosing whether or not to intervene. Although psychotherapists have no greater ability to prevent suicide than other members of society, they are, nevertheless, in a more privileged position and are more likely to be faced with information about their patients' suicidal impulses.

Information technology

Organisations are continually thinking through the implications of technological innovations to ensure the protection of their patients while remaining consistent with their organisational responsibilities. They are obliged to observe the requirements of the Data Protection Act and the Human Rights Act, and there is concern that computers and the way that data is kept on computers might compromise the principles of confidentiality. But, on the whole, organisations attempt to comply with the law on IT.

IT functions can be divided into three areas: the first is the typing of reports; the second is data gathering as part of ongoing audit and evaluation work where individuals would be subject to various parameters to identify their changes and various other empirical measures; the third is the general computerisation of the records of everyone using the services. Organisations generally are obliged and are willing to be compliant with the Data Protection Act provided that the broader issue of maintaining confidentiality is assured. Information, encrypted or otherwise, has to be secure without compromising the reasons why information is kept electronically in the first place—rapid access, research, audit, and multi-disciplinary and multi-agency working. For obvious reasons, organisations rely more extensively on IT than private practice, where usual methods of record keeping might feel more secure. Voluntary and training organisations are also obliged to comply with the law on IT, and they try to limit written records to factual accounts of events: telephone conversations, attending sessions, letters written. The actual content of sessions is handwritten and is kept by practitioners for supervision purposes. Material is written in such a way as to be unidentifiable. Session reports and six-monthly progress reports of the psychotherapy is not usually computerised.

Conclusions

This chapter has attempted to address many of the ethical elements in psychotherapy practice that have relevance to psychotherapy treatment situations as they are practised in organisations. Although, at first glance, there might appear to be significant differences between traditional private practice and the more complex arrangements of psychotherapy in organisations, the result of these investigations reveals a surprising similarity between the ethical requirements in the two contexts. To be sure, organisational contexts—clinics, hospitals, prisons, etc.—are geared up to provide treatment for patients with greater degrees of pathological disturbance that is usually acted out through violence, paedophilia, and other manifestations of borderline personality structures, where the issue of detention and withdrawal of human rights, the necessity to work with multi-disciplinary and multi-agency arrangements, make for differences of degree on key questions. But irrespective of context, the main ethical issues are the same—confidentiality, protection of minors, and prevention of crime. Psychotherapy practice, in whatever context, holds that the duty of care towards the patient is paramount, and this duty includes the keeping of confidence regarding their patient's information, exercising care in the matter of communications between professionals, record keeping and protection of records, and consultation with patients on all matters concerning their treatment.

Acknowledgements

This chapter is the result of several conversations with people who are at the forefront of the debate on ethics in the work of their organisations and professions. I have learnt much from them and I appreciate their willingness to entrust me with their ideas and dilemmas, which, by definition, are in a continuing state of non-resolution. They are all committed to the development of ethical principles in working environments that are complex and difficult. They are also committed to working out the exigencies of collaborative work between professionals from different disciplines. I would like to thank the following: Robert Hale, Lesley Murdin, Vivienne Nathanson, Ginney Riley, Honor Rhodes, and Rosie Wilkinson. I also thank Julie Wilson and Mara Gorli for their good humour while typing the transcripts from difficult-to-hear tapes.

Note

1.   To avoid clumsiness in the usage of terms, this chapter shall define the user of psychotherapy services as "patient", although in some settings the term "client" is used.

PART II
GROUP RELATIONS

Splits, extrusion and integration: the impact of "potential space" for group relations and sponsoring institutions*

This chapter discusses historical sources and developmental links between group relations as a form of activity-based exploration and study and four types of sponsoring institutions that operate group relations conferences: (i) research and evaluation, (ii) clinical, (iii) educational and professional development, and (iv) spiritual. The argument will be made that (a) these four clusters of sponsoring institutions have each uniquely influenced the theory and practice of group relations, and that (b) group relations is an object and a source of ambivalence in the "political spaces" of sponsoring institutions that leads "group relations" to be sources of both creativity and anxiety.

Examples of organisations that form the clusters are:

1. Research and evaluation—the Tavistock Institute, the Scottish Institute of Human Relations;

*This chapter is based on: M. Sher (2009), Splits, extrusion and integration: the impact of "potential space' for group relations and sponsoring institutions. © *Organisational and Social Dynamics*, 9(1): 138–154. Material reprinted with permission.

2.   Clinical—the Tavistock & Portman NHS Foundation Trust, William Alanson White Institute, USA;
3.   Educational and professional development—universities and professional membership organisations that provide undergraduate and post-professional development courses in group relations, for example, Westminster University, Birkbeck College, University of London, University of the West of England, Bristol University, AISA (Australia), OFEK (Israel), AK Rice Institute (USA), Williamson Alanson White Institute (USA), GREX (San Fransisco), Rosehill Institute (Canada), ISLA, (South Africa), Group Relations Nederland, the Bulgarian Institute of Human Relations;
4.   Spiritual–faith-based organisations that offer group relations conferences as a way of exploring roles and their meaning, for example, Grubb Institute, Chelmsford Cathedral Centre for Research and Training.

What is group relations?

Gordon Lawrence (2000), writes that

> . . . [group relations] is the most potent of methodologies because it enables one to distinguish between phantasy and reality. It also enables one, among other things, to judge between truth and the lie; to come to grips between projection and introjection, transference and countertransference, which are the basic "stuff" of human relations. (p. 51)

Group relations is a method of study and training in the way people perform their roles in the groups and systems of which they are members. These can be work groups, teams, or organisations, or less formal social groups like faiths, race, and gender groups. A group may be said to be two or more people interacting to achieve a common task. Group relations theory views groups as tending to move in and out of focusing on their task and adopting a number of different defensive positions based on unarticulated group phantasy.

There are certain features of group relations work that are held in common and are probably subscribed to by most practitioners. These include working with transference and countertransference phenomena, skills in interpreting group unconscious dynamics, working within the boundaries of space and time as well as within psychological boundaries, being clear about working within role and task, working with group-as-a-whole, not individual, phenomena, and capable of generating working hypotheses about group and organisational functioning.

Group relations was the phrase coined in the late 1950s by staff working at the Tavistock Institute of Human Relations to refer to the laboratory method of studying relationships in and between groups. This laboratory method had been developed at Bethel, Maine, from 1947 by the National Training Laboratory, based on ideas of Kurt Lewin on intensive experiential learning. Lewin's group theories strongly influenced the thinking of the early Tavistock staff. This early group of Tavistock pioneers were social scientists and psychodynamically orientated psychiatrists who had been using group approaches to tackle practical wartime problems, like officer selection. They later applied their group-based experiences and approaches to post-war social reconstruction. They drew on many sources: the work of sociologists Gustave le Bon and William McDougall; psychoanalysts Sigmund Freud and Melanie Klein; and social scientists Mary Parker Follett, Elton Mayo, and Kurt Lewin.

Kurt Lewin's field theory provided a way in which the tension between the individual and the group could be studied: "the group to which an individual belongs is the ground for his perceptions, his feelings and his actions" (Lewin, 1947). Lewin considered groups to have properties that are different from their subgroups or their individual members. This finding, and the experiential workshop method of training which Lewin developed, influenced staff at the Tavistock Institute that ultimately led to the development of the first group relations conferences in the 1950s.

Melanie Klein's object relations theory was another important influence, which built upon Freud's theories, in particular, that people learn from early childhood to cope with unpleasant emotions by relying on the psychological defences of splitting and projective identification. The psychoanalyst Wilfred Bion influenced models of group work and group behaviour. In his work at the Tavistock Clinic, and later at the Tavistock Institute, he established that groups operate on two levels, the work level, where concern is for completing the task, and the level of basic assumptions that are meant to ease anxieties and avoid the painful emotions that membership of groups might evoke. Bion identifies three types of basic assumption: dependency, pairing and fight/flight. He reported his work in a series of articles for the Tavistock Institute's journal *Human Relations*, that later appeared as the book *Experiences in Groups* (Bion, 1961).

Since the first group relations conference in 1957 at the University of Leicester, there have been developments in group relations by Ken Rice, Isobel Menzies Lyth, Harold Bridger, Pierre Turquet, Robert Gosling, Eric Miller, Mary Barker, and Gordon Lawrence. In addition to the contributions made by these pioneers, there have been quieter, but significant, influences on the development of group relations made by four types of institutions that traditionally have sponsored group relations work, as described below.

The research and evaluation sponsoring institution

Research institutions apply research and evaluation methods to fields that vary from social policy, production and delivery systems to role effectiveness and knowledge creation. The research and evaluation core culture arises from creating new knowledge, problem solving, improving effectiveness, and efficiency of systems; it is robust, practical, and outward-looking.

The clinical sponsoring institution

In clinical institutions, core influences are identifying and distinguishing normal from abnormal, proposing models of illness and health, pathology, trauma, and growth. Treatment models of "care and cure" are more likely.

The professional development sponsoring institution

Educational and professional development institutions, in the main, develop skills and competencies by culling from the knowledge and experience of other educators and researchers; learning would be derived from deductive methods and transmissive and situational learning, relying more on dependency assumptions of "filling empty vessels".

The spiritual sponsoring institution

In faith-based or spiritual organisations, philosophies around engagement with the cosmos, mystery, the experience of being, faith, belief, and sustainability are likely to dominate.

Experiences of splitting

My role as Director of the Group Relations Programme of the Tavistock Institute involves me relating to group relations organisations around the world. At times, these relationships are friendly and supportive; at other times, they are rivalrous and competitive, especially where established organisations market their conferences in the same diminishing pool of potential recruits. Occasionally, I am invited to direct or be on the consultant staff of these organisations; in turn, as Director of the Leicester conferences, my job is to ensure an international element in staff composition by inviting senior members from those organisations.

To prepare this chapter, I sent a questionnaire to twenty representatives of group relations institutions around the world. The questionnaire aimed to discover how the group relations sections of organisations related to their sponsors, what kind of political and administrative structures existed to do their work, how group reltions fitted in the general culture of the sponsoring organisation, and a question about the continued viability of group relations within the sponsoring organisation. The questionnaire was supplemented by a further six in-depth interviews with selected representatives.

Criticism is often levelled at group relations because of its poor record in evidence-based research and because of its reliance on anecdotal personal narratives as data as the basis for advancing knowledge about group relations. "Absence of systematic research on complex group and organisational processes limits our capacity to advance knowledge in Group Relations" (Cytrynbaum, 1993, p. 42). Researching group relations is acknowledged as being difficult, but it is possible and should be supported. In 2002, Pernille Solvik, a researcher at the Tavistock Institute, undertook a piece of research, "Mapping the market for the Leicester conference". Her research design was a qualitative approach to mapping the market for the Leicester conference by researching individual participants' interpretations of their experiences of the conference. Her methodology was based on two different sources of data: an analysis of conference documents over five years, and telephone interviews with former participants. Solvik's paper established certain protocols for research in group relations and has served as a springboard for further thinking about research. Her paper encouraged me to consider undertaking this piece of research, which is a modest attempt to gather and analyse data to obtain a clearer picture of contemporary group relations and their sponsoring institutions. Without exception, all respondents emphasised the importance of "context" on group relations theory and practice: the role of authorisation in building a group relations facility, the impact of the sponsoring institution's culture and environment, and how group relations has an impact on their sponsoring institutions.

Group relations has to find its place within established organisations—the sponsoring organisation—by bridging the sponsoring organisation's and group relations' main purposes (shared identities and philosophies), and making practical links—administration, strategy, marketing, human resources, and finance. Sponsoring institutions and group relations have grappled with the dynamics of mutuality that come from sharing, supporting, and contending with issues around the respective roles played by each (Gould, Stapley & Stein, 2004; Miller, 1983, 1993).

My own experiences

My task as Director of the Group Relations Programme of the Tavistock Institute includes continuing the development of the group relations programme, despite the fact that group relations is not profitable and seldom contributes to the sponsoring organisation's "bottom line". Mostly, conferences "break even", covering direct and indirect costs and a portion of overheads. Group relations relies on core funding or cross-subsidisation from other business activities of the sponsoring organisation. Despite improved accounting measures, increased number of group relations events, and a rise in the numbers of participants, the group relations programme at the Tavistock Institute was never a profitable business activity. This fact, and the resultant pressures and dynamics within the sponsoring institution, is the basis of my motivation for this chapter.

The Tavistock Institute's commitment to the Group Relations Programme is based on the grounds that the experiential study of group and organisational processes forms an inseparable part of its social science research work; that there is a mutually beneficial cross-fertilisation of research methods, data extraction methods, and knowledge creation and dissemination. Especially relevant is the group relations' connection to the Tavistock Institute's historical roots in understanding and working with unconscious processes (social defences against anxiety) that are necessary for bringing about group, organisational, and social change. Influenced by ideas emerging from the Tavistock in its first decades, and their congruence with other approaches of the social sciences, the early Tavistock pioneers believed that "learning from experience" methods should be applicable broadly to all kinds of social science investigative processes.

Following attendance at group relations conferences, many people are inspired to introduce this form of learning into their home organisations—universities, clinics, institutes, and other public service organisations. In some places, membership-type organisations are established. In addition to developing learning-from-experience events, these institutions sometimes hope group relations conferences would reshape the political, cultural, economic, and social conditions of their societies. Personal experience of a group relations conference often leads to momentous personal learning and, in many cases, to dramatic life changes for individuals.

Group relations as a force for change

A challenging question is how deeply layered are the changes that result from attendance at group relations conferences? Changes in the lives of individuals are more visible—job or career change, marriage, divorce, re-marriage, entering personal therapy, etc. One significant piece of post-conference research (Ginat, 1999) showed that 50% of conference attendees had changed jobs within six months. But what about changes to strategies, structures, and functions in back-home organisations that conferences brochures say might result from conference attendance? Attendees would write after conferences that their deeper understanding of their roles, their intuition, their ability to "read" their organisation's trends, climate, and atmosphere, that come about through their conference participation, had made them more efficient in managing themselves in their roles, in carrying out their responsibilities, and had made them better able to handle difficult situations.

The group relations network

In my role, I keep in touch with many group relations institutions around the world and occasionally I hear about rivalries and contentions. Are these contentions connected with personalities? Or are they systemic? I have wondered about the impact of sponsoring institutions and their organisational and cultural factors on the development of group relations.

Impact

I am grateful to Tim Dartington for first alerting me to the question of "impact" of sponsoring organisations on the theory and practice of group relations. I am using the term "sponsoring institution" to refer to established organisations, such as universities, clinics, research institutes, training and development organisations, and organisational consultancy businesses, that "sponsor" group relations by establishing units or sections within them from which group relations conferences are promoted and delivered. In many instances, there are ideological affinities between group relations theory and practice and the main business of the sponsoring organisation that explain this relationship.

I am also grateful to my friend and colleague, Avi Nutkevitch of OFEK in Israel, with whom I designed and managed the first Belgirate conference on group relations. Both Tim and Avi and the experience of the Belgirate conferences showed how unhelpful it is to regard group relations as a single, distinct body of knowledge or an approach that could be incorporated, packaged, or exported without taking into account the many shaping influences of the "potential space" of organisations, professions, countries, cultures, etc.

I am interested in understanding why group relations flourishes in some places and in others it flounders. I start at home, at the Tavistock Institute of Human Relations, an organisation that is committed to the "integration of the social sciences", that places high value on multi-disciplinary approaches to knowledge creation, understanding and helping organisations and societies decipher and work out their challenges. The Tavistock Institute's *raison d'être* is generating, disseminating, and utilising knowledge that develops from action research and consultancy for the betterment of organisations, communities, and society. The combination of the insights of psychoanalysis and the methodological and research instruments of social science are powerful tools for effecting change at the level of the individual and the social. "Knowledge" is different from "fact" or "information"; it is "wisdom", "comprehension", "realisation", and "intelligence"—states of mind and minds of state (organisations) that often can be more readily observed via narrative than measured. So, what difficulties does group relations have in finding a place for itself and gathering the requisite resources for its functioning? And why does it sometimes attract hostility? These question are asked in the context of the Annual Meeting of the International Society for the Psychoanalytic Study of Organisations (ISPSO) in 2007, at which a version of this chapter was presented: what is the nature of the "potential space" in sponsoring institutions that facilitates or inhibits group relations? How is this "potential space" a source for creativity or anxiety? What are the possibilities and limitations for organisational work?

Research

To help me answer these questions, I asked colleagues in the group relations world for their different perspectives of the "potential space" of group relations and how they integrate their group relations sub-systems into coherent wholes within their organisations.

The perspective from research and evaluation organisations

From research and evaluation organisations, the view is that group relations conference work is a vital adjunct to their core work. Group relations is generally supported internally through their management groups, administration, and marketing units, which enables research and evaluation organisations to respond to the demand for group relations from the marketplace. But group relations also has much loaded on to it. This "loading" might come from both the sponsoring organisation (for group relations to make money) and from the group relations "network". For the group relations "network", group relations carries an "authority" dynamic that might stand in contradistinction to the "spirit of enquiry" inherent in research and evaluation. In other words, the group relations "network" might view group relations methods as standing for an authoritative underpinning of explanations of social phenomena that is incongruent with research and evaluation's "spirit of enquiry" as a way of engaging with data to explain phenomena. Research and evaluation and group relations might differ on the place of "interpretation" to understand phenomena. An interpretative stance, it was suggested, is more appropriate to clinical work than to "spirit of enquiry". By being too strongly interpretative, group relations could compromise the traditional objective scientific observer role. In turn, researchers and evaluators are attentive to the interpretative stance as a means of expanding knowledge and freeing people and systems to innovate. Research and evaluation organisations work through action research, organisational, social, and ecological development, and change consultancy and professional development. Both research and evaluation and group relations agree that knowledge development draws the focus from individuals and psychopathology to groups and mythology. Both research and evaluation and group relations attempt to understand what constructs people are making cognitively and emotionally of their experiences and their environments. Research and evaluation and group relations work contextualises change processes.

But respondents from research and evaluation institutions range in their attitudes from group relations being "outside the mainstream" to being full partners in their offerings. Group relations is considered as carrying institutional heritage. But for group relations to flourish, it needs institutional support. Group relations might be "pulled" into the financial side of the organisation, which could be detrimental to the learning and developmental aspect of group relations and reduce discussions on the strategy and philosophy of group relations—agendas might focus on delivery, not learning. Directors of research and evaluation sponsoring institutions are charged with overseeing all elements of their organisations, that is, the whole, including the group relations part. In the words of a director of a research and evaluation sponsoring organisation:

It is true that there have been times when group relations has been marginalized over conflicts around a disjuncture between skills and approaches relevant to research and evaluation and that which is relevant to group relations. Group Relations is widely considered to have the potential to make a bigger contribution to research than it does. But Group Relations has also marginalised itself! Within Group Relations, it appears that the medical model is more dominant over research models, i.e. holding the view that people will come to Group Relations conferences when they are "ready', rather than actively marketing conferences as worthwhile parts of research and change projects. If group relations is not better in the world, group relations has only itself to answer. Group Relations needs to do more to make itself known and to be more readily available. My hypothesis about Group Relations is that the movement is suffused with a combination of arrogance and shame—arrogance, that group relations should really not have to sell itself; and shame that only 40 or 50 people come to conferences. Group Relations does not have grounds to claim a special status.

To explain the marginalisation of group relations, one also has to consider its own propensity for splitting, resulting from "excessive reliance on charismatic leaders, resulting in a sense of inclusiveness and in a potentially destructive orthodoxy" (Cytrynbaum, 1993, p. 40).

Perspective from clinical organisations

Responses from heads of clinical sponsoring organisations suggest that generally their programmes in clinical work, some of which include organisational development consultancy and research, influence, and are influenced by, group relations thinking. They stress the contribution of psychoanalysis to group relations in their organisational consultancy work. They rely on mixed models of integrated psychoanalytic and general systems theories perspectives and applied group relations work. But they also acknowledge that group relations work, on the whole and with some exceptions, is a valued, but not well-integrated part of their institutions. Their councils and boards rely on the international reputation of group relations, but they do not know much about group relations and, in many instances, are sceptical of it, either because it is "too applied" or because it is "too psycho-analytical"!

In some instances, the relationship between group relations and clinical institutions resembles a "boarding house" model in which the parts operate separately, and exist commensally, accepting and tolerating one another, but not thinking much about each other. There is a certain element of disjointedness in their relationships. For clinical institutions, the paradox is that both elements—group relations and the sponsoring organisations—are important to each other for their identities. There are other mutual benefits, such as some cross-referrals and cross-selling. These organisations certainly have an ideological affinity between their different parts, in so far as these parts represent connections between the social (and the systemic), the interpersonal and intrapersonal traditions. In this sense, there exists a symbiotic relationship in which both parties benefit from the reputation and traditions of the other. These benefits are sometimes consciously acknowledged and sometimes not.

Heads of clinical institutions believe that the future of their partnerships with group relations will improve because group relations is applied, developing new knowledge about groups, systems, organisational work, and society, and taking this knowledge and applying it in novel ways. They think there is a robust future for their partnerships with group relations because group relations is capable of reorientating itself and inserting itself in modified forms to work with people in different work sectors. For people who do not necessarily appreciate the methodology and language, group relations is capable of translating itself into the language of the client system and applying complex concepts to everyday organisational and social systems. Clinical institutions, on the other hand, cannot easily change on their own: as one head of a clinical organisation said,

> It seems that clinical and single-discipline organisations have been designed to remain stuck. They are set up to be self-contained institutions. They tend to remain unrelated to universities or to other organisations. They seem helpless to think through what is happening to them. They are subject to splitting and projective mechanisms and overall they seem to be maladaptive. They have difficulty defining their mission and how to develop appropriate leadership for the task in relation to the outside world or marketplace.

These difficulties might be another source of ambivalence that clinical organisations (and, indeed, other types of sponsoring organisations) and group relations bear towards one another—that each part serves as a reminder of what the other part is failing at and cannot see.

> Sponsoring institutions and group relations have to find ways of giving leadership to each other on the basis of maintaining high standards of professional work that is relevant to the world at large. Clinical sponsoring institutions and group relations have to ask themselves whether they have enough common interest and shared values (studying the unconscious and the 'future of the unconscious') to help them to survive.

Perspectives from professional development organisations

Professional development organisations, often organised as voluntary or membership organisations, find themselves in greater difficulty because they often identify with a model of practice that becomes enshrined as "establishment" or "founding father", and any deviation from that model is considered heretical. In "membership" organisations, it is evident that group relations conferences are developed within established policies and it is expected that they will be self-managing, but they often fail to co-ordinate with their sponsoring institutions' financial and marketing policies.

Education and training organisations have deeply embedded cultures and strong commitments to group relations as a philosophy and way of engaging with its task. In so doing, these sponsoring organisations function with an inherent conflict between "market forces" and their "cultures". This conflict is true of most organisations, but group relations organisations, it is suggested, seem to ignore it by getting caught up mainly in internal dynamics and the expense of an outward-looking, demand-led stance.

In "membership" sponsoring institutions, group relations conferences are usually at the centre of their activities and their actual delivery of programmes is naturally focused on the learning needs of their members: for example, seminars, social dreaming matrices, journal publication, reading groups. Consequently, many "membership" training sponsoring institutions can be described as having a strong dependency culture, religious fervour, and a culture of charity that significantly influences the delivery of group relations. Conferences are often presented in the language of the "faithful", who are loyal to a fantasised psychoanalytic/Tavistock purism with appeal to those who identify with that approach. Marketing is based on similar identification (i.e., not too "commercialised"). Most successful marketing is done through word-of-mouth or through personal relationships with potential members. Each conference's marketing activities begin by "reinventing the wheel", resulting in repeatedly marketing with limited resources and depending on the goodwill of staff for recruitment to conferences.

In these sponsoring institutions, group relations conference staff roles are highly sought after and are a central political focus with considerable competitiveness. Innovations in group relations conference work contribute to envious attacks from the "establishment" and, ultimately, might threaten the host organisation. Presenting group relations work in traditional ways, excluding all other offerings and models, leads to a closed system. Attempts to include political and organisational dimensions—"to play a socially responsible role, taking up current issues in society"—have not been very successful in professional development organisations which remain inward-looking, attending to the needs of their members.

The future of "membership" professional development institutions will depend on whether they are able to establish realistic financial infrastructures that engage with pragmatics beyond purist "psychoanalytic/Tavistock group relations models". Group relations in these organisations will be influential if they "help their members extend themselves intellectually and participate in developing new ideas and be stimulated by them for themselves and for others."

Perspectives from spiritual or faith organisations

Sponsoring organisations emphasising faith, belief, and spirituality seem to take a different view of their relationship to group relations. For instance, their managements are prepared to tolerate and supplement financial losses. Group relations conferences are not required to generate surpluses; they are not "cash cows". In spiritual sponsoring organisations, group relations is considered an essential part of their work streams and is included in all their courses and conferences, in their "applied" work of research and consultancy, and organisational role consultations. Group relations conferences and courses come together under one management and relate directly to other work streams. Their research and consultancy clients are expected to send their people to their group relations conferences. In other words, group relations in spiritual sponsoring organisations seems to inform everything they do. This high level integration between group relations and the sponsoring organisation's other activities is evident in their ongoing processes of hypothesis making and testing that emerges out of their regular research and consultancy work and gets used in formulating the shape of their forthcoming conferences. Their annual group relations conferences, therefore, form a central part of the organisation's internal learning and the conferences, in turn, explore implications of the rest of its work for the year ahead.

The philosophy of belief, faith, and spirituality organisations forms part of their consultancy, experiential learning, and research work. Their spiritual philosophy concerns wholeness and group relations is conceptualised as part of the whole; the presence of the Divine is considered active in the here-and-now, and this makes for a unique contribution to their work in group relations. These are cross-organisational principles in "spiritual" sponsoring organisations. The aim of group relations is to understand how people have created what they have created, which is a salutary exercise in freedom for people who are expected to manage their own accountability. At the heart of their philosophy is the struggle of working with the tension between freedom and accountability for what people have created themselves.

Conclusions

Conceptualising "group relations"—whether it is part of, or indistinguishable from, its sponsoring organisation—raises questions and challenges about the relatedness of group relations to its host organisation. These questions concern the primary task of both. Responses I received often referred to "controversy", "unrest", "political implications", "disagreement and debate", in both group relations and in sponsoring organisations. Respondents described tensions that exist when group relations work is the primary task of the organisation, for example, a group relations membership organisation, and when *group relations is the method by which the sponsoring organisation's primary task is achieved*, for example, a research and consultancy organisation. For instance, in some organisations, the group relations method ("to further the exploration and understanding of conscious and unconscious processes") is turned into the primary task of the sponsoring organisation, and its original aim is then moved to a secondary task, that is, "to contribute to clients' development and change". Method gets confused with aim. One respondent wrote, "I am not clear where the group relations part of our organisation ends and the rest of our organisation as a whole begins". Loss of organisational direction and internal controversy seems to result from conflating the aims of the sponsoring organisation with its group relations part. This conflation might lead to a subversion of the sponsoring institution's primary task.

Putting it another way, there is a tension between two main categories—the general and the specific. The general category is an "imported" Tavistock group relations programme that holds one or two group relations conferences during the year, and people yearn to be on the staff of those conferences. It is doubtful what contribution that conference makes to organisations or to society; an analysis of the delegates who have attended over the past twenty years shows that they attend group relations conferences for professional development reasons in order to improve their consultancy skills or their CVs. On the other hand, there are group relations conferences that aim to contribute learning and understanding of specific organisational and social issues: conferences on abuse in the family and children at risk, life on the road, relationships between members and executives of local government, confronting collective atrocities, health system conferences, conferences on the mood of the nation, the north–south divide, art and society, authority and passivity among unemployed, etc., these conferences are well funded and well attended and have an impact on clients' organisations. In the confusion between primary task and method, people are seduced by fantasies of individual progress up a status ladder and are less attracted to do the work that "contributes to developments in client systems and society".

This is the trap I think that group relations and sponsoring institutions fall into—caught between their attachment to the genericisms of group relations conferences and the struggle to find the specifics that address the needs of specific client systems.

The following excerpt from a respondent highlights problems of the group relations "network":

People in the group relations "network" tend to see organisations that offer group relations conferences and training as doing only group relations, not research, consultancy or anything else. This suggests that people in the group relations network tend to have part-object relationships to organisations that provide group relations conferences as part of their offer. Because issues of authority lie at the heart of group relations, transference feelings and fantasies are stimulated that prevent people from perceiving those organisations carrying out other activities, like research, organisational consultancy or clinical work. The group relations "network" by definition is dispersed. It belongs to neither academia, clinical services, the world of politics, nor the realm of faith and spirituality. Group relations does not fit neatly into any one of these social domains and does not constitute a domain of its own. So, being part of "the group relations brand", encourages fantasies about organisations that have highly visible group relations businesses and people hope to deal with their own isolation and marginality by in their minds "possessing" the group relations sponsoring institution, as if they have a right to it; as if they can "own" part of it, as if it were a "part-object", i.e. group relations split off from its sponsoring institution's other business.

This, I believe, accounts for the discomfort some sponsoring institutions feel towards their group relations "part". A cultural dissonance is created in these two perspectives, which might affect splitting, extrusion, and integration in the relationships between group relations and sponsoring organisations.

Acknowledgements

The paper on which this chapter is based appeared during the celebrations of the Tavistock Institute's sixieth anniversary and is testimony to the intellectual vigour of the Tavistock Institute, which continues to refresh and develop its intellectual traditions. A number of people contributed to the thinking out of that paper. In particular, I acknowledge the contributions of Fiddy Abraham, Eliat Aram, David Armstrong, Anke Baak, Gaby Braun, Ken Eisold, Amy Fraher, Bob Hinshelwood, Bruce Irvine, Karen Izod, Willem de Jager, Ilana Litvin, Carl Mack, Rose Miller, Jean Neumann, Allan Shafer, Phil Swann, Kathy White, and the continual support and help of the members of the Tavistock Refresh Group.

CHAPTER FIVE

Group relations conferences: reviewing and exploring theory, design, role-taking, and application*

Introduction

I n November 2003, a four-day residential conference on group relations conferences for group relations conference staff members
was held in Belgirate, Italy, organised by Avi Nutkevitch[1] of
OFEK, a group relations organisation in Israel and Mannie Sher[2] of the
Tavistock Institute of Human Relations, London. The primary task of
the conference was to review and explore the theory and design, the
taking up of roles in, and the application of, group relations conferences. The Belgirate conference, as it came to be known, was intended
to be a "space" of the kind that is not normally available during group
relations conferences themselves. It was intended to review and
explore dilemmas and questions that lie at the heart of group relations
work. The absence of sufficient opportunities during conferences to
explore these questions is a constant source of frustration and guilt. It
is an abiding principle in group relations conferences that staff work

*This chapter is based on: A. Nutkevitch & M. Sher (2004), Group relations conferences:
reviewing and exploring theory, design, role-taking and application. © *Organisational
and Social Dynamics*, 4(1): 107–115. Material reprinted with permission.

79

through their own particular conceptual and other issues, just as conference members are expected to do. This principle is related to, and is in the service of, the undertaking by staff to do everything possible that promotes the conference's primary task and of furthering the learning of the dynamic relatedness between individuals, groups, organisations, and society. The Belgirate conference was, therefore, designed as a particular structured opportunity for reviewing, exploring, and learning more about the different aspects of group relations conference design, dynamic, and delivery. The conference was conceptualised and designed as a "transitional space" for new learning that would contain traditional forms of scientific activity, such as lectures and discussions and experiential "here and now" activities, like the "Taking up roles" event. This blend of modes had its difficulties and complexities, but it also provided potential for creative learning and exploration.

OFEK and the Tavistock Institute joined together to produce and sponsor the Belgirate conference. The two organisations and their leaders had enjoyed long-term close working relationships in developing group relations in their respective countries. Their working relationship and their close personal relationship, as well as the physical facilities that their organisations were able to provide, facilitated the creation of the Belgirate conference. The choice of the venue was related to the fact of it being mid-way between the UK and Israel, and was facilitated by an Italian who is also a member of OFEK. The decision to hold the conference in Italy was welcomed by the Italian group relations people.

Boundaries and their political meanings in the Belgirate conference

The Belgirate conference was open to anyone who (a) had previously taken up at least one conference staff role (administrative, consultative or directorial) and (b) where the conferences they had attended were based on the Tavistock–Leicester model. These two elements had political and conceptual meanings. It established the Tavistock–Leicester model of group relations conferences (GRCs) as the prototype group relations conference, as distinct from other types of experiential conferences. This forced individuals and group relations organisations around the globe to face questions of identity, as well as allegiance to the Tavistock–Leicester GRC model. The two conditions of membership mentioned above made explicit a definition of the boundary of inclusion and exclusion around the Belgirate conference and, by extension, around the international group relations network. Eligibility criteria, that is, having had a previous conference staff role, were boundary conditions that were actively implemented in more than one case by the management. These decisions helped preserve the primary task of the conference: not learning about GRCs, even though this was an important by-product for many participants, but, rather, reviewing and exploring the theory and practice of GRCs from within a boundary, termed in the conference the "group relations network".

Data

Invitations to the conference were sent to all group relations organisations and other organisations sponsoring GRCs around the world, about thirty in all. These organisations responded positively to our request, agreed to identify their members who had previously taken up staff roles in group relations conferences, and forward our invitations on to them. Applications were received from individuals from twenty organisations. Fifty-two participants attended the conference and their distributions reveal meaningful data about the characterisation and political dynamics of the group relations network. For example, participants came from eleven countries (Australia, Denmark, Finland, Germany, Israel, Italy, Netherlands, Spain, Sweden, UK, and USA). Significant by its absence was France, which, despite being very active in initiating and producing experiential conferences on authority and leadership, declared that it no longer considered itself as part of the international Tavistock–Leicester group relations network. Of interest here is that participants identified themselves as members of nineteen different group relations organisations, indicating a sense of belonging that is served by their membership of group relations organisations. There were instances where people did not reveal any association with a group relations organisation, and there were some statements of mixed allegiances that perhaps reflected complex and ambivalent relationships towards group relations work and towards individuals' local group relations organisations.

Gender, age and role distributions

Thirty-two females and twenty males attended the conference. Forty-nine out of the fifty-two were over forty years old; thirty-four were above fifty.

Previous conference roles

Twenty participants had previously taken up director and other roles; twenty-six had been in consultant roles, and six had been in administrator role only. We were struck by the number of people who had been in administrator role, pointing to the importance that this role has in group relations conferences.

Structure and design of the Belgirate conference

Our basic assumptions in regard to the work of exploring the various elements of the primary task of the conference rested upon the existence of an international network of group relations organisations and individuals engaged in group relations work. These influence, and are influenced by, each other, nationally and internationally, consciously and unconsciously. We were keen to design a conference that would contain an international dimension through the presentation of papers by members of the network, representing different aspects of the international scene—nationality, religion, geography, gender, and race. Colleagues from seven countries were invited to present their work on a variety of applications of group relations conferences.

There were five major elements in the conference, each dealing with one aspect of the primary task. The design involved moving progressively from more structured events to less structured and more experiential ones.

1. *Theory of group relations*: Theory of group relations was delivered via a lecture entitled: "Learning from experience and the experience of learning in group relations conferences". The lecture was followed by small group discussions. Allocation to groups was done by the conference management and reflected a more structured intent.

2. *Structure and design of group relations conferences*: This topic was explored via a lecture entitled: "Structure and design of group relations conferences: issues and dilemmas". The lecture was followed by small group discussions on pre-assigned topics (small study groups, large study groups, institutional event, review and application groups, and staff meetings).

3. *Taking up roles in group relations conferences*: This event was experiential, in which the participants explored the impact of various identity-related variables such as nationality, religion, geography, gender, and race, on taking up roles in group relations conferences. The process of exploration in this event relied on "here and now" experiences of the conference itself to further the work of the event: that is, the groups that formed engaged with each other in their representations of the different variables. The groups worked on their tasks by using the conference Directorate (the two managers and the two administrators) for consultation and for engagement, via dialogue and interviews.

4. *Application*: Exploring the nature of application of group relations conferences was achieved through eight parallel presentations by participants of their own work, followed by a plenary meeting.

5. The conference programme included a space first thing each morning for "morning reflections", in which dream material emerged to shed light on important dynamics of the conference.

Roles in the conference

The Directorate comprised managers and administrators. In addition to the lecturers and presenters of papers, other roles included chairs and convenors of the different sessions and these roles were distributed among the participants. Altogether, twenty-one participants held a variety of roles in the conference. This design, and the fact that we designated ourselves as "managers" and not "directors", reflected our view that the conference should constitute a meeting of colleagues to pursue a common task. Additionally, we wished to distinguish this conference from a regular group relations conference. We hoped to produce a blend of traditional scientific and experiential modes of working that would enable creative learning to take place and simultaneously contain the dynamics that might emerge. During the design phase of the conference, we were anxious because of the conference's unique conception. Mixed traditional scientific and experiential methods of work usually produce complexity and tension. The challenge was to find a creative and containing balance.

Emergent metaphors, themes, and issues

Chicken soup

This metaphor appeared in a dream in the first "morning reflections" event. Associations included: what kind of "soup" did the conference organisers prepare for the participants? Some participants felt "thrown into the soup". The conference was said to be like "Jewish soup".

Associations to the dream concerned the nature of the conference and the relatedness between the participants and the conference. Chicken soup is traditionally regarded as the "Jewish medicine" for all problems, administered by an all-loving Jewish mother. Did the conference represent health-giving regenerative chicken soup or the more negative aspects of benign coercion, submergence in a "Jewish soup / conference", suggesting loss of autonomy, control by the ubiquitous Jewish mother and guilt for rejecting life-giving sustenance?

Criticism of the structure: participants felt forced into a structure that did not always feel productive. People were faced by the painful realisation that they had made a choice to join something about which they had only vague notions. This made them feel entrapped and confronted by their responsibilities for having decided to participate, followed by an internal struggle, on the one hand, to make the best of their experiences, or, on the other, to remain locked in opposition. These two lines of engagement with the conference, both personal and in relation to institutional identity, persisted almost until the end of the conference.

London Transport Underground map

The features of a good design are simplicity and applicability. "Underground" competition and rivalry in the group relations network were forced into the open. This metaphor emerged in relation to the discussion around the design of this conference, in particular, and group relations conferences generally: what is innovation and what is conservative tradition? The metaphor seemed to represent the durability of the Tavistock–Leicester model of group relations conferences, in so far as they contain the two basic elements of good design—simplicity and flexibility. The actual London Transport Underground map of 1931 was the first to incorporate diagrammatic principles of using only vertical, horizontal and 45° lines, even though the spatial relationships between stations on the map did not match reality on the ground. As new lines were developed over the years, they were easily slotted into the existing design. This model of underground map-making was adopted by about 150 underground systems throughout the world. The metaphor of the underground map was present in the questions of whether the Tavistock–Leicester model was actually out of date, or whether it contained the basic elements from which adaptations and new learning events could be built. This metaphor reverberated throughout the conference, ushering the conference into the underground/hidden or unconscious dynamics of the group relations network. Thus, for example, which countries and group relations organisations now held the mantle of leadership and innovation?

The institution of group relations "in the mind"

The Belgirate conference provided an opportunity for map-building of the group relations network, of the institution of group relations that individuals and group relations organisations hold in their minds. Maps are only representations of reality, not reality itself, but, at the same time, without maps, adaptations to reality cannot be made. In this respect, the Belgirate conference started the process of articulating and drawing the map both of the institution of group relations, with its more obvious overt and conscious elements, and the unconscious elements of relationships and relatedness among its various "stations", or international group relations organisations.

"Is the friend dead or alive?"

A participant dreamed of a friend lying down in a house, apparently suffering a heart attack. The dreamer is worried, rushes outside to hail an ambulance, but fails to find one. He comes back inside to find the friend is up and well. The dream might have touched on the internal process of the conference, with the management under attack and a fear that management, and, therefore, the conference, could be fatally damaged. The dream was presented after a day of continuous attack on the management and represented the well-known phenomenon of management being both an object of continuous destructive attack and needing to be protected and preserved. Criticism of the management was at times difficult to contain and to manage. We were familiar with this phenomenon through our work in GRCs. Yet, this conference was unique in that we had to manage a process involving colleagues, many of them our compatriots and good friends. We had to face situations suffused with the dialectic of support and competition, of envy, and of gratitude. The dream might have represented unconscious attempts to manage those impulses simultaneously. At another level, the dream could have represented ambivalence towards the Tavistock–Leicester group relations conference model by those asserting that it was outdated, conservative, and too authoritarian. On the other hand, anxiety about the continued existence of group relations led to strenuous efforts to preserve it. The dream might have represented the perennial dilemma: is the model dead or dying? Or is it alive and well?

Eric Miller's death and the issue of authority in the group relations world

Eric Miller headed the Tavistock Institute's Group Relations Programme for over thirty years and came to symbolise both the theoretical underpinnings and the practical design and structure of the Leicester model. The issue of professional authority in the group relations world had been exposed by his death. One reference to this question was pointedly made by suggesting that there was "no longer a Pope, only two Chief Rabbis". On one level, this statement obviously referred to the two Jewish managers of the conference, who took leadership by mounting this conference. But, on another level, the implication was that, from hereon, there would be no single great man running the group relations world, but rather joint or co-operative leadership. However, the question of leadership is usually accompanied by competition. Now that there is no "Pope", would the "sons" fight among themselves for leadership, for power and influence?

"Birth order". In aspiring for leadership, "birth order", that is, dates of establishment of different group relations organisations, was manifested powerfully in the role-taking event, where all the American AKRI participants "just happened to find" themselves in one group, "not by design", they claimed. Should the "firstborn" (AKRI) be regarded as the natural inheritors of the authority and leadership mantle? Feelings consequently ran high, because a relatively newcomer organisation, OFEK, the "newborn", took its own authority to team up with the Tavistock Institute and conceptualise, establish, and run this conference. Perhaps it was the personal relationship, the common ethnicity of the two conferences managers, that played a part in forming the basis of this particular partnership? Though these were important factors in forging this relationship, another significant factor might have been related to the nature of the relationship that was developed and maintained between the Tavistock Institute and OFEK, that is, the loyalty that the two organisations held for each other over the years, which moved from dependency to reciprocity and interdependence. This hypothesis touches on interesting historical developments of the various "offspring" group relations organisations in relation to the "parent" Tavistock Institute organisation.

Being "chosen"

A major element concerning involvement in role-taking was the idea of being "chosen", which appeared to be more significant than variables, such as gender, religion, and profession. It emerged that for many participants, perhaps all, becoming a staff member in a conference depended upon "being chosen", either by a director or by a sponsoring institution. In addition to the potentially painful narcissistic issues involved in being chosen or excluded were questions of unhealthy dependency, the degree of freedom in the work, genuineness, and authenticity. Failing to attend to these dynamics could lead to corruption of the learning process, implying that group relations, like every other human endeavour, has the seeds of its own destruction within it. Moreover, the notion of being "chosen" can be played out in the arena of organisational relationships in terms of which organisations are chosen by other organisations for joint ventures, a dynamic that was powerfully present in this conference.

The nature of staff meetings

In order to explore various dilemmas regarding structure and design of GRCs, the participants were asked to divide into various groups representing major GRC elements: small study groups, large study groups, inter-group event, institutional event, review and application groups, and staff meetings. The staff meeting group attracted the largest number of participants (twenty); the other groups attracted between four and twelve. It was clear that the nature of staff meetings is a major undiscussed element in GRCs. Questions were raised regarding the primary task of staff meetings, the need to keep firm time boundaries, as in other conference meetings, and the kind of work that needs doing. It was clear that the nature of staff meetings is relatively unexplored. The large interest by participants in the "staff meetings" group suggests a need for further work on this issue.

Authority lies within the network

The question of how this conference came into being reverberated throughout the conference. It was only towards the end of the conference that it was fully understood that the organisers of the Belgirate conference took their own authority and made the conference self-authorising. This creative self-authorising process was acknowledged by the participants, not from a competitive position, but from the realisation of the power of an idea. It was realised that the authority to act in the arena of world group relations would not come from "above", but, henceforth, would lie within the network.

Concluding thoughts

Deciding to hold the Belgirate conference along the lines discussed in this chapter shaped the emergence of a group relations network in which authority is considered no longer to lie with a single individual or a single organisation. The initiative leading to the formation of the conference depended on taking leadership in the relatively undefined world of group relations. The large number of participants from many countries made this initiative a success. It reflects the need— supported by participants at the aftermath of the conference—for the development of more conferences of this kind.

Note

1.   Avi Nutkevitch at the time of the conference was the Chairperson of OFEK, The Israeli Association for the Study of Group and Organisational

Processes. He is a practising psychoanalyst and an organisational consultant.

2. Mannie Sher is a Principal Researcher and Consultant of the Tavistock Institute, London, and Director of its Group Relations Programme. He is a practising psychoanalytical psychotherapist.

CHAPTER SIX

From groups to group relations: Bion's contribution to the Tavistock–"Leicester" conferences*

Introduction

Bion's interest in exploring primitive anxieties and defences in the individual extended to the group. This aspect of exploring the primitive in groups was taken up and developed by his colleagues in the Tavistock Institute, working in particular on the ever-present challenge to memory and desire, to the very human wish that everything should revert to the *status quo ante*. Elaborating on the obstacles to group and organisational learning, and overcoming them, formed the core work of the Tavistock Institute. Understandably, the nature of defences against anxiety offered the chance that new, often surprising insights would be generated.

The purpose of this chapter, therefore, is to rediscover Bion's thinking in the light of my own development and of current changes in institutions, organisations, societies, and networks. In the face of

---

*This chapter is based on: M. Sher (2003), From groups to group relations: Bion's contribution to the Tavistock–"Leicester" conferences. In: R. Lipgar & M. Pines (Eds.), *Building on Bion: Branches. Contemporary Developments and Applications of Bion's Contributions to Theory and Practice* (pp. 109–144). © Jessica Kingsley, London, UK. Material reprinted with permission.

current widespread scepticism about the transfer of psychoanalytic ideas to group processes and other situations where group formation and group behaviour are important, I have often wrestled with issues of application of group relations thinking. Bion considered that psychoanalytic approaches to understanding groups should be limited in the main to groups that had the task of self-examination. Although Bion sometimes made analogies with other types of groups, quoting Freud on the army, the church, and the aristocracy, the language of Bion, and the group he appeared to have in mind, was the psychotherapy group, the group that, by definition, Bion believed would recover from clinical illness through a process of self-examination and self-discovery. What are we to make of Bion's colleagues' attempts to transfer his ideas to other types of group situations, such as working groups, for instance? Bion was surprised in the interest aroused by his articles on groups that led to the publication of *Experiences in Groups* (1961). We have an early indication of Bion's interest in "sovereignty and power" in small groups via his regret at not having discussed these subjects in the book, but he also reveals his scepticism on the subject by declaring that "sovereignty and power" do not develop to maturity in small groups (1961, p. 7). Was he talking about small groups *per se*, or about small groups of psychiatric patients who, as a group, we might expect to have difficulties in the area of self-actualisation and with sovereignty of the self? In the small group, rivalries can be understood, but in a large group they might be more difficult to deal with.

As a practising psychoanalytical psychotherapist, I have been impressed by the fact that the psychoanalytic approach, as Bion asserted, whether through the individual or through the group, is dealing with different facets of the same phenomena. Bion's major contribution here was that the psychoanalytic approach to the individual and the psychoanalytic approach to the group are two methods that provide the practitioner with a rudimentary binocular vision. When these phenomena are examined in individual work, they centre on the Oedipal situation related to the pairing basic assumption. When the phenomena are examined in group work, they centre in the Sphinx and they are related to problems of knowledge and scientific method (Lawrence, 1997). These views appear to presage later work on groups and organisations that was taken forward by Bion's colleagues, such as A. K. Rice of the Tavistock Institute. *The Experiences in Groups* papers were written before Bion's analysis with Klein, but were not published in book form until after. What was the real significance of the sentence in Bion's "Introduction" (1961, p. 8)? "My present work, which I hope to publish, convinces me of the central importance of the Kleinian theories of projective-identification and the interplay between the paranoid–schizoid and depressive positions".

Without the aid of these sets of theories, Bion doubted the possibility of an advance in the study of group phenomena. At once, we realise that, even though relying on psychoanalytic thinking and utilising terminology usually associated with pathology, Bion was turning his attention to phenomena in the broader universe outside the clinical one, providing us with the keys to develop group relations and the Tavistock–Leicester conferences.

In the journey from groups to group relations, deducing attitudes and articulating them applies as much to the perception of the observer of a group's attitude to other groups as to the group's behaviour that is based on its thinking of what the other group's attitude towards it is. This is the case for group thinking shifting to intergroup dynamics, which Bion's colleagues in the Tavistock Institute used to develop theories of group relations. Bion's summation of the theories of group dynamics, that is, their complex emotional episodes, suggests the presence of the "other" in group life as much as it is present in the emotional life of the individual. For instance, Bion describes discernible trends of mental activity in the course of the group "doing" something. In other words, the members of the group assemble in order to co-operate in the achievement of a task. The group, therefore, is orientated towards an outer reality involving other groups that might also have an interest in the group's task. Co-operation is necessary and depends on a degree of sophisticated skill in the individual who has developed mentally through experience and learning. This is known as the work group; its activity is geared to a task, it is related to reality, its methods are rational and scientific. Its characteristics are similar to those attributed by Freud (1911b) to the ego. The observer of a work group will be able to comment on work-orientated attitudes and activities of the members and of the group as a whole, but any interpretation of these will leave much unsaid. Work group activity will also be obstructed, diverted, and, on occasion, assisted by certain other mental activities that have in common the attribute of powerful emotional drives.

Bion's ideas on group mentality emphasised the individual's contribution and the individual's responsibility to modify and take back their contribution to group mentality. Nevertheless, Bion lays responsibility on the group for what happens, not the individual. He is trying to understand the dynamic of the group as a whole, and he hopes that interpretation will stimulate the group to do something. This is the challenge for any aspiring group relations consultant or other interventionist in group dynamics. Will interpretation be sufficient to remove impedimenta to a group's or organisation's functioning, and if so, what should be the form of interpretation in different contexts? It was left to others to transform Bion's methods and make them more focused on work relationships. The Northfield experiment contained different points of view. Therapy was intended to be found in the therapeutic community and the psychoanalytic study of groups at the Tavistock (Miller, 1990a,b).

Bion for me

Soon after returning from my first membership experience of a "Leicester" conference in 1974, the supervisor of my group psychotherapy practice at the Tavistock Clinic, Robert Gosling, himself a close colleague of Wilfred Bion, said that he supposed my way of thinking about my group of patients would have been changed forever by my "Leicester" experience. I remember the relief I felt at Dr Gosling's acknowledgement of my rising confusions about group relations and my role as group psychotherapist. So began a quest to find ways of bridging competing models, one centring on the pathology of the individual patient and the paired relationship with a therapist, the other also attending to individual pathology, but using the group-as-a-whole dynamic that included the psychotherapist. My gratitude to Dr Gosling in helping me make that transition prompts me now to complete the circle and reflect on my first experience of directing the "Leicester" conference. In doing so, my recollections of Dr Gosling nearly thirty years ago are of his encouragement to be as open as possible about the swirling, chaotic dynamics of the group, and to use my feelings stirred up by the chaos to deepen my understanding of the group and to find effective ways of sharing that understanding with it. In that spirit of openness, I decided to include in this chapter parts of a daily diary that I kept during the Leicester conference. I hope, thereby, to place before the reader the unique experiences that form part of the Director's role, and I hope consequently to reveal something of the power of projections that the membership and staff grapple with, how these get "sent" upwards in the hope that they will be "dealt with" or resolved "up there".

My personal experience of directing the
Leicester conference and links to Bion's theories

In April 2000, I directed my first Tavistock "Leicester" Conference. I had directed other, shorter group relations conferences, but never one as long as the Leicester Conference—fourteen consecutive days with a one-day break in the middle. I was anxious about my first attempt at directing this conference, whose participants and staff would be well versed in group relations work. So high was my anxiety that, of the staff group of ten, I had "unconsciously" selected eight who were ex-directors of working conferences. Another measure I took to contain anxiety was keeping a daily diary to record my thoughts, experiences, and feelings, and to set a reflective distance between the conference experience and myself. This helped me to think about Bion's ideas on groups and to use them to give meaning to the chaotic feelings that seemed to be part of the role. I will refer to them here in order to make the link between theory and practice of group relations more cogent and to define the steps from Bion's groups to the Tavistock group relations.

Day one: pre-conference staff meetings

Members of staff arrive today and there is a congenial and friendly atmosphere, tinged with mild irritation with the new arrivals for disturbing the relationships between members of the Directorate that had formed during the previous two days. They arrive one-and-a-half hours before lunch, wander about uncomfortably, not wanting to intrude too much in the preparations that are going on in the office. We are under pressure to complete and print papers in time for the first staff meeting at 2.30 pm. Some members are expecting the meeting to commence at 2.00 pm so they are relieved to have the extra half hour. So am I, because this means that I have sufficient time to get through the agenda. A few thoughts to bear in mind: arriving staff members will be helped to deal with conference members' feelings about crossing the boundary into the conference institution by the way I, as Director, facilitate their entry into the staff group. From the vantage point of the Director, one catches glimpses of fascinating projective processes that move about the different parts of the conference. I see this enormous "tsunami" of institutional anxiety roaring towards me. It can be called "controlling the Director". Members and staff are evidently anxious about this new Director, one who makes mistakes of commission and omission, adding to their fears about the safety of the conference. I also discover that both my words and my silence have power. So, there is power from the role and there is anxiety from the role. What models do I have to draw from? They suddenly all depart and I am left alone to learn that tolerating anxiety and mistakes maturely is necessary for the job, and to do that without splitting and blaming others or oneself. That is a requirement of the staff too—they may want to have a perfect brochure and timetable, a Director's perfect opening address, but they would also walk all over it if they had a chance. We all—staff, directorate, and director—have the job of balancing knowledge, feelings, and thoughts, but in my role I must be alert to the tendency for the different parts of the system— the Training Group, the Large Study Group and the Small Study Group systems—to get me to favour them, that is, their wish to split the director; I also need to bear in mind my tendency to forget parts of the total system, like when I omitted the Training Group from the agenda of the staff meeting!

I am reminded of Bion's (1961, p. 161) assertion that the basic assumptions of a group seem each in turn to "share out" between them the characteristics of one character in the Oedipal situation. However, in the conference these characteristics are interwoven between the members, the staff in their different sub-systems, and the Director. The membership is said to contain the "alternative conference leader", except that s/he is hidden, at the beginning certainly. The hidden individual is the leader, and although this appears to contradict the constantly iterated statement that the Director is the leader, "the contribution is resolved through oedipal fantasies of destroying or replacing the work group leader, because he arouses a dread with which a questioning attitude is regarded". (Bion, 1961, p. 162). The conference being "the object of enquiry, itself arouses fears of an extremely primitive kind". The attempt to make a rational investigation of the dynamics of the conference is perturbed by fears, and the mechanisms for dealing with them are characterised by splitting and attacks on the Father/Director.

Day two (start of the conference)

In the morning, staff of the three sub-systems (Large Study Group, Small Study Group, and Training Group) meet in their respective groups. My confusion about my two roles, director and consultant, soon is apparent. I feel bad because it shows my lack of experience and this has consequences for carrying out the task of learning about managing oneself in different roles. This confusion occurred several times and, although it can be understood in terms of the conference dynamics, I am concerned that too much emphasis may be given to "dynamics" and not enough to the limitations of my competence. To be sure, I have several good moments too, believing I remain on task and in role and help to advance the learning. "Wolfgang" enters the conference lexicon to refer to the dangers of the Large Study Group that lies waiting for the Director to trip up. A few Germans, led by a Wolfgang, are making ready to form the opposition. For others, the position is simple: "If Mannie Sher can direct, why can't I?" In the working conference staff meeting there are rumblings about competitiveness between staff members who unconsciously wish to take my job, but also wish for me to be a clear-thinking and dependable director.

Oedipal dynamics are present, but I wonder: if "father" is already dead, the unconscious wish must be to promote someone to replace him, leading to sibling rivalry, more than Oedipus. But here, too, I am less certain, thinking rather along the lines of Bion's and Lawrence's (2000) ideas on Sphinx, focusing on organisation, leadership, and the personification of the ideal in the person of the leader so that the fantasy can be made manifest—having a good, sound Tavistock Group Relations conference led by a competent director. The converse of this is the fear of being caught in the grip of the "dead ancients", an out-of-date Tavistock and a moribund methodology. It is the fear of being identified with a dead past that I believe gets into me. In the opening plenary later this afternoon, a member asks whether the staff could say when they are being management, when they are being consultant, and when they are being personal, suggesting an attempt to exercise control over chaotic feelings in the first gathering of the members. This must be the challenge of today and of the whole conference: can ambiguity, ambivalence, multiple roles, diverse emotions and thoughts be tolerated and managed successfully by the membership (and the staff) when the Director appears unable to do so himself? I have just remembered! I did not make introductions in the first pre-conference staff meeting, nor did I mention in my introductory remarks to the plenary that "conference time" would be according to the clock in the foyer! First major institutional boundary problem occurs. One of the buildings is locked when the members arrive for their Small Study Groups. One consultant is alone with one female member for ten minutes before the others arrive. The members had a field day criticising the Tavistock and the Director: "Isn't anything reliable any more?"; "Doesn't the Director know what is going on?"; or "Is he deliberately misdirecting us?"; "The staff too either have no knowledge or are in chaos".

Day three

I feel better today after reflecting on the awfulness of yesterday. I sleep well but do not remember any dreams. The day begins with the first sessions of the large study group in which a member demands that I apologise for my mistake of yesterday. There are attempts to play down the error, mostly from men who say they should have been more alert and reliant on their own direction-finding abilities. But later comments about impotent/withdrawn male consultants suggests an attack on the traditions, roles, and primacy of the Tavistock Institute and the Leicester Conference. The "mother of all group relations conferences" has lost its appeal and other organisations around the world are vying for the title and believing it is within their grasp. The men show off, but real competition is between the women. The men present intellectual, flashy images of war but are, in fact, taking flight from their experience of the Large Group. It appears the Large Study Group does not know what to do with me in consultant role, perhaps fearing that if they annoy me in this role, I might retaliate against them in my Director role. The imagery of the Large Study Group has elements of the Divine Comedy, replete with Circles of

Hell. The group resembles a spaceship under command of ground control that has placed the ship on automatic pilot following a computer crash. The "cock-up" of the Director might have liberated them, but more likely sent them into space. Bion states that the group, eager to allay the anxiety state of its leader and exhausting itself supporting the leader, is the duality of basic assumption dependency. Coping with its dependency on an anxious leader consumes the group's energies that might be devoted to the realities of the group task. Another mistake! In the intergroup plenary meeting, I announce the end of the intergroup event would be on Monday at 3.30 pm instead of Sunday at 6.00 pm. I am annoyed with myself because of these mistakes. I had not cross-referenced the different timetables. It is unbelievable that there are two timetables, each with errors. I should have checked them and double-checked. There are details in the timetable I should have changed, for example, there is no rationale for having two-hour intergroup sessions in the evenings. In fact, every argument points to having the evening intergroup session the same length (one-and-a-half hours) as with all other sessions. Another problem lies in managing the reporting of the sub-systems—small study group, large study group, and institutional event—in the limited time available in the general staff meeting. The programme is too tight and I am concerned that staff will not be able to hold up for two weeks with this kind of pressure. Some are suffering from backache and others from colds. Today I bumble less and I think I hold to the boundary of reporting, thinking and processing reasonably well, utilising the explicit and implicit communications to extend our understanding of the conference and its sub-systems. But feelings of contempt and arrogance, unlikeability and scorn are apparent in several group sessions today. These feelings seem to be held mostly by American members and consultants, and the depressed dispirited feelings held mostly by European women.

Day four

I do not run the general staff meeting well because:

1. Too much time is spent preparing for the hand-over (feedback of information regarding the training group was satisfactory). I should go over the hand-over material and make myself more

proficient in it. And this is the horrible truth—I did not have the intergroup event in my mind; it was not on the agenda. Where are your planning, notes, agenda items, purpose, and time allocations? Because of the lack of leadership, the meeting drifts until a frantic D has a temper-tantrum. Your staff want you to lead. (See your note on Day 3 on the group exhausting itself supporting their anxious leaders.)

2. Time-keeping. I had changed the time of the staff meeting from 7.30 pm–9.30 pm, to 7.30 pm–9.00 pm, and then, at D's request, and with everyone's agreement, we finally agreed the meeting should meet from 7.15 pm–8.45 pm. At 8.45 pm K, who had agreed to the change of time, said she thought the meeting was due to continue until 9.15 pm! She was following the old timetable, about which I am so resentful. I had inherited it, and did not think to go over it very carefully and examine every event, every session, and every detail and decide whether they were right for "my" conference. S asked why the intergroup event at night should last two hours when every other event lasts one and a half hours. It only adds to the confusion, he said. I did not know the rationale for it and yet I took it into "my" conference without question.

There are other mistakes in the conference timetable tonight and K helped me correct them. She suggests that in future at the beginning of the pre-conference staff meeting, I should take the staff through the timetable detail by detail. My anger and despair about the timetable and the mistakes I am making make me want to stop working. It is late. I am tired and depressed, but F persevered and, with K to help, we complete the revisions to the timetable successfully.

Discussion about the conference co-sponsorship is good, but also makes me aware of how little substance there is in the co-sponsorship. Our co-sponsors could do more to promote the conference. Few applications came via our co-sponsors. It seems that the Leicester conference is not in people's minds. The isolation of the conference makes it vulnerable. This point helps me to realise why I am so disengaged from the reporting of the intergroup event. As the Director role is on the boundary of the two co-sponsoring organisations, my experience of the intergroup event, I feel, reflects the absence of relatedness between the Tavistock Institute Group Relations Programme and other group relations organisations. There is a kind of virtual relatedness in which working at developing relationships seems optional.

This is strongly reflected today in the Small Study Group subsystem, which seems divided along the lines of English-speakers and non English-speakers. The non English-speakers appear to work harder on seeking to base their knowledge in their experience of having less understanding and, therefore, having fewer expectations than English-speakers. Bion is clear that the agreeable emotional states in the group that make the individual "feel better", and the disagreeable emotional states that makes the individual "feel worse", are kept isolated from each other and from the individuals awareness that these agreeable and disagreeable feelings might have something to do with the individual's membership of the group. Putting it another way, the members of the group privately search for locations of social concern; they find it difficult to ask for help and they cannot comprehend how to manage limited resources.

Day five

A satisfactory day. Things go well in all sectors: training group, large study group, small study group and intergroup events, but we do not have time to review the intergroup, which has two sessions today. At coffee, I hear concerns expressed about a member who seemingly is unable to comprehend the effect of his behaviour on other people. There is some concern about him becoming a casualty, but I look out for him and see that he seems to be getting along satisfactorily. S has him in his intergroup territory and he reports that the member is fine, but experiencing high levels of anxiety.

There are Jewish/black/refugee/colonial/slave issues floating around in the conference, but these are not well articulated. Either the Jewish theme has been overworked or the conference has difficulty dealing with the presence of two Jewish members of staff who are said to look alike. Themes around the International Jewish Conspiracy are present, but are not easy to deal with. Perhaps this masks feelings about the change of leadership at the Tavistock Institute from a true British tradition to a racially hybrid one from the colonies. The development of group relations institutions in the world and the role of the Institute in providing leadership raises issues of power and sovereignty in which "The Tavistock" is held in a semi-permanent iconomatic position, that is to say, "The Tavistock" group relations model is regarded as necessitating change and is also criticised for changing. In any event, the message from the membership appears to be that they seek safety in the Small Study Groups from their experiences in the Large Study Groups—saying that they do not like what they are learning, especially about the individual's connectedness to the group. One particular non-PC piece of learning concerns the attraction of aggressive men to certain women.

I am struck by the relationship with tradition that is imprisoning and freeing, and how bound I have felt by it in taking up the role of director. The big one centres on whether the conference must be held at the University of Leicester in order for it to remain "the Leicester conference". There are other issues that require immediate attention: emails (provide facilities for them); the gates to the garden (unlock them and make the Botanical Gardens accessible as a pathway and a place to relax in); the barman (ensure he does not organise the party for members on the last night).

Day six

Today is difficult. It starts with O wanting to be helpful, but "rushing" at me with warnings about casualties unless my staff address the negative transference. In spite of having discussed this issue with my staff several times and believing that they are doing so satisfactorily, I still feel burdened by this message. Once more, I feel I am not doing my job properly; nevertheless, I resolve not to burden my Large Study Group colleagues with this message. I recall Bion's reference (1961, p. 31) to the effect of his presence in a group, that is, even though he desists from talking about himself, the group seems excessively curious about him, a curiosity that for the group turns into Bion "forcing" himself upon it.

> However irrelevant it may appear to be to the purpose of the meeting, the [group's] preoccupation with my personality certainly seemed to obtrude itself, unwelcome though that might be to the group or to myself . . . We are constantly affected by what we feel to be the attitude of a group to ourselves, and are consciously or unconsciously swayed by our idea of it.

Despite my resolve to keep the message to myself, five minutes before we go into the Large Study Group, K asks me why I am looking worried and I tell her and the others of my concern about the consequences of not dealing with the negative transference. The effect of this comment produces "memory and desire" in the staff group and limits their spontaneous participation in the Large Study Group. I, too, find myself unable to complete my sentences, or to think clearly during the session.

I tell the barman that for entertainment on the last night of the conference, I would prefer the membership to approach the conference administrator for assistance and not him.

Day seven

We are approaching the end of the first week. The changes in the timetable, the end of the first week, the day before the break, all produce tension. There are signs of the membership collectively preparing for the break through various consolidations of their learning. In particular, women appear to be struggling with identity conflicts. One female member is upset at being seen as sexy, because, she claims, it impedes women's progress in the world of work. The issue for women appears to be facing the consequences of claiming their sexuality and the breaking up of women's solidarity. Other themes express longings to belong to one's own group or culture and the difficulties faced in achieving this through membership of the Large Group. The Large Study Group breaks out into multi-cultural themes with tunes and poetry used to express national and cultural feelings. The membership appears to need to refind traditional and familiar roots as it gets ready for the break. There are a large number of people who have not yet spoken in the Large Group. I wonder whether the non-speakers are "holding" the question of relevance of the conference. There is also a question of whether the conference is a British or International conference, and whether ethnic differences and multiple roles can safely be talked about. I have an uneasy thought that if a significant part of the conference cannot raise ethnic, national, and cultural differences, might it be a reflection of a director who might not have fully dealt with his own ethnic, racial, religious, and national issues. Today we had the Working Conference plenary. The lesson, as always, is preparation—knowing what is happening and where everyone is, in what role, every minute of the day. Think ahead and plan, revise, and decide. A key issue is to limit the number of roles one is carrying. Today at the Conference Institution staff meeting (the total staff group), I attempt to report on the state of the Working Conference staff (all staff except the training group staff), believing that as director of the Working Conference I should know what is going on everywhere. But being at that moment the director of the total conference system simply makes it impossible and I grind to a halt. O suggested I should delegate. I asked E to report, which he does willingly and well, and things go smoothly. I ask myself why I did not delegate the task in the first instance and I link the Large Study Group's concern about the pernicious consequences of colonialism, the group's fear of its own power, and preserving the male consultants for future roles to Bion's statement about Saint Augustine and the individual's relationships with the State. Saint Augustine in The City of God postulates a heavenly city in which the relationships between individuals become harmonised through each individual's relationship with God (Bion 1961, p. 129). But, he continues, this is an example of the work group changed in order to maintain contact with the basic assumption—in particular with the dependent basic assumption. Saint Augustine is concerned to defend Christianity, but in the process he is alleged to have undermined Rome's capacity to defend itself against a real external enemy. Leadership in relation to the work group must be taken forward confidently. Consensus leadership does not work in all situations. The group gets anxious and angry and the work task is defeated tonight. Clear vision, determination, and confidence to act are required without losing the capacity to consult with others.

Day eight (free day)

A successful day! Time to gather together and relax. I prepared for meeting with the university's conferences organiser about the gates to the Botanical Gardens. No problem. She comes to the meeting with the solution already in hand. The porter will open the gates at 7.45 am and lock them at 10.00 pm. Problem solved. Question: What prevented the solution being available earlier in the week? Decide to stay in tonight. Good decision. Went shopping with L, giving us a chance to talk. Return and talk with K, who has suffered a family bereavement. She has decided to stay as consultant and continue working in the conference. I am relieved. I cannot deal with another thing like that right now. The next week is before us and we have an important boundary to manage: the Institutional Event. I wonder what preparations have I omitted.

Day nine

I feel fine as all the staff reassemble for the second week of the conference. Everyone is present and they seem to have made good use of the free day—some went home, some stayed in and toured the area, or simply relaxed. K has decided to stay on in the conference and I am relieved, although she wondered whether she would be distracted and not available mentally for work. But she is OK for now. I feel admiration for her determination and her sensitivity. Gender relationships are revealing a pattern—men and women seem to be increasingly relating to each other, but women-to-women relations appear absent. Is open ambition between women hidden? Male and female sexuality manifest differently—men in the conference are described as denying their sexuality and relying on polished intellectuality while women avoid open competition but "sleep their way to the top". A visible male–female pair in the membership has formed. Their behaviour is challenging and disturbing, but I cannot understand it. I wonder whether this pairing expresses hope or is a flight. Feeling surprisingly asexual myself, I am inclined to think that this is flight from a more difficult kind of intercourse, that is, global, political, and religious dynamics as they are reflected in the authority roles in the conference.

Day ten

We are in the institutional event, now working in public and the drama of my "mistake" on the first day and subsequent mistakes are still reverberating around the conference. The membership is preoccupied with questions of whether it was a genuine mistake or a ploy by the staff to gauge the membership's response. The confusion resulting from the first mistake has been compounded by a second in the plenary of the Institutional Event when I am reported to have combined the Training Group and the Working Conference into a merged "membership". I know I referred to both separately in my opening address, but it is possible that, in reply to a question, I might have inadvertently referred to the availability of consultancy to "the membership" in general. The sensitivity of the Training Group members to their new status and their wish to retain a distinctive identity needs to be recognised. Only the day before they had become transformed into consultants to the Review and Application Groups.

Competition within the staff group is an issue regularly referred to, but not fully discussed, partly, I guess, because I do not want to have to deal with staff's feelings about my competence. O supports me, but when she spoke to a member about competence, meaning his, I took it to mean mine. I must look up the difference between competence and mistakes.

A point from the Large Study Group: it is a salutary lesson that when one speaks to a feeling or a thought, one discovers it exists but is suppressed in people's minds until a consultant's remark brings it to the surface. My remarks over tea to a member were obviously discussed in her small study group, which in turn were reported in the general staff meeting as the Director favouring a member. Today I was freer in my associations and the transference to me as Jewish and South African. Fantasies about pairing with the Jewish male consultant, the "international Jewish conspiracy" fantasy, more people engaging and "joining" the Large Study Group—all this is evidence that the group's improved competence. The Large Study Group consultants are beginning to "enjoy" the membership.

Day eleven

There are issues relating to directorship that need considering—experience, seniority, and confidence, holding the boundaries and keeping to task. These qualities allow for the proper management of the conference task, which is to allow opportunities for learning from experience to take place. It is a conference of the mind. The realities of the conference: interaction, daily habits, administrative practicalities, are subservient to the primacy of the mind. This is the only conference method available with this kind of emphasis. Thinking thoughts are essential requirements for this type of work. It is an art, a skill, and a science. The point I am making is that it cannot be taken lightly, ignored, or dealt with inconsistently. Otherwise, confusion and madness enter. Responsibility means sticking to one's role under all conditions, that is, to keep thinking and to offer thoughts even when under pressure, to avoid sarcasm and frivolity, to ponder and deliver carefully and helpfully. Of course, one does not always think or feel this way, as with S's warning that staff are not paranoid enough. Watch out for what is happening, especially the subtleties, and pick them up. Look out for connections, relationships, who is doing what to whom, who represents whom or what. Watch out for niceness. As for transference feelings, they are the essence of the experience: that which exists in members' minds regarding authority figures and each other. Hold several people's interventions in mind at the same time. And make it real.

At the Tavistock Institute, group relations continues to be developed and articulated. Theory and practice are closely linked and this linkage forms the basis of the Tavistock approach, in so far as one can be said to exist, that is, that change takes place principally as a consequence of the mutual engagement of the consultant and group. In other words, extending Bion's assertion that the transference can be used to discuss the group's attitude towards the consultant and the consultant can state in words what the attitude is, the purpose of the statement is to illuminate what is taking place within the boundaries of the engagement.

Day twelve

Today misgivings about the membership's capacity to learn are heard. I feel a pang of self-criticism, an unwelcome reminder that the Director might have done more to ensure an easier path to learning, for example, created a different conference design, appointed different staff, or selected a different membership. Had the Tavistock Institute miscalculated in the appointment of myself as Director of the conference? On the basis of my feelings, I am drawn once more to Bion's view that the conference is quite unable to face the emotional tensions within it without believing that some sort of higher authority is fully responsible for all that takes place (Bion, 1961, p. 38). But as the end of the conference draws near, members become more anxious over unfinished business and they appear to have to identify others who would either appear to have learnt less than them, or find a culprit to blame for not better facilitating their own learning.

Day thirteen

The end of the conference is in sight and today there is a plethora of nautical and religious imagery—the conference feels like a large ship with no one at the helm; a Noah's Ark containing a sinking hope; a rudderless ship; the conference arranged around religious festivals: Easter and Passover, suggesting questions about which orthodoxy would prevail. Once again, anxieties are expressed about the safety of the Tavistock Institute, and there is anger towards the "ancestors" for not bequeathing a safer structure. I feel somewhat confused over what boundaries I am meant to manage—a Tavistock Institute boundary or a boundary around a group relations community? The issue of succession is inevitably in the air and there are anxieties over whether or not that, too, will pass safely. It seems to me there is a parallel between the perception of the membership towards the Tavistock Institute that mirrors a general perception that the nexus of containment has passed from organisations to networks. Today, personal relationships more than formal employment contracts sustain work. The death of organisations means the loss of ancestors, and the membership ask themselves: "Why are we here?"

Day fourteen

Despite continuing challenges to the authority of the staff and complaints about unfinished business (e.g., competition between women was not explored), there is evidence of learning having taken place, especially in the sense that most individuals had felt themselves meeting up with the group collective unconscious, while still maintaining individual differences. Today there is much poetry and many metaphors and dreams in evidence, suggesting it is easier to integrate diversity now without exaggerating it. The staff feel that events are ending well, that important personal growth has taken place. They believe themselves to be holding the right container. I feel I have come through. It has been an absorbing, complex conference and important learning has taken place by members and staff alike.

Day fifteen

A question that I had pondered before the conference, and again within it, is: how does the working conference reflect contemporary organisational life? Is there relevance between the conference and the members' back-home situations? Or, is the conference a haven? A spa in the mind? It is a common view that the design and the theory of group relations conferences exerts a pull to the personal away from the system. A narcissistic culture develops, more focused on the "me", and when staff interpret group transference towards the consultant, they are regarded as unfriendly and spoiling their fun. Staying in role makes one "bad", yet, paradoxically, learning to stay in role is what people come to the conference for. The conference is a container and its success can be measured by the extent that diverse role relationships can be explored without losing one's inner core. Towards the end of the conference, more links are being made to members' organisations. Some groups try working with leaderless teams, but discover that leaderless teams kill each other.

The members ask for our honesty and complain that they get cover-up instead. Can one have a public role with integrity? Or, do conference staff experience the collapse of their consultant roles? Group relations conferences hold values. If we are not honest, members will push us to be integral. People come to conferences with hopes and dreams, but also to deal with the crazy images in society. Group relations is an important network of relationships to help people keep afloat in a schizoid world. It seems likely that the group relations network, not the group relations organisation, is central in this. The network evokes loyalty and trust. If the conference institution can be trustworthy and loyal to its members, then pairing with the director, not replacing him, becomes a possibility.

From group therapy to group relations

Bion was concerned to further the application of his theory of functions to the theory of thought processes. He starts from Freud's idea that thought fills the gap between tension and its discharge, that is, that thought is an experimental version of activity; thought is a way of dealing with frustration. According to Bion, at primitive levels of development no distinction can be made between the material and the psychological and the frustration will either be evaded or modified.

Bion published *Experiences in Groups* in 1961. Earlier, these papers had been published in the journal *Human Relations*, the journal of the

Tavistock Institute of Human Relations. Subsequently, in his impressive canon of published work, Bion referred to groups in his papers, discussions, and seminars. This is often forgotten. As David Armstrong (1992) points out,

> I believe it is possible to trace in this later body of work lines of thought which complement, modify and extend the ideas presented in Experiences in Groups, and the relative neglect of these lines of thought by practitioners in "group relations" contributes to the sense of self-inflicted theoretical and methodological atrophy which seems to surround those who work in this field. (p. 261)

Bion's ideas on groups were incorporated into the thinking of the Group Relations Training Programme of the Tavistock Institute of Human Relations. What Bion would have done if he had developed such working conferences is unknown. We do have his observations in a letter to his wife from the time he took part in an American conference in 1969. (Bion, 1985).

> ... Ken Rice, looking white haired and older, was the same as ever. It soon became evident that R. S. was very nervous, as this was his first experience as Director of the Conference. He was scared stiff of A. K. R. and self, though I did not get wise to this, or its extent quick enough or I would have tried to keep my mouth shut. After the plenary I was so unfortunate as to be talking when the meeting ended and the Staff walked out. I had not realised that according to the real rules of Groups – as laid down by Ken – he insisted on split second termination of each meeting, and by the time I had finished my sentence the Staff had disappeared round the corner and I couldn't find where they had gone ... It ended with my being very depressed and inclined to pack my traps and clear out. (p. 129)

The working conferences now have a substantial history since their beginnings in 1957. The original formulations of Bion on small groups have been extended by learning from new events to explore the social processes in groups of different sizes. As it is, thinking about Bion's hypotheses is suffused with "memory and desire", to borrow his own phrase, which have their roots in past experiences of this kind of work and the various psychic and political defences that are inevitable with the process of institutionalisation that has been necessary for development of the group relations educational method.

Traditional group relations training, based on Rice's interpretation of Bion on groups, focuses on power and authority. But what is left out? Knowledge/science is necessarily a public activity and, thus, involves the group, though it is also the group that resists it. Thoughts require groups. It might be that there is a taboo about K (knowledge) in groups that cannot be broken. The idea that "thoughts are just there" might be impossible to be recognised. Basic assumptions, therefore, can be thought of as defences against something apprehended. It seems that Bion's personal relationship to groups was that he seemed to want to escape them, but remained fascinated.

Bion thought of group therapy as having two meanings:

- the treatment of a number of individuals assembled for special therapeutic sessions: an exploration of the neurotic trouble of the individual (Bion mentions that sometimes this turns mainly on catharsis of public confession);
- a planned endeavour to develop in a group that lead to smoothly running co-operative activity; the acquisition of knowledge and experience of the factors which make for a good group spirit.

This sense of the good group spirit was important in terms of the task he undertook in setting up a training wing in the Northfield military psychiatric hospital. His first task there was to ask what part neurosis played in the problems of a group and what would this mean in terms of timetable and organisation. He linked the fact that 300 or 400 men gathered in the unit had the benefit of therapeutic value of military discipline, good food, and regular care. He was convinced that what was needed was a kind of discipline achieved in a theatre of war by an experienced officer in command over a rather weak battalion. He saw there was a need for urgent action and for the psychiatrists in charge of the wing to be responsible in the way that officers in the field are responsible when facing issues of life and death; psychiatrists had to know what it was like to exercise authority and sustain it. The psychiatrist in authority would realise that his task was to produce self-respecting men socially adjusted to the community and, therefore, willing to accept these responsibilities whether in peace or war. Bion's reference to the need for discipline foreshadows his idea on the need for structures in the mind. The well-functioning group links with his notion of the optimal social environment.

Therefore, neurosis is a problem of the group, not only of the individual. Bion works constantly with the paradox of the disturbed group treating itself. The "transparent wall" enables the group to observe itself by stepping outside the frame. Within the enclosed space, neurotic behaviour can be displayed for the whole group to see, behaviour that is not clouded by the influence of others or by self-deception. Members of the group see themselves through the observer's eyes. This move outside the frame fractures the boundary of the group and enables seeing the inside of one group by being in another group. It is not enough just to be enclosed in a "one-group-identity". A transparent space is three-dimensional—time, place, and inner world.

Bion had seen the danger coming from defining neurosis as a disability of the community, not just the individual. How does the group help its members to adjust to the distress of society? How could it help people to choose to find something bigger than them when they do not appear to have choice? The thing to treat was the social. Bion's genius lay in risking his authority and status on this innovation, that is, to help the men to choose to join the war.

The value of Bion's experiment and his major influence in group relations lay in the possibility of training the total community in interpersonal relationships. By approximating to this theoretical construct, members of the training wing (seen from outside the framework) could look with detachment and growing understanding upon the problems of its workings. Bion's skill, and that of the men in the training wing, was an availability to look at the phenomena in their group in a manner that nobody had done before. By attending to the boundary, and giving the attention to see the space, though the space would not change, the perception of it from outside the framework opened possibilities for relearning and undoing the neurosis. The link here to group relations is self-evident.

Bion imposed certain basic regulations upon the men in the military hospital as a prerequisite for developing and studying group forces. In particular, the daily parade, which was "the first step towards the elaboration of therapeutic seminars (1961, p. 16), had both an overt and covert intent. The expressed intent was for making announcements, etc., and the veiled intent was to allow the men to step outside as detached observers of the group's behaviour. Bion invited the men to move from the individual to a communal position and become spectators of their own experience. Bion appears concerned to ensure that the men become responsible for both their own behaviour and for examining it. Bion might have been acting intuitively and seeing this work as the beginning of group relations, that is, treating the parade as a therapeutic seminar. Or did that all come later? Whatever it is, it is clear that at a practical level the experiment failed, for it was eventually shut down because of the men's behaviour and leaves the impression that Bion might have been construed as subversive. Bion had challenged his officer colleagues' assumptions about their men as cannon fodder and attempted to find and receive greater respect for them. There is a sense in which Bion was encouraging a form of "mutiny", but his position was strongly in favour of transition, where men moved from being in a "patient role" to a "soldier role". He did not suggest radical social transformation, but that men be encouraged to think about the role they take in response to a particular task.

Bion himself was disappointed in institutions. He was deeply affected by the perceived failure of the hospital on the death of his first wife, and his preoccupation with the causes of despair in collections of people might reflect something of his own past. It is possible that flight from institutions was the only way he could gain greater freedom to explore what institutions were really involved in. Bion was interested in helping groups to achieve tasks and not in group relations.

Bion was puzzled by when men obediently follow orders. He claimed it had to do with their training and discipline, in which the army hierarchy is also construed as the enemy and the men collude with this process. Hierarchically ordered sanctions are powerful. Consequently, although those accompanying Bion might have felt that he was giving them power, the question remained as to how they were to use it. Discipline and fear were also controlling factors in the lives of the men. They themselves wished to exercise it when complaining about patients who skived, yet it was also clear that for these particular men, obtaining co-operation by exercising sanctions had failed; the men were no longer frightened by what could be done to them. This might have led Bion to consider that you can only make soldiers by getting men to think voluntarily of being a soldier. It cannot be achieved through fear or discipline.

"What then of love?"

Can men be loved by officers to become soldiers, and is the struggle one of love and hate, expressed as fear/punishment? The struggle is between Bion's love of truth, based on the rigour of reflecting and thinking, as opposed to the co-operation achieved by discipline, fear, and punishment. Bion believed that men co-operate willingly because their officer loves them; the officer can then be free of guilt; otherwise, if men act only under coercion, officers might be guilt laden.

If new forms of leadership were emerging in the army, was there a new model of followership? Certainly, there were major changes in society because of the war. Sexual mores were changing and many women now worked at what would have been implicitly construed as "men's work". But how much of the respect that Bion indicates an officer should have for his men is synonymous with love? It is perhaps implicit to look at what is there, that expresses a concern for the well-being of the individual and encourages him to use his freedom to look at reality. Bion was part of a generalised set of processes going on in the army about new ways of discovering leadership.

Bion's "loving concern" might well reflect his experience of human wastage in the First World War; wastage based on contempt. He is now saying that men have a capacity for making a fuller contribution: indeed, of making the choice about their contribution. Bion's crusade was to see men as capable of reflecting and thinking and making mature judgements and decisions for themselves. His task was to provide those men with the opportunities to do that. "Loving concern" might well equate with Bion's "intuitive sympathetic flair" (1961, p. 22). Bion saw clearly that psychological means are needed to deal with psychological disturbances. He believed in the validity of working with groups in this way, and group relations for Bion might have included group interpersonal relationships. Bion seemed preoccupied with what needs of the individual could only be satisfied in a group, suggesting that the choice was between social-ism and narcissism; that it was possible to have thoughts in a group that are not possible alone.

The group-as-a-whole: group mentality

In my role as director of group relations conferences, I am concerned about the question of whether the behaviour of an individual is

representative of the behaviour of all, a common view in group relations methodology. Are all guilty of the cruelty in the group? Do those
who are silent give consent? Negative evidence is that the group
supports what it does not repudiate.

The director occupies the nexus between a number of layers of
emotions of the conference and is, therefore, in a unique position to
serve as a measure of "conference mentality". From this vantage point,
the director can postulate or interpret the "conference mentality".
Doing so causes difficulty to individuals in pursuing their aims,
because, ultimately, group culture is a compromise formation between
group mentality and individual desires. For staff and members alike,
the director, through "interpreting" conference unconscious process,
shifts the tone from "bewilderment" to something like the possession
of compass points adding direction to phenomena. Multiple systems
are being studied in group relations conferences, and it is, therefore,
important to provide the evidence of how working with unconscious
dynamics has been achieved, and why we, to a certain extent, are
indifferent to "outcomes", therapeutic or otherwise. I was aware that
working with basic assumption material seemed to make me more
detached. This emerges as the other side of something quite depressed,
feeling "left stranded", unable to convince myself, suggesting connections between scientific creativity and the role of depression in this.
For the director, patience is significant, adopting a long time scale,
bracketing out action and outcomes; these are ways of managing
depression, preparing to receive the "significant fact", reparation and
"giving things their due", allowing something to emerge and attending to minute particulars. Whether group therapy or group relations,
tolerance of frustration has to be taken to an extreme.

To Bion, the group was a phenomenon that was greater than the
sum of its parts. For the group relations conference director, the total-
ity of events in the conference-as-a-whole needs to be discerned and
described, and, in particular, their unconscious representations. The
director's interpretations are intended to make links between the environment containing the conference and the conference's ability to
"know", both consciously and unconsciously (Lawrence, 2000, p. 155).
He must take the conference, the groups, and the individuals in them
beyond immediate phenomena. Directors should not be too rooted in
structures that need to be more open and fluid. The conference and its
groups are concerned about the failure of leaders and the attempts to

find a substitute that satisfies. I found that, at times, I had come to be experienced by the conference as someone harmful who acts against the interests of the conference, and the conference consequently came together in order to put an end to my interventions. Members may seek family-like characteristics in the conference, but it is not the same thing as a family. The director of a conference is not the same thing as a father of a family, although at certain times I felt I was expected to be "parental"—providing a containing framework—while managing a projection that told me that I was experienced as an adversary of the conference. But I found, in fact, that an interpretation in one session appeared to be enacted in the next. As the conference passes from one culture (fight/flight) to another (pairing) and back again, group behaviour changes. In the fight/flight culture, it was difficult for individuals to pay much attention to what I said or did. In the pairing culture, it was difficult for any individual to sustain a conversation with me. For the director, the two group cultures (fight/flight, pairing) make the job more difficult and the conference cannot easily receive his contributions.

Group relations work is about the mystery of communications that rely on the mechanisms of projective identification; the group's silence might be due to its envy of its consultants; that the death instinct exists in groups and is destructive of their task, for example, as when the group does not let on that anything has been understood. Envy prevents it being known, but something goes in. The group, after all, might want to hang on to its insight. Group relations is concerned with the language of rebellion; if the individual rebels, will it make any difference? Daring to rebel against prevailing numbing norms leads to an alteration of the emotional field of the group. Rebellion in the conference might not make any difference, but we are interested in what kind of statement enables the individual to shift the culture of the group.

Group relations conference work is a method of investigation of the interactions and behaviour of several interdependent sub-systems, each one interested in, and curious about, the other groups and their internal functioning, and simultaneously participating in an investigation of the dynamics of the conference-as-a-whole. This curiosity and desire to engage sometimes is at variance with the group's unconscious aim of group self-preservation. For example, a group's preoccupation with absent members could be due to anxieties about the group fragmenting. In a group, it takes some time before individuals cease to be dominated by the feeling that adherence to the group is an end in itself.

Group basic assumptions conflict sharply with the idea of a group met together to do a creative job. The paradox appears to be that basic assumptions are both preserving and disintegrating. What makes a group worth preserving? Surviving "at all costs" might represent a heroic delusion. In a group relations conference, which is, after all, committed to learning, it might be better to ask whether a basic assumption exists about learning in a group. As an example of Bion moving from group therapy to study groups and group relations, he states (1961, p. 66),

> The attempt to use the group as a seminar was intended to keep the group anchored to a sophisticated and rational level of behaviour, suitable to the fulfilment of the aims individuals wished to pursue; it was as if without some such attempt this procedure would lead to the obtrusion of a kind of group that was a hindrance of the conscious wishes of the individual. That attempt failing, there began to emerge the group that is dominated by the basic assumption of unity for purposes of fight or flight. If you can only fight or run away, you must find something to fight or run away from.

Given the high level of objection from members at group relations conferences about staff's strict adherence to punctuality, it is well to remember Bion's question (1961, pp. 86–88): "When does the group begin?" Does the group begin at the stated time? When it assembles? When the group is in the mind? What is it that begins? What are the group phenomena which do "not begin", but continue and evolve? The dilemmas about being in a group are always present in the mind. Does beginning mean "beginning to attend" to these ongoing phenomena? Attention is a psychological act that continues indefinitely.

These challenging questions shock many people at a group relations conference for the first time—there is no formal agenda, the group does not appear to "do" anything. What is group relations about? The contribution of group relations is that it is concerned with both the external world—what is "out there"—*and* the internal world of the group—what is "in here". Unconscious phantasies have neither beginning nor end; they are timeless and the members are invited to address these dilemmas.

Conclusions

Group therapy is a setting for individuals to seek help for their psychological problems. They might expect to receive that help from the group therapist, from other members of the group, and from within themselves. On the other hand, group relations conference work addresses the strivings of individuals in groups only in so far as they reveal group-as-a-whole dynamics. In group relations, groups study the behaviour and mental life of the group-as-a-whole, that includes conference staff and the director, and this study of the human mind and human systems is furthered by group-wide and system-wide interpretations. Group relations evolved into an enterprise in which individuals learn about the formal and informal roles they take or are given in groups; it is not about the public scrutiny of individual personalities for improvement in social and personal functioning.

In group relations, members seemingly behave as if they are conscious of themselves as individuals, but unconscious of themselves as group members. Interpretations offered by consultants provide meaning to the group's and conference's behaviour. In the group, we are unconscious, but as individuals we can become conscious of what is going on. But even sophisticated individuals can be swept along by group process. Individuals have "minds"; the group has to work to find its "mind". Mind can be said to exist in a group if the group is ready for it to exist, that is, if it is ready to receive the interpretation.

Group relations work often faces groups with the fear of their annihilation. Leaders deal with their fear of annihilation by not admitting ignorance. Group pressure often directs the leader to be omniscient and make the group feel secure. Group relations work shows how groups defend themselves against unpleasant feelings by splitting and isolating themselves from the rest of the conference in order to avoid the conjunction of certain feelings. Group members, feeling unsafe, long for an omniscient leader who can think for them and make them feel safe. On the other hand, being with the group is also a survival mechanism. Individual group members often feel they can never get it right. Whatever position they are in, there is always another that seems more attractive. Membership of a group means making the best of a bad job. We are part of the group and it is the group that counts, whatever we experience individually. The basic assumptions are all delusions of certainty, security, and survival.

We live in a world where risk is an endemic part of productive forces. The risk is of breaking the existing conceptualisation of the group. Sticking with the group is like sticking with the past. Therefore, being different threatens both the individual and the group. Basic assumptions offer a paradox: surviving, but without thought or the capacity for reality-testing. By staying with what you have got is like going for broke. But a new choice may also fail. Either way it is a gamble. That is the essence of learning from experience in group relations conference work.

Acknowledgements

A number of people have contributed to the thinking out of this chapter. In particular, I acknowledge the contribution of the Bion Reading Seminar (1994–2000) established by Gordon Lawrence and Jon Stokes, and its members David Armstrong, Peter Goold, William Halton, Paul Hoggett, Colin James, and Judith Szekacs, the members of Anton Obholzer's seminar at the Tavistock Clinic on Consulting to Institutions, and to the members of my Sunday morning workshop for consultants (1990–1999).

PART III

ORGANISATIONAL DEVELOPMENT AND CHANGE CONSULTANCY

In search of the "structure that reflects": promoting organisational reflection practices in a UK health authority*

Introduction

A growing number of authors emphasise the role of public reflection as the basis for learning and change at all levels in organisations (Moon, 2000; Raelin, 2001, 2002; Reynolds, 1998; Siebert & Daudelin, 1999; Smith, 2001). These authors take the view that differences between reflection *on* action and reflection *in* action constitute an important locus of learning in modern organisations. They identify critical locations where learning at individual, group, and organisational levels feed and sustain each other. They also note that current reflections on "reflection", at least in organisational and management studies, have two main limits. First, they often elaborate on the theory and principles of organisational reflection without addressing how this notion can be put to work in practice. Second, even when they are practically orientated, these authors often

*This chapter is based on: D. Nicolini, M. Sher, S. Childerstone, & M. Gorli (2004), In search of the 'structure that reflects': promoting organisational reflection practices in a UK health authority. In: M. Reynolds & R. Vince (Eds.), *Organising Reflection* (pp. 81–104). © Ashgate, London, UK. Material reprinted with permission.

describe experiences that focus on reflection at the individual level rather than at the organisational level. Reynolds (1998) notes that these two limitations tend to reinforce each other. The meaning of reflection is often restricted by an individualised perspective within individual problem-solving activity. However, the reality is that in most situations the individual alone cannot address or solve meta-organisational problems. Such a restricted view of reflection, however, neutralises its capacity to produce learning and change. Individualised, private reflection is incapable of reaching, exposing, and affecting the institutionalised assumptions and logic that regulate organisational action, and it is also at risk of being a sterile effort, given that individuals alone are seldom in positions to make substantial organisational changes (Raelin, 2001; Vince, 2002a). Reflection can become an opportunity for personal growth and organisational transformation only to the extent that it is public, sanctioned, participative, and authorised. Effective reflection and questioning organisational assumptions works well when it is a legitimated organisational process and an "integral part to organising, rather than the province of individuals" (Vince, 2002a, p. 67). Certain organisational conditions have to be put in place for the sum of individual reflection practices to become a trigger for wider organisational change.

The issue is how to make this happen in practice. What strategy should be used to promote reflection at the organisational level? How are personal reflection, group support, and organisational change to be bridged? Can reflection be part of a stable and self-sustaining feature of organising? How does a "reflecting organisation" become established without attributing anthropomorphic features to it while bearing in mind that reflection is centred on people?

In this chapter, we shall discuss how these issues were addressed in the context of a far-reaching three-year project aimed at introducing reflection as a legitimated and stable practice among a group of middle managers of the British National Health Service (NHS). We shall start by reviewing the organisational conditions that triggered the initiative. We will then describe how a group of managers and consultants established a large organisational development-based change management initiative that led to the design of a programme that combined elements of the organisational development (OD) and critical action learning traditions. We will describe the programme, entitled the "Cross-boundary Management Development Initiative"

(CBMDI) in some detail, discussing the attempt to combine the creation of several reflection action learning sets (RALS) into a structure that would connect them into a larger and more powerful whole: the "Structure that reflects". Finally, we will reflect on the outcome of the project, on its successes and difficulties, and on what it tells us about the use of reflection in organisations and on how to render such practice "organisational".

"Dumped on from above and reviled from below"

Being a middle manager anywhere has always been difficult, but it was especially so in the British National Health Service (NHS) of the late 1990s. Since its foundation in 1948, the NHS has been beset by difficulties deriving from its considerable size and its inherently complex status. The NHS is, in fact, the largest employer in Europe and even after the significant restructuring of the late 1980s it still counts a workforce of more than a million. The size problem is compounded by its fragmented and inherently contradictory nature. Like any other public health system, the NHS has to align and reconcile the conflicting interests and expectations of a number of constituents, such as patients, health professionals, government, and taxpayers, who all hold different and often discrepant priorities. At the same time, the anxiety-raising nature of the work encourages the creation of institutional defences, rigid boundaries, and projective mechanisms that significantly hamper any attempt to collaborate to accomplish a common task or to steer the organisation at all (Menzies Lyth, 1970, 1990).

These conditions were further exacerbated during the 1990s when the nature, functioning, and cost of the NHS became one of the most important issues in the UK political arena. Health is one issue that substantially moves voter sympathy, and it was the one that probably decided the change of government in 1997. During this decade, the health service experienced the highly controversial introduction and demise of a strict internal market regime that was replaced by the new Labour Government with a system based on a combination of local delivery management and commissioning organisations, regional co-ordination, and centrally monitored performance standards and cost control. Operating under the double scrutiny of the government and the press, towards the end of the 1990s, the NHS prepared for a major restructuring that would affect virtually each of its components except a few major specialised hospitals. The complete redesign was intended to create a network of medium-sized organisations, called *primary care trusts*, which were meant to be responsible for the delivery of all community health services at local level and were to be co-ordinated by regional health authorities. The government's intention was to create a system that would be more "patient centred", that would increase integration between health and social care services, would reduce "red tape", maximise the return of the extra funding provided, and produce tangible service improvements for the public (Blackler & Kennedy, 2004).

Set against all these changes, management at all levels, but especially middle managers, were anxious and exhausted. This was hardly surprising. The literature abounds with examples of middle management bearing the brunt of major organisational restructuring, and the conditions were particularly harsh for this group of managers (Dopson & Neumann, 1998). For example, over a period of five years, the organisations involved in our project, which eventually became the Hertfordshire and Bedfordshire Strategic Health Authority, went through *seven* partial or total mergers. The extensive shake-up of organisational roles, jobs, and responsibilities generated a situation of winners and losers. Some managers were regarded as "not up to the job" for the next reorganisation and were not offered new appointments. Others opted for early retirement. Overall, management felt unsupported in this process, "dumped on from above and reviled from below", as one of the voices from the service put it (Wall, 1999). Research into middle management's perceptions, revealed that they felt they were "not listened to, not recognised nor appreciated by colleagues, and especially not by superiors" (Pattison, Manning, & Malby, 1999). For many, things were not making sense any more, morale was declining, and there was apprehension that the proposed changes would be cosmetic. New ways of working had to be found and new skills acquired, especially how to manage under conditions of rapid change and organisational turbulence.

Building on seesaws

Against this background, in 1999, the Human Resources Director of the West Hertfordshire Health Authority approached the Tavistock

Institute to obtain assistance in designing an initiative aimed at supporting middle managers to cope with the impending changes and turn the difficulties they were experiencing into opportunities for personal and organisational learning. The HR Director spoke on behalf of an already established "grass roots" group of managers called the Organisational Development Forum (ODF). The ODF was composed of a number of managers who had set themselves the task of promoting a proactive approach to the management of ongoing changes, and especially in the setting up of the new primary care trusts.

Prior to the HR Director's contact with the Tavistock Institute, the ODF had carried out a needs analysis that revealed that local middle managers

- did not want traditional forms of training;
- wanted training that made sense of their experiences and would help them to cope better;
- wanted to explore new ways of doing things, because "the old ones were not working any more".

An interesting dialogue ensued that would become the major source of learning for this level of management. The Tavistock Institute consultants, following a well-established path in the OD tradition (e.g., Cummings & Wolrey, 1996), suggested working with the ODF to establish it as a driving force in the management of change in the Health Authority. The aim was to obtain the necessary endorsement and mandate from the higher echelons of the organisation so that the ODF could co-ordinate local changes and support the process through the use of well-known tools of the "planned change" tradition. The HR Director, on the other hand, was sceptical of the capacity to engage with the NHS in this way. As she put it later, "although I recognised this was the right way of doing it, I knew that I could not engage with our chaotic organisations in such an ordered way. It was not possible to work at an organisational level in that environment at that moment".

Two different concerns were at work here. From the beginning, one of the main concerns of the Tavistock consultants was to avoid colluding with the pressing urge for action. During the first round of exploratory interviews, we often heard the claim that "we do not have the luxury of developing strategies while Rome burns". Pettigrew, Felie, and McKee (1992) note that the highly politicised context of the NHS generates a self-perpetuating process in which continuous crises and panics lead to endemic short-termism and over-reaction that generate yet more crises. In this context, responding to serious challenges through swift "resolutions" and poorly planned actions becomes part of the problem instead of being part of the solution. The Tavistock consultants were especially wary of this risk, which they were trying to expose and counteract.

The HR Director, on the other hand, was tacitly aware of an opposing risk, which was the endemic difficulty in the NHS of getting anything done that crosses any sort of boundary. Her major concern was that the Scylla of mindless action in the NHS is inevitably matched by the Charybdis of inaction and failure of empowerment. Possibly as a form of defence against the persisting chaotic conditions, managers at different levels and locales developed a tendency to wait for direction, maintaining a fantasy that people "at the top" would somehow know what they were enduring and would come up with solutions. The HR Director's concerns were, in many ways, confirmed by the inconclusive attempts of the progressively shrinking ODF to obtain any form of substantial endorsement beyond vague and inconsequential general expressions of interest. In spite of months of contacts and discussions with different parts of the organisations, the middle managers were still without any form of support. No initiative could be jump-started for lack of approval from the elusive "top" of the organisation.

Working with an organisation that shifted between mindless action and paralytic inaction, we were faced with an intriguing question of how to address change "in the middle" in an organisation in transition. A body like the NHS has many parallel and loosely coupled decision-making bodies. People attend these meetings one day and are not part of the organisation the next. Strategic initiatives fail because much energy is dissipated in attempting to set them up. We wondered what other forms of interventions could be used in place of neat and tidy, but unfeasible, OD architectures that could hardly be built on such shaky organisational ground. We struggled to find approaches for useful interventions in what was an organisational seesaw, an environment in which the next "tide" of change would profoundly alter the terrain we were building on. We had no answer on how to proceed without abandoning our basic belief that no real impact on change-related issues could be achieved without obtaining the necessary organisational support and legitimacy.

Working with the structure that is . . .

The HR Director, the few remaining members of the original ODF group, and, eventually, also the Tavistock Institute consultants concluded that in order to move ahead on the design of the intervention, they needed an approach that would closely follow the contours of the fragmented organisation. The major pressing need of providing active and visible support to the middle managers had not been fulfilled. Given that a top-down approach was not feasible, the group turned towards a model that was different to traditional organisation-wide consultancy: action learning and critical reflection.

Action learning

According to Revans (1980, 1997) action learning (AL), like the OD tradition, stems from Kurt Lewin's emphasis on the importance of real life issues as a source of learning. Unlike the OD tradition, however, which is mainly focused on large scale and systemic changes, action learning often operates with a bias toward personal learning and tends to take individuals in reflective action learning sets as the main locus of learning and development. It is difficult to refer to action learning as a unified corpus, given the broad variety of practices that are collected under this umbrella term (Boshyk, 2002; Marsick & O'Neil, 1999). On the other hand, it is possible to say that the action learning tradition is more focused on initiating change through personal development, but it makes large-scale changes difficult to obtain. While OD is focused on modifying the power–knowledge dynamics that keep existing practices in place, action learning intervention has a more agile and plastic architecture. Action learning is less threatening and more amenable to local adaptations that increase capacities to produce significant change effects.

Critical reflection

Given the aims of the interventions and the conditions under which we were operating, we were interested in the particular variety of action learning practice that has been defined as the "critical reflection school" by Marsick and O'Neil (1999) and Cunliffe (2002). To the belief of the action learning movement that the starting point of all learning is action, the critical reflection school adds its insight that participants also need to establish a dialogue and reflect collectively on the assumptions, beliefs, and emotions that shape practice.

Therefore, we developed a practical working hypothesis that an integrated action learning–critical reflection approach would deliver the two aims of the project:

- to sustain middle managers in their efforts to cope with change;
- to produce significant results in cross-boundary methods of working in this part of the NHS.

As there were profound differences between this approach and the original aims of this intervention, we decided to test the validity of the approach by running a preliminary round of ten "consultation syndicates" with about 100 middle managers of the health authority. Consultation syndicates are a form of structured group activity mutated from the group relations tradition (Coleman & Bexton, 1975; Coleman & Geller, 1985). In the consultation syndicates, participants address in turn an issue of their choice in a one-to-one coaching situation; the rest of the group and the facilitator remain in attendance. After a set time, the process stops and the group reflects back to the "inner pair" their considerations about the conduct of the interaction and its outcome. In this way, a second order of learning is generated for both the consultant and the consultee. At the end of the session, the facilitator comments on the overall experience, so that another layer of learning is added.

The consultation syndicates run in the CBMDI programme were specifically aimed to provide a first response to the support needs of the middle managers and to test in the field the validity of the approach and the reactions of participants to this novel (for them) experience. In this way, we could both respond to the expressed needs and gather data for the design of the next part of the initiative. The consultation syndicates were favourably received by participants and were widely endorsed as feasible ways to proceed. Three major themes emerged as topics for the subsequent part of the project.

1. The roles that senior and middle managers would play in managing the changes demanded by the New NHS Plan.
2. The nature of the working relationships that would develop between the professions and disciplines to implement joined-up forms of management that had traditionally been competitive.
3. The challenge of improving inter-agency and inter-sector collaboration both within the NHS and between the NHS and social care systems.

The participants said that in their particular environments organised and sanctioned reflection activity would have a powerful counter-cultural effect. "The best way you can support us", they said, "is by developing a blame-free climate of listening where people can publicly discuss and review novel ways of working. We do not need solutions, we need space to think."

The consultation syndicates, however, emphasised another aspect with which we had been wrestling in the first phase of the project, which was the need to address the power conditions that would allow the result of reflection to be implemented to produce organisational effects. Consultation syndicates are, in fact, different from action-orientated group reflection practices in that their main aim is to use reflection to open up issues and feelings, not to address problems. When used in isolation, they could lead to frustration because participants would still have to carry the responsibility for sorting out the issues raised without the support of their "comrades in adversity" provided by the reflection action learning sets (RALS). Although consultation syndicates were introduced as a "taster" of a different approach to personal and organisational development, it appeared that the empowerment issue could not be put in the background and had to remain high on the agenda.

Establishing a structure to reflect

To summarise, in order to fulfil the expressed aims of the project to support middle managers of the health authority to cope with the changes they had to face *and* to turn their change efforts into meaningful learning opportunities, we needed to devise a new approach. This approach would combine the practical advantages and contextual appropriateness of critical reflection and action learning with the wisdom of managing change that comes out of the OD tradition. Because the two traditions have elements of both learning and action, as well as some contra-indications for our particular situation, we felt the only way forward was to explore a hybrid model. However, examples of hybrids were difficult to find. In spite of their common roots and the recognised need for action learning to link with, and extend to, other forms of "search conferences" and "whole system change" methodologies, the two traditions rarely meet or are put together (McLaughlin & Thorpe, 1993; Morgan & Ramirez, 1983; Pedler, 1997b). Therefore, we designed our own "hybrid", the "cross-boundary management development initiative" summarised in Figure 1 and described in detail below. The design of the programme was based on a simple principle: we would use the flexibility and simplicity of the architecture of a reflective action learning set and combine it with the OD prescription of the need to create the necessary leverage that would support participants in their change efforts.

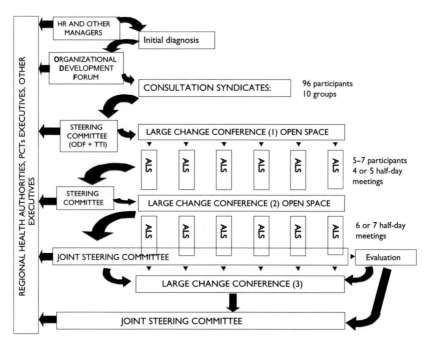

Figure 1. Diagram of the "cross-boundary management development initiative".

If legitimisation and empowerment were impossible to obtain as a preliminary condition for the start-up of the intervention, building such influence would become one of the aims and, ideally, the outcome of the project itself. To achieve this effect, however, participants would need to make up more than a number of loosely coupled cohorts. They would have to form a network and the project as a whole would have to become an actor-network within the organisation. The design of the project, therefore, had to be developed on two separate but related levels. The first would be the level of the reflective action learning set in which the middle managers could reflect and learn how to cope with the ongoing changes in their organisations. The second level would involve the sets establishing a dialogue among themselves and constitute a "structure that reflects" that would create the necessary conditions for the changes they were planning to take root in their organisations.

The overall design of the programme

To achieve this goal, the "Cross-boundary management development initiative" was designed to have three large whole community change conferences (one at the beginning, one half-way through, and one at the end) interspersed with half-day monthly meetings of reflection action learning sets. The sets, six in all, were facilitated by two Tavistock consultants, met over a period of twelve months, and lasted half a day at a time. The objectives of the "Cross-boundary management development initiative" (CBMDI) were to provide a space for senior members of the participating organisations to

- reflect on their experiences of changes in their organisations,
- develop more effective cross-boundary management practices,
- establish ways for exchanging learning and experiences.

The project was managed by a steering committee led by the HR Director and comprising three members of the original ODF and the Tavistock team. The steering committee met regularly during the programme and acted as internal client and referent for the programme. Members of the committee collaborated to define the aims of the programme, to identify and convene participants, to design and review the first two whole community change conferences, to monitor progress, and to design the outline of the evaluation process. They also assisted in the efforts of the programme participants to engage with the rest of the health and social care systems.

The first whole community change conference

The CBMDI programme started with a whole-day conference held at a venue symbolically located at the centre of the catchment area of participant organisations. The conference aimed to:

- introduce participants to the history, rationale, and overall design of the programme;
- help participants identify and agree themes and practical issues for reflection, action, and learning around cross-boundary management practices;
- start forming reflection action learning sets;
- plan the next steps for the sets and for the community as a whole.

In order to establish in practice the principle of reflective conversation and action as a guiding principle of the whole initiative, the first conference was designed using a particular type of large group intervention—open space.

Open space is a variety of large group intervention developed by Owen (1992, 1995; Bunker & Alban, 1997) and constitutes an especially energising and mind-opening approach to large group interventions. Its main characteristic is to be mostly self-organised by participants and to rely significantly on their willingness to accept responsibility for what does or does not happen. Unlike other events, in which sessions are decided in advance, open space sessions are proposed during the large group meeting by anyone who cares about an issue. The open space technology, therefore, helps participants to tap into their creativity by eliminating some typical sources of anxiety (producing something nice and tidy, finishing on time, or using all the time) and encourages them to focus on the process and not only on the outcome.

During the first conference of the CBMDI, we ran three sessions of eight parallel self-organising discussion groups. Participants were asked to clarify their chosen topic with a view to establishing an Reflective Action Learning Set, to start exploring what was potentially interesting and what could be done about it and/or learned from it. The results of each group discussion were summarised on one flip-chart and posted on a board in the large room. Once all the sessions were finished and the flipcharts were posted on the board, the facili-tators negotiated mergers between themes and groups. Participants were then asked to sign up to one of the resulting groups. In this way, participants formed six reflective action learning sets that met in the last session of the day to explore whether or not their topic was a feasi-ble theme for a long-term reflection activity. If they agreed the theme was feasible for them, they planned the next steps: for example, dates of future meetings and how to stay in touch with one another.

The design of the first conference gave a clear signal on how per-sonal and organisational development was going to be approached. While many participants felt energised and empowered by the oppor-tunity to take full control of their own development needs, others acted out the prevailing dependency culture, were disorientated by the low level of direction and structure, or simply left the conference and the programme. Overall, however, the conference successfully established from the outset the notion that whatever work would be conducted within the reflective action learning sets would be part of a larger structure managed by the steering committee. This awareness provided the necessary containment of anxiety raised by the work of the reflective action learning sets. In spite of this, there was still ample evidence of paranoid feelings towards the steering committee, but these were soon dealt with and the reflective action learning sets got on with their reflective activity.

Reflective activity in the sets

Following the first conference, six reflective action learning sets were established around the following themes:

1. Manner and style of communication with colleagues and staff.
2. Managing the complexity of cross-boundary working in relation-ships with and between individuals, teams, professions, organi-sations and sectors.
3. Moving towards a shared vision in a constantly changing complex organisational environment.
4. Creating smooth transfer of patients across services.

5.   Increasing understanding of negotiating/managing change across professional boundaries.
6.   Power, empowerment, and influence for doing things differently.

The number of participants in each reflective action learning set at the initial meeting varied from a minimum of six to a maximum of eleven. However, the numbers quickly settled to around 5–6 members per RALS, which is the normal recommended size for RALS. At the first meeting of the RALS, after signing up to individual learning contracts, members of the RALS proceeded to clarify the objectives of the RALS, set the ground rules of their work, and agree ways of communicating with the steering committee and other sets.

With these steps, the members gave practical meaning to the notion of "critical reflection". The reflective action learning sets interpreted this notion of critical reflection in four different ways and used RALS as

- spaces to reflect,
- resources for reflection,
- spaces to act,
- resources (tools) for action.

The RALS used all these modes of interpreting critical reflection in practice and often shifted from one to the other during the programme and at times during the same session.

The RALS as a space to reflect

Members interpreted RALS first and foremost as spaces to reflect on cross-boundary issues affecting their everyday working lives. One of them called these spaces "a haven of sense-making, while everything else is crazy". Reflection, here, meant a combination of containment and challenge that allowed participants to engage in personal and organisational development. Structurally, the meetings subdivided into three or four time slots and ran according to agendas agreed at the start of each meeting. The presence of facilitators combined to create "safe environments" in which participants were able to report on their practical management and organisational issues and make sense of them by engaging in conversation with the other set members. The activity, therefore, unfolded in terms of "public reflexive dialogical processes" (Cunliffe, 2002), which is difficult and painful work. In this way, participants recognised how they had been affected by certain situations or events, worked out why this was so, and explored what this told them about their own practical ways of constructing their working reality and about their organisations. With the help of the facilitators and the active support of their colleagues in the groups, participants were then encouraged and often challenged to make links and connections between events that offered new explanations and meanings. They also had opportunities to establish connections between their own experiences and those of others, a reassuring exercise for managers who frequently complained about their deep sense of isolation at work. The process led to establishing new connections and new possibilities of seeing, being, and acting for the person raising the issues and the other RALS members.

This way of approaching critical reflection was both powerful and problematic. It was powerful because, as participants clearly stated, this way of learning was perceived as "a form of conversation *in* practice as opposed to a conversation *about* practice" (Gherardi & Nicolini, 2002). Themes and issues emerged directly from actual working life, feedback was frank and, at times, merciless, but always delivered by peers who had a deep understanding of both the organisational and emotional conditions of the presenter. This led to the collective production of non-judgemental, non-competitive arenas that allowed participants the freedom to explore new ways of being that would generate different ways of behaving. Consequently, the process of learning was profound and meaningful for participants because the situations they were describing were messy, deeply emotional, unstructured, unplanned, and had a driven quality about them. These situations were, however, problematic and a cause of anxiety for both participants and facilitators. Theories that equate learning with clear-cut and ordered processes whose outputs can be measured for efficiency and added value, that is, where learning has been equated with production, have been deeply introjected by staff of the NHS as, indeed, is the case with most organisations in the Western world. To the extent that learning and training are framed in terms of the prevailing logic of production, they are perceived as legitimate realities. On the other hand, the form of developmental activity carried out within the RALS has peculiarly been orientated towards the production of a "no-thing". Although this form of training and its value was never discussed, and, in fact, some members preferred it to other structured forms of training, this element of producing a "no-thing" rendered attendance at the RALS a source of guilt. This created a problem for the facilitators, who felt caught between the dilemma, on the one hand, of responding to the needs of participants and following reflection processes wherever they would lead, and, on the other, of producing a form of activity that would be properly reportable and accountable.

The RALS as a resource for reflection

The RALS were used as resources for reflection and opportunities for learning. Members of the sets would describe situations—processes and practices—that reflected the values, expectations, and assumptions of their organisations. These descriptions presented opportunities to explore tacit assumptions and their consequences. For example, at the start of the programme, one of the RALS was visited by the person responsible for designing the evaluation of the programme. Due to a miscommunication, the person came into the group at the wrong time, that is, crossed a boundary without being invited, announced, or authorised. This triggered a range of reactions which became the object of reflection in the following session and helped the participants to see connections with a number of broader organisational assumptions and (mal)practices in relation to crossing professional and team boundaries. The incident turned into an opportunity for reflecting on the nature of boundaries and their functions and their effects on the people crossing the boundary and the group that has its boundaries transgressed.

The RALS also planned and implemented a number of activities to support the reflection process on cross-boundary issues. For example, some of the sets invited members of different organisations to attend set meetings to explore together the nature of the boundary between their organisations and their perception of boundaries as dividers instead of connectors. The ensuing discussions ranged from a mutual understanding of similarities and differences, to the identification of ways of bringing down barriers between them. In some cases, a more proactive approach was adopted. A manager in an organisation would be identified and a RALS member would arrange to "shadow" that manager and spend a day with their "alter-ego across the boundary". The results of the shadowing were then fed back to the RALS and discussed at length.

Finally, RALS operated as reflectors for participants and helped them explore in depth their assumption and feelings about the issues under discussion. The facilitators encouraged reflection of assumptions and feelings as part of the main task of the programme and then modelled "appropriate supportive critical behaviour" (O'Neil, 1997). Halfway through the programme, the facilitators made their approach "explicit" through a short presentation on the reflection process. This was designed to enhance the critical capacities of the RALS members and to emphasise that the acquisition of reflective competencies was, in fact, one of the desired outcomes of the programme.

The RALS as a space to act

Although we were wary of the potential contradiction of pressing participants to enter a "production-orientated" style of reflections, from the beginning it was accepted that participants would be involved in personal or organisational change initiatives that would constitute a significant source for reflecting. Sets were, therefore, used to support, devise, monitor, and review personal action plans and to discuss anticipated relevant cross-boundary events in their organisations. Several participants identified personal or organisational change objectives and used the RALSs to elaborate plans, to discuss progress, and to reflect on successes and failures. This activity was sometimes interpolated with broader reflections on power and change. Some of the sets chose to deepen the understanding of this topic by establishing joint study sessions or by accessing short training sessions that had been offered as a resource to all RALS at the beginning of the project. By studying "power" dynamics as they emerged and manifested in the participants' change efforts, they were able to understand both the nature of power and how power operated within their organisations. This, in turn, empowered them to "work the system better", that is, to make progress in their change programmes.

Other RALS participants used the meetings as opportunities to obtain support to steer changes that were already happening in their organisations. Topics ranged from interventions to address difficulties individuals were encountering, difficulties with collaborators or superiors, ranging to more complex situations, such as managing the closure of services and organisations and team mergers. In these cases, RALS were used for support, enrichment and a critical voice during planning and reviewing stages. When RALS members were involved in organisational planning, they used the RALS to explore scenarios, understand power dynamics, and engineer participation and consensus-building. They tapped into their previous experiences, reported to the RALS, allowing their colleagues to learn collectively from their experiences and make connections with their own situations. RALS activity involved the copious use of flipcharts that were summarised and circulated among members of the RALS and retained as a collective memory aid.

The RALS as resources (tools) for action

The sets were used as tools for intervention. In some cases, two participants of the same set identified common issues, such as a common boundary that they believed needed to be made more permeable. This challenge was then addressed with the support of the rest of the set. In another case, a whole set worked together to intervene on a complex organisational change initiative. In this case, the RALS took on the character of a *de facto* local OD initiative, as illustrated by the following example.

During the open space session at the beginning of the project, a group of four people from the same organisation decided to work together on their cross-boundary issues involving the smooth transfer of patients across services. These people formed a set and proceeded to investigate and map existing transfer processes and their obstacles, alternating this with reflections on the nature of the barriers they were encountering. Once a draft was completed, they contacted all the actors identified in the transfer process map and explored with them the reasons why patient transfer was not smooth. Positions on the map where forces and interests had been identified and intersected, and which prevented a smooth transfer of patients, were marked with "cockroaches", a very powerful image that helped to capture the imagination of everyone involved. Discussions were, henceforth, framed as attempts at eliminating the "cockroaches", that is, to identify practical ways to remove obstacles to smooth patient transfer. By mapping the territory, the RALS had, in fact, changed it. The reflective exploration activity allowed the set to build the necessary relationships and support and what followed was a change process and new procedures for patient transfer. Most importantly, once news of the set's activity started circulating through the organisations, the set members were contacted by local directors who invited them to present their work at higher level meetings. This constituted both an acknowledgement and an endorsement of their work and their bottom-up empowerment strategy, as well as a further source of influence for the set in support of their activity.

The second whole community change conference

The second conference took place during the fifth month of the initiative, about half-way through the project. The conference aimed at establishing connections between the RALS and engaging with wider organisational contexts by communicating provisional results of the programme to a group of "key decision makers", whom it was hoped would champion some of the initiatives pursued by the sets. The design of the second conference included a sharing activity between the sets, a consensus-building activity on how to turn the collection of six sets into collective change agents (How can we work together? What can be done to make our learning experience more relevant and make a difference in our health and social care systems?), and finding a space for suitable forms of engagement with key decision makers. In the view of the steering committee, this conference was designed to mark the beginning of creating the "structure that connects". Things, however, went very differently from what had been expected.

The key decision makers simply did not turn up, and the few who did turned up without being able to make any commitment beyond a personal one. In many respects, this was a manifestation of the same conditions that fostered the programme and shaped the CBMDI initiative, that is, the fragmentation of responsibilities and accountability. The same processes that made it impossible to establish clearly identifiable authorising points in the organisation to support the use of a system-wide OD approach and the absence of a culture of reflection made these managers ignorant of the relevance of their presence for CBMDI participants. This signalled that the programme as a whole had been less successful in self-empowerment than had been the case for the individual sets. Finally, the lesson for the steering committee was that "engaging" with a whole system such as the NHS meant acquiring different models to those mutated from companies in the private domain. We shall return to this point below. Overall, failure of key decision makers to show up was a powerful demotivator. The signal they sent was a painful reminder of the difficulties and high levels of resources necessary to accomplish anything in the organisation. The lesson of the key decision makers' non-attendance was a very harsh reality check.

Following the second whole community change conference, the steering committee, by now constituting its own reflective space, concluded that the attempt to create stable connections by making people meet to discuss and identify a common aim and action plans, had been probably too ambitious. Nevertheless, feedback from the RALSs revealed that participants viewed their reflections as part of a larger programme. They felt that synergy between the groups was important to support the legitimisation of their reflection activity and to create the conditions to implement the change agreed at set level. The steering committee decided to explore in practice another way of creating connections among RALS, that is, by a method of representation, which was a more time-consuming, but more reliable way than the model used at the second large conference. Accordingly, sets were asked to nominate representatives to join an expanded steering committee whose aim would be to collate the learning and recommendations arising from the RALS and present them to the organisations that were part of the CBMDI.

The now enlarged joint steering committee met twice in the last third of the programme. In the first meeting, representatives briefly shared the recent learning from the RALS and reflected on the causes of the low level of satisfaction with the outcome of the first large community change conference. They noted that what had happened in the conference was an accurate mirroring of their everyday experience of organisations in states of unravelling and where "engaging" meant tiresome and painstaking work. They agreed that the programme would have to build its own legitimacy by establishing relationships with other initiatives and agencies, especially across the health–social care services boundary, by disseminating the results of the sets' work. The joint steering committee also agreed to take responsibility for contributing to the design of the evaluation process and of the third, final, large community change conference, a task that was carried out at a second meeting. During the meeting, representatives of the sets discussed and approved the idea of working together to invite managers "one level up" in their organisations to the third large change conference.

The third whole community change conference

The third whole community change change conference took place one year after the start of the project. Because of the reluctance of external managers to confirm their attendance, this time the steering committee decided to prevent another failure and, based on their learning from the second large change conference, opted for a reduced agenda. This third conference was aimed at sharing the learning between sets, agreeing how to connect with other initiatives, and discussing what to do in the future. Sets were given one hour before the meeting of the first session to summarise what they had learnt. Groups used a range of methods to communicate their experiences, from slides to artefacts, from flipcharts to anecdotes. The second session was used to reveal the early outcomes of the evaluation process. Finally, the sets met to explore hopes and desires for the future, both for each of the sets and for the programme as a whole. The results of this latter session were taken up by the joint steering committee that met in the afternoon. The joint steering committee decided to remain in place after the conclusion of the CBMDI and to own and disseminate the results of the evaluation process and to support the promotion of new initiatives. These included the possible establishment of a programme of RALS-facilitated training that would allow members of the CBMDI to extend their experiences to others in the organisations.

Discussion

Reynolds (1998, 1999) suggests that critical reflection is characterised by a number of specific features that set it apart from individual-centred methods of understanding reflective activities in organisations. Critical reflection is about questioning organisational assumptions. It pays attention to power relations in all its forms; it is democratic and forward-looking, that is, it focuses on expanding the ways of making sense of work in all its aspects and of the ways of talking and acting in the organisations (Blackler & Kennedy, 2004; Reynolds, 1998, 1999; Vince, 2002b). By addressing and monitoring these aspects in all phases of our project, it was possible to prevent some of the known shortcomings of the more individualised approaches to learning. These shortcomings include tendencies to operate within existing managerial agendas and assumptions; to frame change in individualistic and heroic ways, to become "isn't it all awful" forums that provide psychological support to participants, but do little to address the root causes of organisational problems (Pedler, 1997b; Vince & Martin, 1993).

The CBMDI project was a practical test of the working hypothesis that tools, designs, and techniques of the two related traditions of action learning and organisational development can be combined in order to promote organisational reflection and individual and organisational change. (Morgan & Ramirez, 1983; Pedler, 1997a). The effectiveness of this approach was encouraging, although certain aspects require further development.

The evaluation process of the CBMDI, based on a number of focus group interviews with project participants, their managers and colleagues, revealed positive, deep, and long-lasting effects at both individual and organisational levels. Most participants reported that the programme had given them new tools to manage themselves more effectively in their roles, such as improved practical understanding of partnership working, cross-boundary management, working with the power dynamics of the organisation, enhanced delegation skills, and applying reflection techniques as everyday managerial tools. As one participant put it "the RALS changed my way of managing". Some organisational results were short term and tangible, such as new cross-boundary innovations; others were long term and intangible. Two participants said that the programme helped them stay in the NHS. A rough calculation revealed that costs to the organisation in recruitment and training new managers at their level of seniority was equal to cost of the CBMDI itself.

The most relevant aspects of learning lay in the province of tacit and aesthetic managerial and organisational "knowing" (Nicolini, Gherardi, & Yanow, 2003). Statements such as "the most important thing about this programme for me was that I could finally say aloud: 'Folks, I made a mess!'" were heard in different forms and on different occasions. We believe this pointed to the success of the programme in establishing a "structure that reflects", that is, a cognitively and emotionally protected space that allowed participants to experiment with new ways of being at work. Additionally, the programme contributed to the development of a culture of organisational reflection and individual development within it. The evaluation process confirmed that the programme, through its design and facilitation practices, created a "social space" that functioned as a "zone of proximal development" (Engeström, Miettinen, & Punamaki, 1999; Engeström, Virkkunen, Helle, Pihlaja, & Poikela, 1996) and a "holding environment" (Winnicott, 1965), which allowed for organisational and individual development to occur. Critical to this was the recognition of the power of emotion and the search for a balance between support and questioning. The overall design of the CBMDI and the facilitation practices established a setting that was both a source of anxiety through its questioning and reflecting practices and a container of anxiety. Emotional support was a key element in the life of the sets, and it was successfully channelled outwards, thus preventing the groups from becoming self-pitying groups. Because of the inevitable anxiety that learning and change arouses, critical reflection needs to be sustained by practices that guarantee emotional containment (Bion, 1985a; Vince, 2002b). Emotional containment is indispensable to making "standing back from daily pressure" possible, allowing new meanings to emerge in conversation, and allowing for experimenting with new ways of managing in the organisation.

The CBMDI showed how reflective activity deeply questions existing organisational assumptions. This was achieved by promoting a critical stance through the use of questioning practices and providing alternative theoretical tools for thinking, and through the design of the project itself. The critical dimension of the reflection activity was rooted in the sustained attention to issues of power within the RALS and in exposing the unsaid and unsayable assumptions of NHS organising processes. Such effects were achieved by using open space technology in large gatherings, by shifting responsibilities for the outcomes of the large change conferences on to participants of the RALS and by legitimising a no-result as a possible outcome.

Critical to the attainment of these results was another aspect mutated from the OD tradition: the acceptance of democratic principles in all phases and aspects. Democracy inspired (a) the content of the programme emphasising power, politics, and authority as central issues for the RALS activity, and (b) the overall design and conception of the initiative, including the role of the steering committee. Early in the project, the steering committee declared that it would only establish the conditions for learning, but not "manage" it. This aspect of the process would be the responsibility of the participants and left to their discretion. The programme had no elements of programmed training, a praxis that is common in certain strands of action learning. This position arose out of recognition that, in addressing the complex issues at stake, the real source of expertise lay with participants. The CBMDI project was built on the principle that others in the organisations were involved in a learning experience, too, not only RALS participants. In fact, we (the authors) now believe that some of the difficulties encountered by the steering committee, and described in the previous sections, might have derived from its early failure, despite its good intentions, to live up to these democratic principles and accept that it, too, was a participant in the reflective activity. (Was it anxiety? Was it resistance?) In order to make the programme an authentic instance of critical reflection in all its elements, all the participants should have endorsed the reflective practices used in the RALS, including the steering committee and the evaluation team. Had they done so, several of the difficulties could have been addressed differently and more positively. Herein lies a powerful practical lesson. Designing organisational reflection activities and promoting them in such a way that exempts the sponsors from being part of the reflective practices deprives them of the experience of learning, and exposes a paradox of reflection being promoted at one level and denied at another. Inevitably, this will have practical repercussions and will be played out by the participants as they pick up and enact this inner contradiction.

A key ingredient of the programme and its success was the recognition of the centrality of the distribution of power as a critical aspect of all organising processes and especially those concerned with development and change. By attending to questions of the distribution of power in all the forums of the programme, participants were able to deepen their understanding of its nature, manifestations, and ways of operating. This provided them with a new awareness of their own capacities to influence power and gave them a set of practical tools to "work the system better", thereby enhancing their capacity to intervene in producing and steering change. As the evaluation revealed, several participants said that the project had enabled them to see their organisations as systems they could influence.

This bottom-up empowering strategy was successful, but had its limits. As the previous sections illustrates, the empowering process worked well at individual and set levels, but was less successful at the organisational level. While we successfully managed to create structures and places *to* reflect, the effort to create the structure *that* reflects, that is, to sow seeds of a reflecting organisation, proved far more challenging. It is true that one of the outcomes of the project was the establishment of a joint steering committee, which constituted a potential future source of influence in the organisation that might collectively increase top managers' sensitivity to cross-boundary issues and the value of reflection.

The project was fraught with difficulties, but there were lessons to be learnt.

First, our original idea to put in place a collective actor, the "structure that reflects" that would constitute a pressure group within the organisation, was maybe too ambitious. We believe this was due in part to our over-optimistic time frame; one year was too short to trigger broader organisational effects.

Second, difficulties stemmed from the particular characteristics of the multi-set arrangements. In the CBMDI multi-set project environment, energy tended to be generated within sets. Normally, establishing boundaries around sets is critical to the generation of energy, but, nevertheless, it is still possible to channel this energy outwardly by having set members using the group as a base for launching new ways of being and doing. However, the set remained the reference group and source of identity for participants. We observed many times that the sets, and not the project as a whole, was the more important source of identification, the focus of participants' care. As one said, "In the RALS there is a high level of energy. When we attempt to connect with the chaotic system outside, this energy gets drained, sapped. We return to the RALS to recharge." Put in other terms, a certain level of "insularity" is necessary and inevitable for this model to work, although efforts can be made to prevent this insularity from becoming counterproductive. In order to develop a common aim and goal and turn the collection of sets into a "collective actor", one has first to overcome this centrifugal force. The fact is that the more each set develops its own history, language, and priorities, the more sets become effective at empowering and energising their members, the more work is required to identify the broad aims of the project to work collectively at organisational levels. On the other hand, disregarding the centrifugal forces of sets and trying to appeal to individuals does not work, as we found in our second large change conference. In short, a multi-set project is much more difficult to mobilise than a single aim change-orientated coalition. For the same reason, the shift between contributing to the set and to the "structure that reflects" might not be perceived by participants as having consequences, in so far as sources of energy and motivation in the two are profoundly different. Pedler (1997a,b) suggests that in order to increase the power of RALS "the Set may have to be larger than usual" (1997b, p. 261). It is clear that a "set of sets" cannot reproduce the same mechanisms that glue small sets together, because large groups behave and perform in very different ways. They are much less efficient as "holding environments" (Winnicott, 1965) and are, in fact, anxiety-producing situations. Participants will have to be convinced to turn their primary attention, responsibility, and caring concerns away from their initial focus, themselves and their "comrades in adversity" in the sets, and redirect them outwards to their organisations. In short, RALS are powerful ways to begin the process of critical reflection and change, to "unfreeze the organisation", but they might not be the best way to bring the change to fruition, unless the sets are recast as small "action research teams".

Our *third* source of difficulty is related to our attempts to "engage with a system" such as the NHS. Some of our difficulties were due to the particular local circumstances, such as turmoil in the organisational environment and top management "merry go round" created by the various mergers.

Our experience in this project, however, suggests that some of the difficulties might have been the result of a misleading notion of "engagement", based partly on a fantasy of "wholeness" and "imagined stability" that might have hampered our action instead of helping it. The notion of "engagement" provides a powerful language for addressing the necessary relational and political activities for a programme like the CBMDI to connect with the rest of the organisation, but it also fosters the image of the organisation as an integrated whole that speaks with one voice and with which it is possible to negotiate, that is, to "engage". French and Vince (1999) and Vince (2002b) note that "imagined stability" and unity is at times endorsed and supported by corporate rhetoric within a political process aimed at steering actions and change in a particular direction. By colluding with the fears and anxieties generated by a change perspective, by sustaining the fantasy of the existence of a unitary organisation capable of supporting projections and solving all problems ("the organisation could, if only it wished"), sources of resistance to change are powerfully increased. As Vince puts it, "The avoidance of the power relations that inform attempts to manage change, limits managers' abilities to find ways of enacting their authority that are inclusive and open to view" (Vince, 2002b, p. 1206).

In highly politicised organisations such as the NHS, the notion of a unitary, stable, and coherent organisation is only a fantasy, albeit a useful fantasy that helps contain anxieties. This fantasy is somewhat nurtured by the UK government, which, for generations, has tried to "put the system under control" using planned, rational approaches that assume the existence of a ordered, unitary organisation. Members of NHS organisations, in fact, deal with totally different daily experiences of loosely coupled organisations in which the existence of multiple perspectives, interests, and ways of representing the world creates inevitable linguistic and practical contradictions, inconsistencies, and paradoxes (Law & Singleton, 2003). In this context, "engaging with the system" can only mean establishing partial connections, transient ties, and negotiated alliances with one or another of the existing and emerging constituencies. It follows that establishing temporary connections, learning and becoming skilled in knowing when, with whom, and how to connect, and when such connections become an unnecessary burden and should be dropped, is not only legitimate, but is also a sign of managerial strength and wisdom. Many participants of the CBMDI learnt that their job was not so much to get rid of dilemmas, ambiguities, and problems, but to accept that these are integral to their managerial work. Consequently, the results of the project suggest that in order to promote empowerment from the bottom up, innovative and flexible strategies will need to be adopted, and innovative and flexible ideals and expectations regarding the meaning of "engagement" need to be embraced.

Summary and conclusion

In this chapter, we have described the role of public reflection as a basis for learning and change at individual, group, and organisational levels. Most reflective activities focus on individual and not on organisational development. Our experience of the CBMDI suggests that reflection works at individual and organisational levels if it is public, sanctioned, participative, and authorised. Working with a large group of middle managers in the UK National Health Service, we developed a large organisational development-based change management initiative that combined elements of traditional OD and critical action learning traditions.

Despite the size of the NHS and the conflicting interests that are its main characteristic features, and the massive changes in the shift to PCTs, the programme provided the managers with new skills and tools for working with the realities of a fragmented and politicised organisation. This was achieved by devising a model of reflection that emphasised the importance of learning from real life issues. These were embedded in the three phases of work: consultation syndicates, large change conferences, and reflective action learning sets. Working together with a steering committee that formed an internal referent group, these elements represent a unique combination of critical reflection and action learning models of the organisational development tradition that created the necessary leverage to support organisational change efforts across a wide spectrum.

The CBMDI programme demonstrated that it is possible to create a hybrid model combining critical organisational reflection that questioned organisational assumptions and the individually focused learning activities of reflective action learning sets. At the same time, the programme also highlighted a number of issues that emerge from such a hybridisation and that will need further consideration. The programme was evaluated for effectiveness and evidence of change in cross-boundary partnership arrangements. Everything pointed to critical requirement for learning being an awareness of the power of emotion in the search for a balance between support and questioning. Winncott's idea of the "holding environment" and holding to democratic principles and ideas about the distribution of power were especially relevant.

The programme had its limits, from which much was learnt. These included resisting having an over-optimistic timeframe, recognising that RALS would generate insulating forces that would be counter-productive in addressing organisation-wide issues, and the mythical sway of ideas of engaging with a system, the NHS, that is presented as a stable integrated organisation only through corporate rhetoric to achieve political ends. Coming to terms with this fantasy enabled participants in the CBMDI to become skilled in knowing when, with whom, and how to connect, and when such connections become burdens and need to be dropped. The CBMDI helped reformulate the meaning of engagement in ways that promoted managerial effectiveness.

CHAPTER EIGHT

Hopes, fears, and reality in a merger of two charities*

Introduction

The decision to merge two organisations—however much determined by economic factors—contains the hope that the new organisation will combine the strengths and overcome the weaknesses of the old ones. Those involved in making the decision often feel undermined and distressed by the resistance and antagonism they encounter when the plan is made known.

Boards and executives, preoccupied with planning the shape of the new organisation, often fail to understand or take into account the anxieties that are aroused in the organisation. These are concerned with threats to identity at various levels: actual job loss, old relationships, and the implications of changing organisational identity and values. Executives and senior managers are prey to the same anxieties and might well focus their energies on omnipotent fantasies of "getting it right"—as if, thus, all pain could be avoided—rather than on containing anxiety and working through the inevitable difficulties.

---

*This chapter is based on: M. Sher (1997), Hopes, fears and reality in a merger of two charities. © *Journal of the British Association of Psychotherapists*, 32(2): 45–57. Material reprinted with permission.

The case material of this chapter comes from the merger of two charities working with elderly and disabled people, but the issues discussed—especially the need to attend to the human factors—apply to other forms of organisational change.

Background of the merger

Two charities serving an ageing ethnic population decided to merge because, by merging, they believe they stand the best chance of survival as an effective charitable service. Both charities serve the same population of elderly and mentally and physically disabled clients and their families with help-in-kind in their homes, short- and long-term residential care, and professional social work assistance and counselling.

Helping organisations, like commercial ones, have to be financially viable. Unit costs in the 1980s were rising alarmingly, which, together with a diminishing sponsorship population to support their work, compelled the leadership of both charities to search for solutions. The similar nature of the two organisations' work and clientele made the idea of a merger sensible. Discussions between the two boards were held and most staff were excited by the prospect. Job security was a major concern for the management groups of both charities: savings, it was said, would be made through natural wastage, and a "no redundancy" policy would be adopted. This later turned out to be impossible to support. Leadership, management, and staff tackled the task of the future merger with logical and practical objectives in mind and ignored the effects of new boundaries and new relationships on people's anxieties. As with most mergers, implementation was rushed when caution would have been better advised. As time passed, the board and senior managers wanted to go faster, to take months, not years, but by then it was their motivation, not their staff's. Winning people over and integrating teams was neglected.

Merger: general considerations

A merger is usually defined in its organisational or behavioural sense, and relates to the subsequent merging, or fusing together, of some or all of the central functions of the two organisations. Mergers are seldom defined in terms of omnipotent hopes that the future must be better than the past, that everyone will gain equally, that envy and competition will be successfully controlled, or in terms of threats to people's identities, separation anxieties due to people relocating, old relationships given up and new ones established, or the old chestnuts of who will win and who will lose. Thus, in our example, all the central functions of two charities were fully merged into what would become effectively a new organisation, which we shall call Golden Years. Like so many mergers, this one, too, was the outcome of a struggle for the hearts of staff and their clients, their financial supporters, and the community at large.

Most organisations grow by assimilating others; they also mature, decline, are disinvested, and so grow into something else. The boards of both pre-merged organisations operated on an accretion model, that is, by putting one organisation together with another, the expected result would be a combined improved version of the former organisations. In reality, boards seldom conceptualise a totally new entity. They utilise the skills and resources of the old organisations, while essentially creating a new entity. They seldom operate on a morphotic model, which relies on the shaping and forming of new organisational systems through organic transformational growth; merging and being merged are normal stages in the life-cycle of many organisations. Mergers are usually looked at from the point of view of strategy, economics, and finance. These disciplines seek to answer the essential questions which any board might ask. What size should we be to achieve our purposes most effectively? Should we diversify or concentrate, expand or consolidate? Will clients of the newly merged organisation benefit more than those of the former pre-merged organisations?

However vital these questions might be for the boards of organisations when they consider joining forces with another, they address only one side of the merger process—the longer term strategic positioning of the organisation in an essentially external field. They fail to address the more immediate internal question of how best to organise the merging organisations in the short term so as to deliver the longer-term goals—the question of how to ensure the people make the merger happen successfully.

This neglect of the human variable is cause for concern. The literature on mergers concentrates on the financial and business aspects— very few on the human aspect (Adams & Brock, 1986; Ginzberg &

Votja, 1985; Heins, 1987). At Golden Years, the merger ought to have been successful according to financial criteria; the sense of frustration that the management and staff felt six months after the merger could only be attributed to the neglect of the human factors involved.

By the term "human factor", we mean the full range of leadership, organisational, interpersonal, and unconscious factors—in both merging organisations—that require to be addressed and effectively managed in order to make the merger work in practice. These factors come into play through all stages of the process, from planning the merger through to executing the implementation. Once the merger is agreed, there remains the common problem of meshing together into some kind of harmony two quite distinct organisational cultures—two separate management teams with different systems and styles of management. It is at this stage—the post-merger stage—that many of the unexpected difficulties surface.

At Golden Years, problems arose as a consequence of very simple acts by key personnel at the pre-implementation stages, often quite simple acts of commission or omission which were misplaced, misunderstood, and which started an irreversible set of quite destructive organisational dynamics. The human cost to the merging organisations could have been lowered if sufficient attention had been given to them in advance.

Our argument on the human factor is this: financial criteria provide the necessary, but not sufficient, preconditions for a successful merger. Once the organisations have been merged, it is then almost entirely dependent upon the human elements within the new organisation to make it live up to expectations. Unless the human element is managed carefully, there is a serious risk of losing the advantages that the merger could bring to the new organisation.

Planning the merger

Why did we go after them? [one party in the merger]. There's the obvious reason: to provide the same level of service at reduced costs. But we could have achieved that through some other means, maybe for less effort. If I'm honest, the real reason is that there is something tremendously satisfying about taking over an organisation and being seen to have turned it around in a very short time. (Chief Executive, Golden Years)

This is the stereotype of the decision to merge. In it, the larger and stronger of the two merging organisations has a set of well-defined merger objectives derived from its corporate strategy. Armed with these, the task of scanning for suitable targets devolves on to a small number of key people—maybe the chair of the board, CEO and senior directors—who identify likely targets. The board will commission lengthy and very detailed analyses and projections on the target organisation, which is then submitted to the board for evaluation. The final decision is depicted as emanating entirely from these analyses— a clinically cold, rational, "business" decision devoid of sentiment, emotion, and self-interest.

The merger which resulted in Golden Years did not correspond to this picture. The reasons for merging were political; the decision was as much emotional as it was rational. The reason was also opportunistic: "It was there and we grabbed it." The larger organisation was at pains to point out, "We do not want this to be a take-over." But it behaved in just that way.

Ahead of all the other reasons for the merger was the importance given to how the community would rate the new organisation.

A merger of these organisations would increase our financial support with the community. (Board Chair)

The general picture to emerge from Golden Years, however, was one of frustrated careers, lost opportunities, and a demotivated climate. The former organisations merged at Golden Years attached considerable importance to their fields of operations and methods of work. These were seen as crucial to expansion of their services and in ensuring there would be proper succession plans for their chief executives. The two boards each hoped the merger would bring benefits: technical expertise, opportunities to work with new client groups, improved management skills, better systems, and help in defining new directions for the new organisation. However, many people at staff level in the two pre-merged organisations were not hopeful that the new management would understand their work enough to invest sufficiently in it.

False assurances played a part in persuading staff to accept the merger. Assurances about a "no redundancy" policy were given to allay fears and to maintain the commitment of senior management, once it was known that the merger was going ahead. Pre-merger assurances are binding in honour only. The new board had gone back on its word and management were having to implement redundancies.

The theme of trust was always present. The two organisations moved towards merger reluctantly. Discussions between the two organisations were based initially on the impression made by the other side: "It felt right, they felt right, but . . . how did we know we could trust them?" Some people were saying privately what everyone felt.

Gaining entry: opening moments in a consultation and their meaning

On stepping out of the lift at the second floor for the initial meeting with the Deputy Director of Golden Years, I was met by the CEO's secretary, who asked me to follow her. The Chief Executive, she said, wished to have a quick word with me before my meeting with his Deputy. The "quick word" lasted an hour, during which the Deputy telephoned around the building wondering what had happened to his "appointment", who, between the ground and second floors, had mysteriously disappeared.

From the Chief Executive, I learnt that Golden Years urgently needed organisational consultancy because the "no redundancy" policy had caused a pervading sense of injustice to reverberate among the staff of his organisation. The smaller pre-merged organisation— and the more wealthy of the two—believed it had been kidnapped; the larger one felt it had made a good "catch", acquiring a "dowry" without exerting itself.

First moments of a consultation often contain vital clues of an organisation's past history, current problems, and habitual ways of solving them. My experience of being ensnared and taken away was probably an accurate reflection of the experience of other people in both organisations, which was that the merger felt more like a kidnap: people had been bullied or seduced into the merger without having had opportunities to work through their feelings of hope of what would be gained by it and anxieties about what would be lost.

The "kidnap" experience illustrated in miniature the characteristic nature of transactions in the organisation. Managers at Golden Years feel cheated by the hasty merger; they "grab" the consultant as a potential resource, a hoped-for adjudicator; he is enjoined as a new member of one team, usually the most powerful, and is reluctantly "let out" to others. In the search for resources at Golden Years, "grabbing" seemed to be a criterion for success. My initial working hypothesis about Golden Years ,therefore, was that the organisation felt shamed by the mistakes of the merger, that the consultant is "kidnapped" in order to acquire the omnipotence which has been projected into his role and to undo the mistakes, and to prevent him from uncovering anything.

Why was Golden Years seeking consultancy?

Golden Years' public image was of a progressive organisation; it had a powerful executive team and was well connected to important backers. It possessed the self-confidence of an organisation that knew where it was going, and a sense that there were few problems it could not handle independently. The organisation was proud of its achievements in anticipating and planning for demographic changes in the community. Consultancy, for the new organisation's executive and managers, was meant to be an opportunity for them to grasp the painful realities of their situation, that is, their burden of making difficult decisions about redundancies, redeployment, shifting budgetary resources, etc.

What was the executive team not addressing? In any relationship involving a request for help, the individual or group requesting help experiences embarrassment and anxiety, which they fend off by making the helper feel them instead. Consequently, it was I, and not the Chief Executive, who was now feeling a sense of confusion and inadequacy. He proudly explained Golden Years' history, its undisputed superior service, its rivalry with sister organisations, and the final triumphant achievement of the merger, which was heralded as an expression of faith in its future—a new streamlined organisation primed to meet the challenges of the next century.

As discussions proceeded with the Chief Executive, who had by now been joined by his bewildered deputy (but not by his co-Chief Executive, who had been the director of the smaller original organisation, and his rival), he hinted that he was himself struggling with the imponderables of an organisation in transition, of the uncertainties of the general environment, and the specific problems of Golden Years' now expanded client groups. Members of his senior management group were behaving aggressively towards one another; staff were complaining that they were not informed of changes, and everyone was demoralised. I wondered aloud to the chief executive and his deputy whether my experience of having been "grabbed" was meant to draw me on to one side of the senior management team and so provide one more resource for that side? Simply having me on their side seemed to serve as a form of insurance against future vicissitudes. The Chief Executive then said that he was really unable to articulate just why he needed consultancy now. He had thought he and his executive and management teams needed a "space" to think about Golden Years, to evaluate the effectiveness of the merger, to plan for the future, and their methods of work, and, importantly, to consider how they managed themselves in their roles within the new organisation and how they would adapt their roles to meet changing circumstances. In this fairly casual way, the Chief Executive unintentionally outlined the brief for the consultancy event that followed.

Managing transformations

Change is an excursion into the unknown, implying a commitment to future events that are not entirely predictable, and to their consequences, which inevitably arouse doubt, anxiety, and resistance (Menzies, 1959). As their consultant, I would be working with the executive and management teams on organic transformations of their organisation. I would be trying to help them take up their new roles and manage transformations in a considered way. At the time, they were reacting to external changes and creating a dependency–counterdependency culture, rather than planning transformations which would involve developing a vision, sharing that vision with others through example, paying attention to their leadership and management styles, especially to their differences, to envy and rivalry among its senior people, and to anxieties about winning and losing.

Staff of the new organisation were complaining about the imposition of excessive controls, such as more centralised management systems. These seemed to be meant to protect the executive and management from their anxieties about an expected surge of new but unrelated work. From the time of the merger, factors such as cost-per-client were discussed interminably, mainly because they are measurable. These discussions created the illusion of certainty as a means of coping with management's feelings about the merger's viability in an eco-environment of larger numbers of people living to an older age and a shrinking financial base to support them. The truth was that the merger had been agreed and rushed through without full consultation in order to rescue one of the merged organisations, which was failing to operate within its financial limits. Pressures to cut costs were building up. The previously promised "no redundancy" policy was now becoming increasingly untenable because there were two contenders for almost every senior post. Some headquarters staff were likely to lose their jobs and their worries were being projected on to the less powerful staff members.

It is commonly understood that good managers are good delegators, but the new executive and management teams had underestimated the complexity of the emotional work required to delegate authority to their subordinates. While the senior management team was grappling with problems of balancing the budgets, some of its other management tasks, for example, supporting their middle to junior managers below them, were neglected. Consequently, when unit managers had problems that had to be dealt with by senior management, they were siphoned off elsewhere. Bureaucratic processes can play a defensive role in organisations. The management, feeling anxious about the merger, and wishing to protect its sense of self-worth in a threatening situation, resorts to a common organisational defence: idealising its own organisation and competence and scapegoating and blaming others, principally, in this case, the fieldwork staff.

As the negative implications of the merger spread across Golden Years, anxiety increased and staff looked to the managers to provide the necessary boundary controls to protect the work. However, if managers are unable to provide proper controls, or are themselves thought of as causing the anxiety, then surrogate managers are sought and the consultant is at risk of being drawn into the role of surrogate manager. But consultancy is a method of collaborating with organisations to help them improve their performance. Staff in the organisation often regard the consultant as a "super manager", able to fix things that present managers are unable to, and as the focus of hope and salvation. Yet, the consultant is there to help members of an organisation understand the meanings that staff attribute to particular events, the feelings they harbour about their work, and the intentions that shape their relationships to colleagues, bosses, and their own ambitions (Miller & Rice, 1967). Consultancy as a support activity enables the consultant to develop a rich understanding of staff's feelings, motives, and purposes, because consultants, by studying their own feelings, can share them with consultees as a means of revealing processes in the organisation that staff members are unable to see for themselves. The consultees can begin to understand their experiences as they really are, and not as they are supposed to be, that is, reducing denial by containing anxiety.

At Golden Years, various aspects of the new culture were considered by most staff and many executive and management members to be negative. The new organisation had been turned into a business by the board, and the language was becoming commercial. Emphasis was given to efficiency and economies of scale. Changes in the culture were happening by stealth and not as a result of debate and consultation, and, therefore, could not be "owned" by the staff. Suspicion and anxiety about the board's and executive's intentions were widespread. Staff lower down the organisation viewed the merger more as a takeover, and feared this process would continue to include other community welfare organisations. Lack of corporate ownership of the changes had resulted in vagueness about the objectives of the merger, low morale at headquarters, poor communications, and, paradoxically, an increase in the number of administrative staff. Change, and the dependency–counterdependency culture produced by it, did not provide for the working through of feelings. The mind transforms events into experiences: treating staff as mindless individuals means that events are simply reacted against.

Discussion

The consultant is perceived as purveying omnipotence and strengthening defences against reality on the one hand, and the overthrow of omnipotence on the other. An organisation is imbued with omnipotent wishes when it sees itself as the only organisation capable of achieving a particular objective.

The theme of merger has within it many elements of omnipotence, because often they are mergers on paper, not properly worked through and accepted by staff. The consultant might be drawn into this and invited to bridge the gap between the fantasy of merger as conceived by the planners and the reality of the merged organisations that have been thrown into disarray. The consultant's job might be seen as "making it happen". This is a very different role to the one of analysing on the ground the difficulties that arise in the organisation as a result of the merger imposed on it. The consultant can easily become a champion of change, falling into omnipotence himself and a messianic role. He can find himself performing many roles for different parts of the organisation, believing he can be all things to all people and forgetting that confusion is inevitable when conflicting roles are held simultaneously, and that his pre-eminent task is to struggle with people to enable them to give meaning to their experiences as they are happening. Filled with the hopes and wishes of the management and staff on the one hand, and struggling to preserve the consultancy role on the other, the consultant tends to carry two conflicting roles at the same time, and, like the organisation he is consulting to, he experiences anxiety. His ego functions, like those of the organisation, are weakened by splitting (Klein, 1975). The consultant is confronted with the organisation's feelings of despair, confusion, and fragmentation, its guilt, and its urge for reparation. In spite of the consultant being available as a container of feelings and wishes, these feelings will still happen. They can be worked with. The drive to make reparation can be motivated by drawing attention to the management's destructive impulses and splitting processes, and steps towards an improvement can be made. Strengthening management is based on enabling it to become more accessible to the split-off good parts of both itself and its staff, for instance, the care functions, which they both hold in common.

The new, merged organisation was searching for a single idealisable figure who could do everything, including effecting the constructive merger of two very different organisations. I found myself merging, too, that is, fusing together diffuse roles: where there were two organisations, now there should be only one; where there were two roles, now there should be only one.

In organisational terms, where there is overlap and duplication of services, personnel, etc., it makes sense to merge the two. But in human terms, the idea of merger is a mad one. If two individuals are merged, the result is not one better individual, but, rather, a bizarre combined object. So, when a merger is proposed, psychotic anxieties are inevitably evoked. There is a genuine threat of loss of identity. The organisation with which one identifies will no longer be the same organisation. What kind of organisation will it become, and will one be able to identify with it? Or there might be a more direct threat to one's identity—one's job might no longer exist or it might be given to someone else from the twin organisation. The merged organisations were promised that there would be no redundancies, but instead bitter quarrelling broke out and, subtly or overtly, staff were forced to leave. Was the no redundancy policy an omnipotent denial of the reality of the merger? Management renege on taking responsibility for unpopular decisions, instead passing this responsibility down into the organisation unprocessed, so that staff have a multitude of roles that they cannot fulfil. The planners seem to want harmony—a single merged organisation that has swallowed up its differences. The managers talk about populations, not people. The consultant, listening one moment to managers talk about population and the next listening to staff talk about people, is drawn into a mad world, where unacknowledged difference is equated with harmony. In this context, harmony is an omnipotent wish, because populations are composed of people, and differences do not go away by splitting. For the consultant, the danger is one of being drawn into the world of splitting (people *vs.* population; procedure *vs.* personal experience) or homogeny (can we live in happy harmony?), rather than the more difficult position that there will always be a disruptive influence from somewhere. In these circumstances, the consultant needs to help the client system move from the depressing "one never gets it right" to the socially depressive one of "one can never get it right" (Moylan, 1990).

Consulting to organisations contains the hidden hope for the consultant to maintain the status quo, to enable the psychic equilibrium of the organisations and the individuals in them to be maintained. The consultant must be able to engage with the organisation's experience of its own unconscious dynamics and behaviour. With Golden Years, the consultant felt he was invited to take up the role of referee, to help the sides keep to the rules, to enable them to merge in a good way, but essentially to make no difference to the status quo. But equally, the consultant's presence also stoked fears of catastrophic metamorphosis, fusion, and loss of identity. In many ways, the perverse nature of the merger, the truth about the new situation and its implications for clients, is unbearable. The consultant is invited to become a referee to perform the useful task of preventing the attacking and defensive manoeuvres of the various teams from becoming too murderous.

The ultimate aim of consultancy is the integration of the organisation's purpose, management, staff, and clients. Splitting processes arise in the earliest stages of an organisation's development. If they are excessive, the organisation can be said to be schizoid in character. In normal organisational development, these characteristics can, to a large extent, be overcome by consulting and interpreting repeatedly the anxieties and defences bound up with envy and destructive impulses. The deeper and more complex the organisation's difficulties, the greater is the resistance the consultant will encounter, hence the need to give adequate scope for the "working through" of competitive attitudes. Where the consultancy fails, it is partly because the pain of loss in some cases outweighs the desire for truth and ultimately the desire for transformations. With psychoanalytically orientated in-depth consultancy, envy and competitiveness diminish, leading to greater trust in constructive and reparative forces, greater tolerance of the organisation's limitations, as well as improved relationships and a clearer perception of internal and external reality. The original fantasy has the two organisations pairing in order to produce a third—a messiah. The consultant avoids colluding with this basic assumption pairing (baP), which has got mixed up with other basic assumptions. Our working hypothesis now is: mergers evoke basic assumption behaviour, because they are explained as necessary responses to change, for example, financial threat. If, however, bringing together of resources and skills of two organisations is construed as creating a new task-orientated organisation which is in touch with the realities of both external and internal environments, it increases the possibilities for the people involved to manage what transformations are necessary by relying on the use of their more mature adult qualities.

PART IV
BOARDROOM EVALUATION

Corruption: aberration or an inevitable part of the human condition? Insights from a "Tavistock" approach*

Introduction

E xamining the subject of corruption from a "Tavistock" systems psychodynamic standpoint reveals refreshing insights into the individual human mind and as it is manifest in collective enterprise. This chapter will describe the concept of *internal object* to explain individual and social behaviour by suggesting that internalised mental images of significant people, events, and ideas have strong emotions and feelings attached to them that influence identity formation, belief and value systems, and, in turn, lead to the construction of attitudes and behaviours. This chapter will also address how system psychodynamic concepts can be gathered and bound into a social theory of group-as-a-whole functioning around the subject of corruption.

Corruption can be defined as:

---

* This chapter is based on: M. Sher (2010), Corruption: aberration or an inevitable part of the human condition? Insights from a "Tavistock" approach. © *Organisational & Social Dynamics*, 10(1): 40–55. Material reprinted with permission.

- a hostile turning away from internal objects,
- exercising leadership in pursuit of an objective that has nothing to do with the work task,
- the erosion of values and standards through noxious processes that have not been foreseen, have not been predicted or worked with until it is too late,
- the undermining of principles on which legality is based.

Turning away from internal objects: attacks on linking

Turning away from internal objects involves the total subversion of one's relation to internal sources of value and sources of goodness. The reason for this psychic primitive turning away is hatred (Bion, 1959; Grotstein, 1981; O'Shaughnessy, 1995), symbolised as H, and an intolerance of knowledge, symbolised by minus K. A combination of H and −K brings to mind the infant turning away from the breast, as one might do at any point in later life, through turning against the unbearable idea that one might have learnt something from our "internal objects", that is, parents, teachers, priests, supervisors, mentors, etc. One's face is turned against them and what was actually learnt from them is reversed. A defiant "I won't learn from you; I will only learn from myself". Corruption is an inversion of reality and the relationship to internal objects. That is what contemporary psychoanalysis (Bion, 1952, 1992; Klein, 1957) emphasises: this turning away is an attack on knowledge. The whole system is subverted. Rather than accepting the system, one tries to get away with whatever one can.

Corruption can be thought of in terms of perversions and the idealisation of violence, untruth, propaganda, and prejudice, exhausting higher levels of value and promoting those things which are the antithesis of ordinary human values. This is a shaky definition because it depends on human values that are socially constructed. In principle, there is no reason why a society should not say that telling lies is a good thing. It depends on whether one accepts that value systems are socially constructed or whether there is something innate in being human—what Freud (1921c, 1923b) called natural ethics, ethics that comes out of nature. One can subscribe to the view that human nature engenders a set of human values, which are probably fairly timeless, based on the innate propensity of human beings to establish human relations: what promotes human relations is ethically good and what subverts and undermines human relations is ethically bad. Therefore, corruption is something that goes against the nature of human beings, attacking truth, honesty, relationships, and acknowledgement of dependence and valuation of those who support one. Subverting human values is different from straightforward wrong-doing and gaining personal advantage from breaking rules or laws because one thinks it is possible to get away with it. Corruption is subversion of the foundation of actual legal systems.

Corruption of knowledge is significant. There is a particular quality about our relationship with knowledge: that things can be known, but the value of what is known is not respected. "I know things, but they are of no use to me. I don't value knowledge; I don't value the evidence of my own eyes. Instead, I value some constructed delusion." Unconsciously, there will be a recognition and an experiencing of what has been done and feelings of guilt. Corruption is the strategy of dealing with that guilt and with the knowledge of one's culpability, and that is to subvert the whole value of knowing things. Criminals know what is right and wrong, but go ahead anyway and deal with their guilt through repression. It is different from those who say, "Well, that might be wrong, but I don't care what is right and wrong." It is subverting the whole moral system. A criminal might not subvert the moral or legal system; they might go against it and take the consequences.

However, in group or collective phenomena like economic trends, something different happens. Markets are prone to episodic bouts of frenzied speculation, "bubbles", which leave financial ruin and recrimination in their wake. The dotcom bubble of 1998–2000 revealed that, for all the sophistication of modern financial systems, investors are as prone as ever to delusions of limitless wealth. Ironically, the best explanation for such episodes—and perhaps even their prevention—might be implicit in the language used in accounts of stock market bubbles over the centuries: they are described as outbreaks of "mania", "mass hysteria", "frenzy", etc. In certain conditions, it seems, investors go collectively insane, the prevailing sensibilities and structures get corrupted, control mechanisms are undermined, and "the markets go mad".

Tuckett and Taffler (2008) treat stock market investors as individuals behaving collectively in herd-type behaviour. They describe stock market bubbles as episodes of paranoid–schizoid behaviour. The recurrence of such events is, in their analysis, entirely predictable: in the dotcom fever, as in the nineteenth century railway speculation, or the "South Sea Bubble", the denial remains long after the frenzy has subsided. Tuckett and Taffler's theoretical framework for corrupted vision, expectation, and behaviour is Freud's (Freud, 1916–1917, p. 357) division in the psyche between the "pleasure principle", which sees the world as we would like it be, and the "reality principle", our acceptance of an imperfect and sometimes disagreeable actuality. The adult mind reconciles this contradiction by adopting either a depressive position state, which acknowledges imperfection and conflict, or a paranoid–schizoid position, in which disagreeable emotions such as guilt and anxiety are repressed and projected outwards. The key to this state is the cultivation of "phantasy objects", which the mind substitutes for a reality that has become too difficult to bear. In the emerging Internet economy of the 1990s, the novelty and excitement of the online world allowed business "gurus" and excitable young investment bankers to persuade themselves, and their clients, that the old economic rules no longer applied. Share valuations at the height of the bubble bore no relation to possible returns and corruption of the system seemed inevitable. As share prices continued to soar, cautious traders either fell in line with the bullish crowd or lost their jobs. The investment community repressed its doubts and anxieties, preferring to believe in the seductive "phantasy" world of unearned wealth. This, according to Tuckett and Taffler, is a "path-dependent" trajectory—one thing leads to another, with the crash inevitable, once the accumulation of anxiety overwhelms the forces that are repressing it.

Tuckett and Taffler's analysis questions a fundamental assumption of mainstream economic models: that investment decisions are rationally motivated by competing, self-interested individuals. These models fall down in uncertain dynamic conditions, such as those created by the rise of new technology, when emotion and unconscious impulses drive decision making as much as any dry reading of growth forecasts. They argue that in bubble situations, banks and financial institutions should be as wary of "emotional inflation", that is, the corruption of thought and emotion, as they are of fiscal inflation. Feelings and unconscious phantasies dominate rational and intelligent professionals. Attractive investments involve guesses about an uncertain future and uncertainty creates anxiety. When there are exciting new investments whose outcome is unsure, investors can get caught up in the "everybody else is doing it and so should I" wave which leads first to underestimating, and then, after panic and the burst of a bubble, to overestimating, the risks of an investment.

Investors in bubble situations continue to think they are behaving rationally, buying into a story that allows them to detach themselves from anxiety and lose touch with being cautious. Rationalised wishful thinking regarding profits then allows them to take on much more risk than they actually realise, something about which they feel ashamed and persecuted, but rarely genuinely guilty, when a bubble bursts. In other words, a semi-delusional state of mind, or corruption, will ensue, rather than admit responsibility, or learn from mistakes.

Collectivising corruption

Our conundrum is: how are individual intrapsychic corruption processes collectivised into groups and systems? The Tavistock total-systems approach (Lawrence, 1979, 2000; Miller, 1993b; Obholzer & Roberts, 1994), based on the group-as-a-whole theories of Wilfred Bion (1961), deals with this critical problem of understanding how individual intrapsychic processes, which each individual has, become collectivised and co-ordinated into a system. Through the study of whole systems, the Tavistock has gone some way to determining how a number of separate minds get to behave as a system at a different level, in this instance, corruptly. Leadership has an important function in collectivising the intrapsychic processes of the individuals into corruption. The leader will try to capture the allegiance of individuals to some particular ideal that is represented in ways that pay no attention to human values, "we are above all that; they have no value to us".

Bion's (1961) group-as-a-whole ideas rest on the gathering up of individual intrapsychic dynamics and linking them to one person, where they are co-ordinated. It is the co-ordination, as well as structural elements, such as the task of the organisation and the way it lays out its roles, that leads to states of corruption. This is an efficient way of explaining social phenomena and their relation to individual psychological dynamics. We want to avoid naïvely transposing from the individual psyche to the group process, especially when we do not understand why so many people in a group allow themselves to be involved in group processes; when, despite having their own individual psyches, so many people follow a leader to destruction.

One answer might be that everyone has the same kind of intrapsychic personality processes, but it is not necessarily the case. Germany, one of the most sophisticated nations in the world, suddenly overnight turned into a Jew-hating, murdering, prejudiced, totalitarian state where thought disappeared and ordinary people were caught up in the group process. One cannot say that the entire German nation had a totalitarian mentality, although people do say that and there might be some truth in it, but there were extremely thoughtful people in Germany who created the pinnacle of philosophy and music and art and cultural achievement. Suddenly, thought collapsed and these most sophisticated people bought into a state of madness. One has to understand how there can be a corruption of an internal world through overwhelming external pressure. This is what Menzies Lyth (1988, 1989) calls "enforced introjections", when mature people are forced to regress to states of primitiveness. When they are in the system, individuals are powerless to prevent "enforced introjections".

The German people became a liberal democratic western nation within a decade. It was not a new generation of people; it was the same people who had been operating the Nazi system, suggesting that changes in the internal allegiance can be very rapid and very profound and are not just concerned with psychological development. Corruption is about bending the means to achieve an end, which, at the time, feels right; something that one might even believe is for social good. This points to the need for new paradigms to help us understand the rapid changes that can occur that reverberate within social dynamics.

Narcissism

Long (2008) provides a useful description of the role that narcissism and individualism play in the rapid growth of greed, consumerism, acquisition, and exploitation. These dynamics promote perversion and corruption through the process of turning a blind eye (Gettler, 2005; Hoggett, 1992; Steiner, 1985, 1993). This affects organisational life as conscious and unconscious perverse dynamics become more evident, leading to corruption. Perversion and corruption are often linked as in those cases where organisation leaders attempt to cover up perceived failures in an attempt to manipulate the share market and provide leverage for a hoped-for recovery. The denial involved in turning a blind eye can become a conscious attempt to disguise reality. "The psychological dynamics of corruption are manifest in greed, arrogance, a sense of personal entitlement, the idea of virtue as personal loyalty, and the inability to distinguish between organisational and personal ends" (Levine, 2005, p. 17). These individual characteristics are eventually expressed as unconscious perverse societal dynamics and they lead to corrupt behaviours within the system.

Following a number of major corporate liability cases over recent years, the law has changed in the direction of regarding organisations as entities that bear responsibility for providing growth and benefits and bearing responsibility for being instrumental when things go wrong. The idea of organisations being imbued with character traits informs the actions taken by organisational leaders and members. When character traits are destructive and dominate the actions of organisational members from within an unconsciously perverse social structure, this is regarded as corruption. "Organised corporate corruption is a conscious manifestation, the iceberg tip of an unconscious perverse societal structure and dynamic. Corruption builds on an underlying social fabric of perversity" (Long, 2008, p. 3), an idea that suggests that a society operates systemically through a dynamic, a state of mind that affects individual and group behaviour. A "state of mind", according to Harré (1984), is a social, not an individual phenomenon. Bion's work on groups (1961) and Lacan (1977) demonstrate the idea of mind as located in the group. When narcissistic, greedy, grandiose individuals are in operation, the organisational system, the "group", can display itself as illusory, self-deceptive, in denial, and exploitative. The development and reward of narcissistic characteristics leads eventually to the creation of a perverse system.

Infant development and corruption

In human development, the baby has its needs met principally by the mother. The baby, in its primitive unformed state, relates to mother, not as a person, but as an object, a needs-satisfying object. From the baby's perspective, mother satisfies its physical and emotional needs and, in so far as mother does that adequately, the baby gives her good experiences; in so far as mother frustrates the baby, it gives her bad experiences. So, the infant learns that mother has to be looked after: "I have to do this in order that she will feel good and she won't do bad things to me".

In later developmental stages, the baby realises there is a father and that mother and father have a relationship which sometimes includes, and sometimes excludes, the baby. A way has to be found of negotiating that triangular relationship. But there are threats posed by father, which we postulate comes from a projection: "I want you, father, to go away, so that I can enjoy this exclusive relationship with mother; ipso facto, I think you want me to go away, so that you can have with mother what I want to have with her, so I'd better hide my true wishes", that is, the beginning of corruption. This scenario links to phantasies about the sources of supplies. Mother is the source of supplies, of good feelings, nourishment, survival, and now there is another figure who is coming into the picture, a rival who poses a threat. Very probably, that is a major source of corruption for the infant, who is more concerned with ensuring that he retains mother's love by manipulating her to be his possession.

Individual and corporate greed

The managers of Enron, Lehman Brothers, and other organisations (see Long, 2008, for detailed descriptions of cases of corruption of Enron in the USA, HIH Insurance in Australia, Long-Term Capital Management in the USA, Worldcorp in the USA, and Parmalat in Italy) can be said to have acted in their roles, but in order to look after themselves only. If we link that to infant development, the baby has not yet achieved the stage of concern for others; it is looking after itself pretty well. Psychoanalytically, the baby's phantasies are of devouring and incorporating mother in order to take possession of her as the feeding object so that the infant would never have to feel dependency and be without. It urgently searches for a sense of oneness or fusion with the satisfying object, which is what can be said executives of these organisations were doing, too. If one has $100m instead of $10m, the fantasy of fusion with the universe is stronger—the fantasy is of never having to want for anything.

The Enron directors believed that they owned, or had a right to take, the money. They believed they were all-knowing, all-powerful, all-wise, and exempt from due process. They saw process as not applying to them, a primitive, infantile phantasy based on greed, of saying it all belongs to me; it is all mine. All the directors were claiming to have genuinely seen the truth and the truth was that it all belonged to them and, as leaders, they corrupt the rest with omnipotent but unrealistic and amoral aspirations. From these observations, it is possible to say that all human systems have both visible, conscious parts and hidden, unconscious parts, and corruption is inherently and potentially part of every system, that everything has the seeds of its own corruption. This takes us back to the baby-and-mother paradigm, with the baby saying, "I want the mother and everything she represents all for me; others cannot have any of it, because if they were allowed to have any of it, they would want all of it. How do I, baby, know that? Because I, baby, know that I want it all too."

Primary narcissism, enter the father, and developing a sense of reality

Winnicott (1950, 1980) and Kernberg (1992) are interested in the connection between child development and morality. Individuals learn about the basics of morality through consistency and continuity of care and attention. The development of morality also involves going through the depressive position (Klein, 1946), in which the infant develops a capacity to recognise and accept mother, not merely as a needs-satisfying object, but as a person in her own right. That right includes mother having relationships with others of her own choosing. This, of course, involves the infant resolving the Oedipal conflict with its father, a prelude to learning about and getting to grips with reality. Emerging into a world of reality and coming to terms with it leads to temptations to take short-cuts back to perfection, and later these short-cuts might include lies, hypocrisies, and delusions.

When the mother looks into her baby's eyes and says, "You are the most darling baby in the world", this is an important experience for the baby to have, so that its normal healthy narcissism can develop. But the baby also needs to understand this is a social convention and, while it feels lovely, it is also somewhat illusory. If the baby actually believes this illusion in a consistent way, it is subject to the most terrible processes. Either it becomes so narcissistic that it is unmanageable, or it becomes so gullible that it is at the mercy of every flattery in the world. So, the infant has to be able to be "deceived" sufficiently to have the experience of feeling loved and wonderful, while at the same time it has to remain sufficiently aware of the illusory pretence. The corruptive process in infancy starts at the point where there is clash between primary narcissism and the dawning awareness of others as people with needs, and when that awareness is overridden by personal omnipotent, narcissistic, or other desires. Developmentally, the child has to work through and give up much, and realise ultimately that it is one among many and that the world is bigger than it. It is possible to argue that elements of corruption are present in the attempts we make to reach back to what we once had and was lost. In other words, corruption seems to be the refusal to adjust to reality and/or the dismantling of previously achieved adjustments to reality. It is almost as if, in growing up, one has to play by the rules and one accepts these adaptations painfully as one moves to the depressive position of recognising others, and then being told, "You don't have to do that, you can drop all these painful adjustments." In Kissinger's memoirs (1979), dealing with the last days of the Shah of Iran, he writes how the influences that provide realistic feedback and being in touch with societal processes drop away one by one, until finally only a fantasy situation is left which feeds a total psychotic delusional omnipotence; being totally out of touch and surrounded by sycophants who all say in chorus, "You are the most marvellous baby in the world, you are the Emperor."

Biologically, human beings start off their existence in a state of fusion with mother's body. Generally, there is no need to struggle for resources because these flow into it smoothly and continuously. From a state of fusion, the infant moves into a state of non-fusion, where survival is dependent on another to provide resources. The infant has to find ways of attracting the breast and acknowledging its value and importance and debt of gratitude to it. The Kleinian approach centres on that struggle. Can you feel grateful to your life support system? Or do you hate it and want to prove that it is of no value to you? In that sense, corruption and devaluing what is valuable can be said to originate in infancy. Corruption has a biological inevitability about it that emerges from the human condition of dependency. But, somewhere, we would have to acknowledge the insertion of socialisation and social values into that process. If corruption has its roots in our biological and social inheritance, then we need to acknowledge corruption, not as an abnormal phenomenon, but, rather, an inevitable part of all systems, and to be watchful of its manifestations. We have to conclude that there is a predisposition towards corruption in individuals, organisations, and society. If the reality principle is about making adaptations and compromising, then there can be difficulties distinguishing between that and corruption. Compromise is about being in touch with reality and making healthy adjustments. When does a healthy adjustment become compromise and when does compromise become corruption? From the moment the baby is born, or even before, the baby is framed within a social system where daily it is irradiated with aspects of the prevailing value system. It is deviation from the value system that is considered corruption.

Corruption in organisations

New organisations form at times when there is a need for them. A particularly gifted person sees the need for a new organisation, then precipitates the need or the idea out and forms a new body. The organisation then builds itself to meet that need and makes use of that which is available and comes to hand. The organisation uses personalities and attitudes or states of mind that are around, that then forms into an organisation that fits into whatever social climate there might be, thus fulfilling a very important social need. Soon after its formation, the organisation acquires accretions of acolytes and others, and from then on, it loses the very quality that caused it to be sensitively in touch with societal processes. These social processes, its *raison d'être*, then become a threat because the organisation has constantly to adapt. So, the organisation becomes more and more institutionalised and more and more defended, and more and more corrupted, by falling into defensive states of needing to protect itself, as opposed to remaining open and modifying and constantly recreating itself.

New movements and organisations start with high ideals. Political parties win on the basis of hope and expectation, but, later, reality intervenes, the parties cannot deliver, and they begin to fudge.

Choices have to be made and we are back to the leadership question. The role of leadership is to be in touch with reality. Leaders might espouse high ideals, but ultimately their enterprises have to be successes. The tragedy in organisations is when work is undermined and decisions are made, not openly on merit or fairness, but secretly on preferences and favours.

Corruption, survival, and paranoid–schizoid mechanisms

The paranoid–schizoid position characterises early infantile develop-ment, prior to the onset of the depressive position, so-called because the predominant characteristic of the infant's mental state is one of acute anxiety about its survival and not having any developed means of defending itself. Paranoid–schizoid mechanisms operate in organi-sations and are central components of corruption in that they remove entirely the process of being in touch with reality and acknowledging others. On the other hand, being in the depressive position, it is possi-ble to see the whole picture better. One can then be in pain about what to do about it. There can be debate-cum-acknowledgement-cum-thoughtfulness about complex situations. Corruption removes think-ing, acknowledgement, and indebtedness, and fosters a regression to primitive mental mechanisms. In addition to corruption being about greed, it is, first of all, persuading others to forget about the ordinary rules of decency; it is about claiming uniqueness. Therefore, one falls into believing that one can act in ways that anyone else would regard as unacceptable or immoral. Thoughtfulness is thrown away and one falls into an omnipotent, oceanic state of oneness that cannot differ-entiate between oneself and other people; you are them and they are you. If one is part of a system that encourages mindlessness and lack of differentiation, then one is protected from guilt that would come from thinking about others and seeing the differences.

Corruption follows an emotional trajectory: excitement at a new idea leading to pleasure, domination of the group by the excitement, then jitters, panic, and blame. The new idea creates a belief that some-thing revolutionary is happening. This turns to euphoria and boom; emotions determine "reality". A paranoid–schizoid state dominates and anxiety that might spell caution is denied. Doubters are dismissed. When the corruption is exposed, panic and revulsion result, then anger and blame, but surprisingly little guilt or learning. Typically, people blame each other for allowing them to be caught up. The sense of reality is still paranoid–schizoid because responsibility is disowned.

The field of emotional finance recognises how uncertainty underpins all investment activity, although the consequent anxiety, doubt, and stress are often suppressed. It also emphasises how reason often has little effect on judgement. Anxiety is dealt with by depressive or paranoid–schizoid states of mind. Applied to corrupt systems, in a depressive position state inherent unpredictability is recognised, in which decisions are made transparently in the service of the task, or they might be hidden in order to favour a few. In a paranoid–schizoid position, the pain of the awareness of hurting others is avoided by separating good and bad feelings. Ideas that feel good excite, while those that feel bad are repressed. This allows people to ignore the consequences of decisions, or to blame others for them. A paranoid–schizoid state is characterised by distrust and constant jittery activity that are manifest inside and outside the organisation.

Corruption implicitly contains an attack on internal objects (parents, and authority figures) that are seen as being hypocritical. People might be persuaded that authority is self-serving and corrupt and uses its position at the expense of others. Authority claims the credit for others' work. Conversely, the fantasy is encouraged that we, too, could have glory, but first authority would have to be overthrown, thereby enabling one to leap magically from dependency into independence. But the fantasy is based on a false set of principles that we can stop authority taking credit for something that is believed not to be theirs. This inversion is an example of the ambivalent relationship towards dependency. Groups in organisations get into states of despair where they feel there is nothing they can do; "Isn't it all awful?" they state. "We just have to wait until the elusive 'top' of the organisation decides to provide more resources." The despair leads to blanket condemnation—"It's the system." This leads to thinking that the organisation is corrupt, that is, "the organisation isn't helping me, so why should I help it, or better still, I will take from the organisation to make me feel I still have power and means of control." If we hold on to the notion of organisation as "internal object", then corruption in organisational settings is about turning against the organisational task and turning against the leadership; having a hatred of the task and a hatred of leadership.

Corruption needs to be contained inside everyone, where one's own experiences and feelings of the corruptor inside oneself can be dealt with. If there is no "cure" for corruption, then it is hugely important to acknowledge that, contain it, and manage it within our systems. We need to acknowledge corruption dynamics in ourselves and in our systems and find ways of managing and containing that, because otherwise we can get caught in what becomes circuitous persecutory views towards corruptors and the corrupted.

Acknowledgements

I have discussed the issues contained in this chapter with a number of people. They have all made helpful comments, which I have weighed and almost always incorporated in some form. I want to thank them for their comments, whether they have been supportive or critical. I do not wish to implicate my commentators, but I want it known that I have tested widely what I say in this essay with people whom I respect as authorities in this field: Eliat Aram, David Armstrong, the late Mary Barker, Ken Eisold, Dione Hills, Bob Hinshelwood, Richard Holti, Johnny Kelleher, Olya Khaleelee, Gordon Lawrence, Jean Neumann, Anton Obholzer, the late Ken Smith, Phil Swann, Kathy White, and many others.

CHAPTER TEN

Psychological and behavioural elements in board performance*

Introduction

Boards and board behaviour cannot be regulated or managed through organisational structures and controls alone; rather, behaviour is developed over time as a result of responding to existing and anticipated situations. It is this very dynamic nature of how behaviour evolves that means that Chairs have responsibility to ensure that their boards take time to purposefully evaluate their behaviour and the implications on the effective functioning of the board.

Behaviour is learnt, subject to change, and dependent upon situational demands such as social influence. Chairs of boards will both influence and be influenced by their vision of the desired direction of the board and the organisation, by the existing and hoped-for strategy of the future, and by existing and actual and anticipated behaviours and demands of others on the board. Susceptibility to social influence

---

* This chapter is based on: A. Gill & M. Sher (2009), Psychological and behavioural elements in board performance. Annex 4. In: D. Walker, *A Review of Corporate Governance in UK Banks and Other Financial Industry Entities* (pp. 139–146). Material reprinted with permission.

is not a characteristic of those who lack willpower; it is instinctive and we are all subject to it (Bion, 1961; Freud, 1921c, 1923b; Lawrence, 1979; Miller, 1993a).

Underlying attitudes and traits, such as physical vitality and stamina, intelligence and action-orientated judgement, eagerness to accept responsibility, need for achievement, and other such typical characteristics associated with those in the roles of Chair, influence the dynamics of a board's ability to work effectively together. But leadership research (Gemmill & Oakley, 1992; Western, 2008) has shown that none of these traits influences leadership ability as much as a person's ability to learn from reality and encourage systemic behavioural change in order that others may adapt their behaviour to meet the demands of the external environment.

Chairs operate at a number of levels—task, group, systemic, and environmental—in order to mobilise others to share a vision of an anticipated future state of affairs and a willingness to collaborate to bring it about. Behavioural maturity of Chairs will include an ability to take the long view, while being clearly mindful of next steps.

Requisite behaviour of Chairs of boards

Recommendations

To be effective Chairs of boards, their behaviour should cover:

1. *Integrating their boards' collective thinking.* This is possible when Chairs excel at seeking and sharing information, building ideas into concepts, analysing and considering multiple perspectives and different alternatives, and can control their individual needs in favour of the common good.
2. *Empathy and enabling openness in board members.* The ability to listen is critical to successful chairing and team dynamics. Listening to what is not being said is as critical as listening to the words that are spoken. An ability to listen engenders trust and respect at the deepest level.
3. *Facilitating interaction.* This requires that Chairs of boards recognise who needs to be in the conversation and facilitate their participation, rather than "managing" the process. This requires that skills and expertise are valued and respected regardless of hierarchy or power dynamics.

4. *Developing others.* Chair behaviour should include active coaching, mentoring, and development of talent within the board, and in particular with new board members.
5. *Communicating complex messages succinctly.* Chairs should excel at disseminating information through written and spoken means. The ability to communicate effectively reduces confusion and frees the board for analysis, exploration, and learning.
6. *Collaborating across boundaries.* Chairs of boards have to navigate multiple boundaries. The ability to identify boundaries and successfully navigate across and within them is critical to creating a culture of collaboration and efficiency.
7. *Continuous improvement.* Good behavioural objectives include continuous evaluation against internal and external benchmarks. The continual focus on improvement is as much a mindset as a behaviour.

The behavioural repertoire and characteristics of the high-performing Chair is extensive: high level analytical and intellectual capability, emotional maturity, awareness and consideration of others and their value, physical vitality and stamina, intelligence and action-orientated judgement, eagerness to accept responsibility, task competence, understanding of followers and their needs, skill in dealing with people, need for achievement, capacity to motivate people, courage and resolution, trustworthiness, decisiveness, self-confidence, assertiveness, adaptability and flexibility.

The demand for these characteristics and behaviours will vary, depending upon the mix and maturity of the business and the other board members. The more transparent the Chair's strengths and weaknesses, the more possible it is to develop and strengthen the repertoire and the more likely that the Chair will be capable of leading enduring success.

Appointing Chairs, non-executive directors, and executive directors

Recommendations

Chairs, non-executive, executive directors, and the board as a whole should be independently assessed at appointment and annually. Full psychological and board-as-a-whole assessment should include assessment of behaviour, experience, knowledge, motivation, intellect, and group dynamics.

Leadership behaviour is predictive of boardroom success and should be given greater weight over industry experience. Assessment reports should be a key part of building an induction and gap management plan to integrate new members and reduce the risks inherent in groups that work together for long periods.

Effective board performance is directly linked to issues of leadership. Organisations and their boards are complex and dynamic, and, therefore, every Chair, non-executive and executive director role will be different. Regular objective review is critical for assessing the appropriateness of particular types of leadership, skills, and experiences of boards.

Assessment is a means of accelerating understanding of the current and future potential capabilities of a board's leadership. It is a process of peeling back the layers to determine individual and group success. Techniques such as behavioural event interviewing, psychometric assessments, work-based tests, and cognitive and numerical reasoning tests considerably enhance the chance of predicting how successful individuals are likely to be in role and what will be needed to help them succeed. Assessment reports provide details about performance, what has been achieved, and how. Assessment provides knowledge about personality preferences (likes to do), ability (can do) behaviour (how it is done), motivation (will do), and red flags (will not do).

Behaviour and motivation are the most predictive indicators of performance in leadership roles in complex organisations (Gill & Sanders, 2009). The challenge with most board level appointments is that there is a limited level of knowledge about individuals, obtained through peer networks, press reports, and performance results, etc., which tend to take precedence over proper objective evaluation of the actual needs of the board and the comparable skills of NEDs or EDs. At individual and board levels, the purpose of due diligence is to create an in-depth understanding of how individuals and teams (boards and committees) will perform within their roles in the context of the organisation's current performance and future business plans.

The assessment of executive and non-executive directors requires that the assessor pays particular attention to the differences between leadership, authority, and power (Obholzer, 2001, p. 201) (see next section). Many organisational leaders demonstrate poor emotional intelligence, behavioural limitations, and the power to block development. Understanding these danger signals is critical to preventing abuse of authority.

Induction and training of Chairs of boards, non-executive direcotrs, and executive directors

Recommendations

As part of qualifying to be a Chair, executive director, or non-executive director, individuals should be trained in how to take up roles, managing role boundaries, recognising the difference between power and authority, and group dynamics.

The role of the Chair is to effectively manage group processes in the board and its sub-committees. Effective group leadership involves holding the balance between satisfying the group's emotional needs and focusing the group on its work. Chairs, executive directors, and non-executive directors need skills in observing, interpreting, and drawing conclusions about what people are thinking and feeling, but not saying: that is, they need to have awareness of below-the-surface dynamics.

The model of the single hero, usually male, leader is outdated. In complex organisations such as banks and other financial institutions, distributed leadership will more likely lead to effective boards (Miller & Rice, 1967). Distributed leadership and diversity of thought increase the probability of superior strategy and decision making. However, with diversity comes the challenge of increased potential for conflict and, with it, "groupthink". To avoid this, board members need to be schooled in group relations, power dynamics, and the behaviours and processes that are required to maximise the intellectual capability of the board. This type of leadership is known as transformational leadership. It requires that leaders have highly tuned facilitation and listening skills and understand the place of emotions in the life of the group. Transformational leaders satisfy the group's emotional needs while also holding it to the work of the board. In our experience, transactional, rather than transformational, leadership is predominant in the financial industry, where high risk, high pressure, and high reward dominate, and also where "anger" is the dominant emotional tone (Burns, 1978; Sorenson & Goethals, 2001).

Transactional leadership

- Transactional leadership with followers is a way of getting things done, setting expectations and goals, and providing recognition and rewards. Transactional leadership is typical of politicians.
- Transactions are typically based on satisfying leaders' self-interest and the self-interest of their followers.
- Transactional leadership fulfils contractual obligations, which creates trust and establishes stable relationships with mutual benefits for leader and follower.
- Positive and negative transactions are reward-based or coerced-based, respectively.
- The assumption is: if the desired behaviour is produced, the contracted reward will be received. The leader clarifies the expectations and the follower delivers, receiving the contingent reward. If the follower does not deliver, and if the leader spells out the penalty for not delivering, then contingent reward becomes contingent punishment: "If you don't stay on target, here's what you don't get."

Transformational leadership

- Transformational leadership engages followers not only to get them to achieve something of significance, but to become "morally uplifted" to be leaders themselves.
- Transformational leadership is more concerned with the collective interests of the group, organisation, and society, not self-interest.
- Components of transformational leadership include individualised consideration, intellectual stimulation, and charismatic inspiring leadership.
- To be transformational, the leader has to learn the needs, abilities, and aspirations of followers and address them considerately. By doing so, followers can be developed into leaders; elevated to higher levels—understand followers needs and capabilities to transform, reshape, and reprioritise them.

- Transformational leadership is intellectually stimulating and challenging followers' basic thinking, assumptions, and models to encourage followers to think about new ways to perform work.

A curriculum for inducting and developing board members might include coaching and practice in leaderless group facilitation, consideration of role and role boundaries, authority *vs.* power and its implications in groups, leadership and followership, and the behaviours and processes that maximise the intellectual capacities of groups.

Power

- Power relates to the availability and deployment of resources and is either task related or not.
- Where power is used without a clear connection to task, the result is abuse—of people, of position, and resources.
- Power is having the resources to be able to enact and implement one's decisions.
- Power is personal and has little to do with authority.
- If personal power is exercised in a punitive, dictatorial, or rigid manner, it provokes either submission or conformity, in which case the system displays stable dynamics, or rage, rebellion, and sabotage, in which case the system becomes unstable and moves towards disintegration. Both stability, with its repetition of the past, and disintegration are destructive of creativity.

Authority

- Authority derives from a shared task; it is the product of organisation and structure, whether it is "external", as in the organisation's sanction, or "internal", as in the mind of the leader(s); authority derives from the task to be done and from the hierarchical structure.
- All authority is exercised in the context of the *sanction* provided by the followership, but any such sanction (or lack of it) must be measured against the primary task of the organisation.
- Giving or withholding sanction for change must be measured against what the change is intended to achieve. If withholding

sanction interferes with the achievement of the organisation's primary task, this should be taken as resistance to change. This would require work on the part of the leadership to address the underlying individual and systemic anxieties.

● Awareness of the presence and workings of unconscious personal, interpersonal, group, intergroup, and intrainstitutional processes among both leaders and followers is essential and addresses issues of "internal" authority.

The optimum size of boards and sub-committees

Recommendations

The optimum size for a board ranges between eight and twelve people. When boards are composed of more than twelve people, a number of psychological and group phenomena—span of attention, the ability to deal with complexity (Dunbar, 1993), the ability to maintain effective interpersonal relationships and motivation—are compromised.

The optimum size of sub-committees is between five and nine people. To ensure quality thinking and effective interaction, sub-committees should have not less than five and not more than nine members. At five, a group becomes more of a team, at seven, thinking is optimised, above nine, the cognitive limit of the group is exceeded.

Research on effective groups shows empirically that small boards are more effective than large boards. The ideal size is between eight and twelve individuals; at this size each member can give a personal account of each other board member (Turquet, 1975). Size is important because there is a limit to the number of individuals with whom any one person can maintain stable relationships. Eight to twelve persons can know each other well enough to maximise their talents and give a personal account of one another. The group's potential to integrate its thinking is enhanced and the potential for dislocation (the feeling of not belonging or not being as important as another) is reduced.

Large boards tend to be contentious and experience phenomena of hostility, dislocation, and "groupthink" that reduce its ability to effectively monitor senior management and govern the business. Hostility in groups is often present in the form of a nameless dread, a threat of something that is around, something that is going to happen. This dread might be expressed through individual silence and unwillingness to talk about an issue in the group context. This group phenomenon allows board members to take advantage of each other through coalition building, selective channelling of information, and dividing and conquering. Dislocation causes participation and commitment to decrease. This effect is typically seen as group size grows beyond 8–12 participants, increasing the opportunity for leadership to be manipulative and political (Hall, 1976).

"Groupthink" is a type of thought exhibited by group members who try to minimise conflict and reach consensus without critically testing, analysing, and evaluating ideas. As a group grows beyond the optimum size, the leadership task increases exponentially, and with it grows the likelihood of groupthink as member's motivation to achieve unanimity overrides motivation to appraise alternative courses of action (Janis, 1972, p. 9; Jaques, 1976).

The main, but often unspoken, justification for a large board is to facilitate the board's resource-gathering. A larger number of directors, it is believed, will translate into more interlocking relationships that might be useful in providing resources such as customers, clients, credit, and supplies. This, however, is not the function of the board, which should be as *steward* for the primary purpose and values of the organisation. A large board has an inherent risk that it has not been formed to act appropriately, but, rather, to avoid its primary task (of stewardship) (Long, 2008).

Sub-committees are meant to provide greater in-depth analysis of a particular topic. Therefore, sub-committees' ability to integrate their thinking and assist boards in creating strategy is critical. For this type of work, between five and nine people are likely to be more effective. Sub-committees spend more time "thinking together" to explore options, analyse data, and seek and process information. Their abilities in the area of "working memory"—to hold information—is key to the sub-committees' abilities to build on knowledge as new situations unfold and impact on their relationships with boards.

Relationships between boards and sub-committees

Recommendations

Chairs of boards and sub-committees should be schooled in the managing the effects of "denial", "splitting", and "projection'.

The role of Chairs of sub-committees is twofold: (a) to gather intelligence on its specialist subject, and (b) to educate the board. Subdividing groups increases potential for political and psychological differences, and for the differences to dominate relationships and for collaboration to weaken.

The role of boards is to position the organisation in its context, and decide on sustainability and direction of the total organisation. Board members have to set aside their identifications with sub-committees, divisions, and sub-systems. Delegating work to sub-committees and then reintegrating their work into the board requires an understanding of dynamics of "parts" to "wholes" and sensitive handling and awareness of the potential for competition and envy. A useful way of understanding these power dynamics comes from the conceptualisation of "denial", "splitting", and "projection" (Carr, 1996; Jaques, 1989; Klein, 1959).

An example of denial, splitting, and projection might be seen in a board's sense of discomfort because it lacks knowledge about a subject, or perceives there is increased requirement to focus extra resources on a particular area of expertise, for example, risk management. This discomfort might be "denied" and rationalised as "all fields of endeavour have specialist areas of knowledge and we can leave risk management to the specialists". "Leaving it to the specialists" is a form of "splitting", and helps boards distance themselves intellectually and emotionally from the difficulties of risk prediction and management. But, together with getting rid of uncomfortable feelings of anxiety about risk and ignorance of the subject, etc., goes another set of feelings—mistrust: "Will the specialists try to pull the wool over our eyes?" Fearing that the specialists will do that, a board might "project" its ignorance, fear, and mistrust into the very sub-committee/s it has created to deal with risk, and accuse them of arrogance, manipulation, and engaging in politics, etc., often leading to a self-fulfilling prophesy whereby the sub-committee actually behaves in the ways they have been "projected into". "Projection" is commonly accepted as the attribution of feelings, qualities, intentions, etc., to others that truly belong to oneself (or to the board, in this case).

When a sub-committee re-enters the board to advise or propose an approach, "projection" will be particularly prevalent and holds considerable sway. The sub-committee's findings might be repudiated by the board because of its unconscious envy of the sub-committee's knowledge and expertise and fear of how that knowledge and expertise might be used against the board. These processes are very subtle and only become apparent over time. Chairs of boards can be schooled to recognise these dynamics before they have time to take hold and dominate relationships between boards and their sub-committees.

CHAPTER ELEVEN

Inside the minds of the money minders: deciphering reflections on money, behaviour, and leadership in the financial crisis of 2007–2010*

Introduction

Our research was directed at the question of why senior, intelligent, and respected leaders from all sides of the finance industry failed to prevent a crisis that some had predicted years in advance. We were interested in knowing more about the dynamic influences—personal and global—on the thinking of industry leaders. For our purposes, "thinking" is also considered alongside "not thinking", the "inability to think", and "hatred of thinking". Therefor, we drafted a set of open-ended questions that was designed to elicit "thinking". As we conducted our interviews with about thirty senior figures, we noted our reactions to our interviewees as a way of deepening our understanding of their experiences of the crisis from their roles.

* This chapter is based on: A. Gill & M. Sher (2012), Inside the minds of the money minders: deciphering reflections on money, behaviour and leadership in the financial crisis of 2007–2010. In: S. Long & B. Sievers (Eds.), *Beneath the Surface of the Financial Industry: Towards a Socio-Analysis of Money, Finance and Capital* (pp 58–73). © Taylor & Francis, London, UK. Material reprinted with permission.

Our hypothesis is that money, finance, and capital serve as "containers" for hidden individual and social meaning. In our examination, we hope to expose the dynamics that contributed to the financial crisis and in what way they shaped the operating paradigms of banks and other financial institutions. Our interview method invited participants to offer free associations and uncensored thoughts, in order that we could access deeper levels of understanding of the below-the-surface dynamics of leadership of financial institutions and the financial industry as a whole.

Our perspective in systems psychodynamics focuses on conscious and unconscious relationships between individuals, groups, organisations, and society as a whole. The unconscious is perceived not simply as a place in the mind of an individual, but as an intricate web of social relations. In this, thinking and feeling are critical aspects of organisational functioning.

We work with the concepts of holism and transference. Holism considers that all parts of all systems affect one another (Tarnas, 1991). Transference refers to the displacement of thoughts and feelings from one person or situation on to another person or situation. Counter-transference refers to the feelings that the researcher or observer has toward his or her subjects. Both might occur in the relations between research interviewers and their subjects: the observers and the observed. Miller (1990a, p. 170) captures the essence of the transference dynamic in group and organisational work when he states that

> ... in the field of human behaviour no conceptual framework is complete without a statement of the role of the observer and his/her relation to the observed. ... Consultants collaborate with clients as actors in understanding and perhaps modifying their roles in the organisations. ... [Consultants] are integrally part of the process, not outside it.

In this chapter, we will examine (i) how opportunities for talking freely to us enabled our respondents to articulate thoughts that are normally set aside or repressed because of pressures of day-to-day work activity; (ii) how these hitherto unexpressed thoughts aroused, had an impact on, and interacted with our feelings that enabled us to offer new and testable hypotheses about the collective fantasies and behaviour of the people and institutions charged with stewardship of the economy. We anticipated that our presence in the research organ-isation would trigger thoughts in areas of organisational life that Bollas (1989) defines as the "unthought known", that is, thoughts that are inchoate and pre-conscious; that everyone is thinking, but will not acknowledge publicly. For example, one chief executive said,

> Following the near-collapse of the West's finance industry we have to re-orient our thinking. Going for the last million and thinking about the quality of our life and the lives of our customers has to be balanced. Levels of remuneration are not the only things in life.

This thought had been at the back of many people's minds and found its way to conscious expression in this interviewee by virtue of our presence as researchers.

In addition, we were concerned that any anxiety and guilt that our respondents might have felt about their roles in the financial crisis would evaporate soon after the crisis passed. We were concerned, too, that the expectation of a "bail-out", the complacent "too-big-to-fail" idea, and the role of government as lender of last resort, would lead to a business-as-usual attitude and the opportunities for learning from the crisis would be lost.

We designed a list of ten open-ended questions that encouraged our respondents to free associate rather than feed us the "company line". Examples of questions are:

> Q1: The vivid language used in the press over the last twelve months has described "bankers" and "city leaders" as "greedy, stupid and socially useless". To what extent do these definitions by outsiders, however painful, describe how you as an insider feel about yourself, your organisation and your industry? What language, stories and defi-nitions do you and other leaders in the financial industry use when you talk about your work and the role that banking plays in society?

> Q2: If the outsiders' definitions of professionals in the financial indus-try paint such an extremely negative picture, how do you feel about the potential influencing role of outsiders in future regulatory arrange-ments? How does the changing nature of banking, finance and regula-tion impact on your role and your hopes and fears for the future?

Our respondents were chosen because of their roles in different parts of the financial system: banking, insurance, accounting, regula-tion, and civil service.

Through the interviews, we found that the experiences of these individuals, their interpretations of what had happened, and their understanding of causality were similar: that, on the one hand, they and the finance industry are indispensable to western liberal democracy, the free market, and civilisation generally. On the other hand, few were willing to admit the extent of their own participation and collusion in the failings of a system that had privileged them. We think the critical difference here is how our respondents believe they might have behaved as *individuals* from how they might have acted collectively. Despite occupying roles with huge authority and powers of control, they absolve themselves individually of accountability; they almost all describe events as being outside their control, whereas their places in the system suggest that had they collaborated more effectively across systems and understood more about the nature of systems dynamics, events in the financial industry and their knock-on effects in almost every walk of life would have come more easily within their collective control. This led us to critically assess the nature of leadership failure when systems break down. We believe that in the finance industry, leadership failure is related to the peculiarities of the material they are working with—money and markets—and the context within which they are working, capitalism and globalisation, especially because these are such large collective systems that are so very different from individual, small group, and single organisational dynamics with which they are more familiar.

Our respondents agreed that banking—"oiling the wheels of western liberal democracy, providing opportunity for growth and dreams"—has changed forever as a result of the near melt-down of Western economies. De-regulation and globalisation have made clearer the divide between the "casino" of investment banking and the "vanilla" of retail banking. The crisis has also paradoxically shown their inherent interdependence. The traditional bank manager, the one who "looked the customer in the eye" and made judgements about reliability and risk, had been lost in efforts to improve the efficiency of High Street banking. Technological advances and the desire to reduce costs and increase profit drove out the traditional bank manager who had played a vital role in knowing where to lend money, a role that was underestimated and undervalued by a banking system that had become global. Traditional retail banking business seemed boring and the new, more lucrative business of investment banking seduced workers by its fast pace and promise of unlimited and accelerated wealth.

> When bankers get to that age where they need a bit more money, where they've just got married, bought a house, things start to get tough. They are dealing with aggressive bankers who poach them, offering them lots more money than they are earning and the promise of more. They are putting up with bad behaviour at work anyway so they think they may as well go and earn more. (Senior Partner, Accounting Firm)

Very few grasped the implications of the rapid rise of investment banking, with its deep pockets and continued promises of wealth. Neither did they understand the increasingly porous nature of boundaries between retail and investment banking.

> My picture of banking has worsened over the years; retail banking I saw as humdrum. But it had a social use. The banker was a person in the community, valued and modest. Technology has changed that; the community element no longer exists. Investment bankers wreak havoc on communities, but have no sense that they are doing this. (Regulator)

Investment banking incentives were high and risks unforeseen. Investment banking became a gambling business and flourished on the thrill of wins with little thought given to the possibility of loss. Gambling self-sustains, with an optimism stoked by the behaviour of leaders of the field.

> In a business, money is the lifeblood; people who work in business know its power and importance; but in the City, money is an end in itself. In the City there is a dislocation in the amount of money earned and effort. It is a form of curse. (NED; Regulator)

Risk managers, the leaders, were saying "It's OK". Industry leaders were behaving as if it was acceptable to take high risks. Thus, many people continued to do what they were dubious about. If money "is an end in itself", it would suggest it contained no meaning beyond itself, or contained many different and contradictory meanings:

> Money isn't motivational to people—it motivates for a very short period. What matters is intellectual challenge, career prospects and being surrounded by other interesting people. Money can however be de-motivating; if you discover you are paid less than your peer group. That de-motivates and is divisive. (Banker)

and

> It's hard work if you don't have enough money—it's hard to get off the ladder once you're on it. You need more and more money to meet needs you didn't know you had. I pursue the things I like; I have a taste for expensive wine; I have a new car every two years; I have children in public schools—I didn't need these things, but I would find it hard to go back to not being able to have them. (Banker)

Our reactions to these responses was incredulity that industry players with reputations for superior intelligence and aggressive drive could now be seeking sympathy for mistakes they had made, their lack of foresight, and even lack of compassion. Were we ourselves victims of a media flurry to tar all bankers with the same brush as villains? Or were we seeing their genuine vulnerability and stunned disbelief? Were they pulling a fast one on us? We felt that our interviews were eliciting genuine feelings of shame and remorse in some of our respondents and that, in many instances, the "chiefs" actually did not see the crisis coming, and, even if they did, they felt pretty helpless. The interviews were turning into cathartic confessionals and we were their confessors; it was as if they were waiting for opportunities to unburden, so cornered did they feel by their own sense of shame and failure and by the chorus of hostility that had been evoked from the media, government, shareholders, and the public.

In addition to the confessional style, the interviews had healing elements in so far as "thinking" could once more find a place. Many of our respondents commented on the value of the experience of talking. They almost all said the interviews were difficult; they felt stretched, it made them think; some were physically and emotionally distressed by the experience, shown in their agitation, stuttering, tears, anger, table thumping, not wanting to end at the appointed time, and asking for second interviews.

Our understanding of our respondents' behaviour and our reactions to them are linked to the development of new financial products that created vast new wealth opportunities for so many people in a short time. Everyone seemed to have got caught up in a manic defence of overbearing omnipotence: "we have created a new order; all the former rules can be suspended; we have conquered unpredictability and the future is ours. We possess it all"—a virulent form of infantile omnipotence and control of the feeding mother. Immediate and infinite gratification leads to the suspension of thinking lest the thinking leads to a critical re-evaluation of what they are doing and which might require a dramatic re-evaluation of their beliefs in themselves and their powers.

The market as God

Our respondents told us about their belief in the concept of the market as a supreme being—the invisible hand that rewards good behaviour and punishes bad. That is how wealth is created and how grace is received. They also said markets are imperfect, but the best available systems. The market is regarded as an impersonal overriding judge of performance; announcements are made and share prices rise or fall. Technologies allow performance management to be rated almost instantaneously. This speed is beyond human comprehension; it distracts and creates a sense of insecurity, causing people to focus on the short term. Instant gratification, not value, becomes the end in itself.

> If disclosure of short term results focuses behaviour on even more short-termism, it is a vicious cycle. The transaction is not valued over the long term and this creates a dreadful lack of trust. (NED; Banker)

In this "short-termist" environment, some regulators said they had found themselves "defending the indefensible". They observed behaviour that was known to be excessive, but they were persuaded that this time things were different. Bankers and regulators became captured by mathematics, believing that because they were modelling risk they could contain it. The regulators, too, were deluded. Group mentality had developed and was embraced. People vigorously signed up to the latest idea, saying "this time is different". The regulators said that "We should not have believed them, but we felt we were up against people's unlimited capacity to persuade themselves otherwise. This clearly happened to us too."

Markets are still the best way we have of allocating resources, but they also generate breakdown! Market failure is inherent, regulation only mitigates it. Failure is a given! The problem has become global and the nature of global relationships is not understood. The true underlying problem is that the system had changed, but people hadn't understood that. The need is for individual governments to make changes in regulation, but they can't work fast enough. It is an impossible job. The market system is the best way for wealth creation, but it contains inherently wealth destruction too. There will always be a problem; therefore safety nets have to be provided, like safety deposits schemes, because systems do collapse. Regulation can reduce the amplitude and frequency of crises, but the regulator is in a difficult job because the players are always changing. The market isn't failsafe. In fact, it's designed to fail, but the bankers believe it is failsafe. They have an infinite capacity for self-delusion. (Regulator)

This "infantile capacity for self-delusion" played on us, too. Some of the most powerful and celebrated figures in the financial world were talking to us and pouring their hearts out about their blind spots, failures, and sense of shame. That filled us with feelings of inverted power—the great confessing to the lowly, grateful for being listened to, revealing their weaknesses as if seeking absolution from guilt. We felt at times as if we were experiencing a form of undifferentiated fusion with some of our respondents, resulting in a destruction of our own thinking capacities and values. We had to work hard to restrain our fantasies of sitting in judgement of our respondents and punishing them. Was this, we wondered, a mirror of a contemptuous judgementalism that some of our respondents themselves projected on to their financial organisations, markets, and customers in their pursuit of omnipotent infallibility and self-aggrandisement? We felt we needed to be watchful of our judgemental and haughty attitudes lest they get in the way of our work and undermine our research roles.

Competition, capitalism, and globalisation

As far back as 1997, senior bankers from the twelve biggest institutions in the world came together, saying, "We are the heart of the financial system. If we get it wrong, the whole system will suffer." They were seeking a way to regulate themselves. In the analysis of the latest crisis, leaders frequently refer to their lack of understanding of the global nature of finance. According to our interviewees, early attempts to create global regulation were flawed because "the international competitive juices were stronger than the collaborative ones." The regulators said that to have a global solution required global co-operation; but authority was national, not global. The regulators felt powerless. Our interviewees described how national interests superseded the bigger systemic demand. Unable to resolve differences, they dissociated from social reality and distanced themselves from their social obligations. Their proposed self-regulation could not occur because they feared that their own jurisdictions would constrain their ability to compete against those countries not present. Despite numerous attempts, the global finance system remained unregulated.

In our research, we have attempted to assess the contents of people's minds: their thinking, their non-thinking, and their hatred of thinking about the financial and banking issues they were involved with on a daily basis. Property as an asset suffered inflated prices around the world in a decade of rising house prices. When prices fell, the financial bubble burst. Sub-prime mortgages in the USA are believed to have been the final straw, but they were not the main cause of the financial meltdown. In conversations with us, our respondents appeared to confirm Goldsmith's (2008) assertions that they inhabited a bubble in which they talked only about their investments. Day-to-day dialogue revolved around investment opportunities. We heard how investment decisions were made solely on "how much this has gone up in the past", not "what is this worth?". Thinking appeared to have ceased and greed had overcome fear. They focused exclusively on the upside and ignored the downside. Prudent risk assessment stopped. They say they were disconnected from the true value of what they were selling. Their organisations were over-leveraged and investment bankers borrowed whatever they could in the home mortgages market. Huge mortgages, often as much as 125% of the value of the property, or six or seven times earnings, spoke of a system drunk on debt. In the complexity of a financial system driving debt, innovation in finance meant intelligent individuals, who should have known better, were maximising returns primarily to satisfy shareholders and some banks were borrowing as much as forty times their capital base. Being caught in the cross-fire of high leverage was the only means of keeping up with other banks. Certainly, most of our respondents struggle to understand the global, social, and systemic nature of the financial crisis. They seldom came up with anything better than headline catch phrases like "trust", "behaviours", "relationships", "interdependence", but these could neither help them really understand what had happened to their industry, nor lead them to effective solutions.

The interviews produced a sense of responsibility in us. It seemed our respondents were making us feel responsible for them, to provide them with solutions. Should we have been clearer about their responsibilities? Our questions about the systemic nature of finance, about the potential abusive power of groups resulted in silence, yet they spoke passionately of "interdependence". How could there be true interdependence without conversation? This left us confused. Some of our respondents spoke of their fear of litigation, not because of wrongdoing, but because litigation would expose them as being found wanting. The lonely leader feared "being found out". As researchers and organisational consultants, we cannot repair the damage; neither do we seek to judge what happened. Our role is to contribute towards thinking about the role of culture, its strong driving force and how leaders manage the impact of these forces on themselves in their roles.

Despite their many words, and everyone—bankers, regulators, civil servants, and lawyers—was articulate, to us they seemed lost. For many, it seems their distress is about their careers ending on a note of appalling indignity, some even facing the prospect of criminal charges; they appear to be saying that they could not believe that they had been found wanting, caught out by such a catastrophic failure. They seemed unsure how to judge their own part in the failure, unsure as to whether their failure should be judged as personal rather than systemic. To what extent did they understand their roles in choices they made and their accountabilities that could have prevented the failure? All the sub-groups had become unconscious players in the dramas of the groups to which they belonged. Everyone seemed at a loss to understand the system beyond their individual part of it. Of course, many do understand, and they plead with us to show they do understand, but they claim that from where they stand, especially as regulators, accountants, and civil servants, there was little chance of being heard. Would we be able to hear them? To be sure, "hearing them" felt as if our response had to be an uncritical acceptance of their helplessness and collude that the crisis was the fault of others. We felt drawn into an "us-and-them" split. Reconciling different views of the causes of the crisis was made more difficult because of the way two sides—financial industry leaders and regulators—lined up.

Certainly, that was how we, the researchers, often felt about ourselves during interviews; our knowledge of organisational and global systems, behavioural dynamics, and organisation and leadership theory had departed from us and we felt sucked into an abyss of inadequacy, feeling that we had lost our own capacity to question, understand, or explain. We felt lost in a world of smoke and mirrors, caught in the countertransference of denial, splitting, and projection (Long, 2008).

Our respondents seemed unable to consider the invisible forces at work; everyone, to a greater or lesser extent, was involved—the borrowing public, corporate customers, investors, shareholders, regulators, the media, politicians. Seemingly, everyone was persuaded that growth was indefinite, ignoring their own often quoted advice that whatever goes up, must come down. Together with our interviewees, we struggled to understand the imponderables of culture, the atmosphere and climate of the sector that had engulfed everyone and forced upon them a way of thinking and acting that no one single agency caused or had the power to stop. After many very good years, the "bubble" had been pricked by mysterious forces that were beyond control of even the "masters of the universe", as banking leaders were described. Even as the crisis unfolded, the competitive forces and denial continued.

> The industry was in "silent complicity"; we were engaged in a "feat of levitation" that could not go on and on. But it went on and we all believed in it. People knew that eventually the house of cards would fall down. Many CEOs felt "we're OK; we will benefit from the catastrophe of others". Many allowed themselves to feel reassured because regulators had approved of the model of banking that did not require banks to hold much capital. How many said it was about to explode? Why were institutions under pressure to increase their leverage? There was enormous pressure from the institutions. Owners, media, shareholders . . . everyone . . . None of them said "stop!". (Banker)

Bankers talk a lot, but say so very little. We felt drawn to want to explain, ask, and challenge our interviewees. If "interdependence", "collaboration", and "co-operation" are the hallmark of other disci-plines and sectors that have been struggling with these dynamics for decades, why does this seem like a new discovery for bankers? As if they have invented something new. We wanted desperately to be heard, yet, the more we leant forward, looked them in the eye, and nodded, the more words would come tumbling out of their mouths. Even our smallest comment or question would result in a stream of consciousness, almost as if they had thought and thought and thought, but had never drawn conclusions.

The banks, the regulators, the politicians, and the auditors knew that banks were running high risks. But risk management in the 1990s and early 2000s moved increasingly toward mathematical modelling and away from human intuition. "Bubbles" of euphoria (Tuckett & Taffler, 2008) get separated from reality; it is a process in which every-one colludes. For Lanchester (2010), capital, capitalists, and capitalism are forces enjoined by emotions, some of which are associated with the universal desire to escape reality and be embraced by a warm sense of control and invulnerability that comes from the unrestricted in-flow of goodness (profits, dividends, bonuses) that are not cali-brated against the direct input of one's own labour. Other emotions are associated with aggression, daring, and challenge that place survival at risk. Normally, the presence of a rational mind with sound ego functioning helps to balance desire with reality and leads to responsible decision making that avoids swings of perception, expec-tation, mood, and behaviour. In economic terms, these swings are referred to as "boom" and "bust". When property markets rose, irra-tional exuberance (Greenspan, 1996; Shiller, 2005) meant enormous amounts of money were piling into the mortgage markets. That was good news for capital, because mortgages offered a steady stream of set-up fees and repayment money and it could expect to take part in the increase in house values as property values steadily rose.

We often felt caught up in processes of idealisation and magical thinking and sometimes we felt persuaded that our own insights into unconscious dynamics might be flawed. Here was the answer and it seemed so simple. Our respondents express desired outcomes, but do not address the challenges of the how to promote understanding lead-ing to wiser policies and action.

One needs to be realistic. There will be more pressure to regulate, demonstrate transparency, accountability and effectiveness. That cannot be done without more awareness of and exposure to, outside interests and influence. Outside influence is necessary otherwise bankers won't be taken seriously. Government, business and civil society must act in concert in making strenuous efforts to enable people to understand and know how the system works, the risks it runs, what it takes to generate value and remain competitive. (Civil Servant)

"Acting in concert" ignores the presence of competition, different levels of power, status and authority. "Better understandings" is based on a rationalist approach to communications and education; we felt pressure was put on us to collude in ignoring group basic assumption that sets its face against scientific approaches and defends against the experience of anxiety-arousing knowledge.

We felt at times seduced by the status and apparent knowledge of our civil servant respondents through their closeness to the hub of powerful interconnecting relationships between the banking sector, government, and society. Their position at this hub had made them aware of the importance of *collaboration and interdependence* as the most feasible way forward for government and society. They spoke eloquently and passionately about these processes. However, as the interviews progressed, we felt the conversations had the quality of a mantra: how everyone and all sectors would benefit if only they would accept the incontrovertible wisdom of *collaboration and interdependence*; on the other hand, their statements often sounded too perfect and ignored the negative dynamics of competition and conflict that are inherent and sometimes dominate relationships between organisations, sectors, and systems. We were left wondering why so little attention was paid to the presence of omnipotence and narcissism alongside the drive for success, corporate social responsibility, identification with community, and other positive values.

Our respondents' positions are too "either . . . or" and do not take sufficient account of the presence of the duality of the dynamics—positive and negative—operating simultaneously and both needing to be understood and worked with. We felt pressured to accept their formulae that drove them towards rigid practices and more theoretical and exhortatory positions.

The driven nature of the speech of our respondents had an obsessive quality. They seemed caught in a balancing act between competing forces in the world of finance—bankers, customers, politicians, and regulators—and yet appeared desperately wanting to be friends with and liked by all. Their obsessive talk seemed a means of protecting themselves from something they could not bring themselves to articulate: the tension between guilt and reparation, their desire to repair the damage that they must have recognised had been part of their lives for many years. Now, with the crisis, it seemed their rationalisations were no longer holding up and no longer holding them up. We wondered about their evangelical speech. Was it a case of them losing, or had they lost faith in themselves and their work, and were now regressing to an earlier faith that had earlier sustained them? Belief in capitalism, in the free market and in deregulation had been shown to be illusory, creating benefits for a few at the expense of the many. Was that the reason, we wondered, why some were now preaching a universal loving faith that incorporated everyone, as if by doing this, they hoped to be taking banking back to its pristine days of doing things only for social good? We had the impression they were bitter and feeling deceived by their profession, their systems, and their colleagues after a lifetime of devoted work "lubricating society", and now it had all come undone and they have no answers.

Bankers everywhere are driven to reduce or even eliminate risk in their investments. Previously, this was done on a basis of trust that developed via interpersonal relationships between lender and borrower. To the relief of bankers and regulators, mathematicians and economists produced all-encompassing mathematical models that dispensed with the time-consuming and subjective assessment that the traditional bank manager had relied on in assessing risk. With new mathematical models it was possible to correlate the apparently uncorrelatable, and this opened up the field to new financial products such as sub-prime loans as a source of collateralised debt obligations (CDOs). These products were spread throughout the global financial system, unsupervised and largely invisible to even well-informed investors.

> Bankers believed this time it's different because we are modelling. Bankers were captured by mathematics—the "quant's". . . . But they failed to price risk in their products and that is the bottom of every problem. "Quant's"—those mathematical geniuses who persuaded banks of their quantification models—said they could price risk and they were wrong! People were prepared to be convinced that risk could be calculated and this led to the abandonment of caution. The longer things seemed to be going well, the more inclined they were to

believe. People's behaviour fed the feel good factor. There was unconscious collusion between the users of the system and suppliers of the
system. The crisis had to happen. Credit card users and bankers
and markets shared the unconscious fantasy—triumph of hope over
experience. (Regulator)

Our respondents seemed naïve; they tenaciously held the view
that because risk had been fully accounted for, the financial crisis was
really an accident, an unconnected series of events. We felt that we
were being asked to sympathise with the victims of an accident, possibly in order to avoid the public's opprobrium towards them as abu-
sers. In almost the same breath, while protesting the "accident" idea,
respondents would say the collapse of Lehman Brothers was through
bad decision making, that banking regulators, through Basel II, deliberately allowed banks to lend without sufficient capital, for example,
Northern Rock, Alliance & Leicester, Bradford & Bingley had all
eagerly adopted Basel II. They claimed that there was no villainy at
play, there were no power games, that the markets were not driven by
selfish behaviour, that there were no wealth gaps, no injustice. Few of
our interviewees even admitted that people had suffered in the crisis.
They could not, it seems, live with the idea that their gains might have
resulted in losses for others.

The dance of false confidence

Most of our banker respondents answered our questions confidently
and self-assuredly. We would have liked to see a little more critical
doubt in their answers. The masters know the rules of the game and
seem only slightly bewildered by the resultant mess and were quick
to pin the blame elsewhere—"the supervisors stopped supervising
and the managers stopped managing"—but there were no answers as
to why. The analytics, they say, were appealing, subjectivity was lost,
and numbers and models reigned supreme.

We need to define the sort of system we want and the behaviours we
want. We got too complicated—management got focused on analytics,
not management. Regulation got focused on analytics, not supervision. Supervision stopped—everyone was looking at the numbers. In
the past supervisors came to see us, they looked us in the eye and

judged whether what we were saying stacked up. These were informal and subjective judgements. This has been lost. The regulators too got focused on models and analytics—they stopped talking and listening. We got obsessed with numbers and quality of algorithms—we stopped being human beings. (Senior Executive, Banking)

What was not being "human beings" defending against? Seeking risk-free perfection? Avoiding the ordinariness of work and inevitability of financial cycles? Understanding and preparing for the cycles had been rejected as a process and growth was made concrete. Our respondents were torn between intellect and feelings. They were in touch with feelings mainly when describing the feelings of others. They were good at analysing them, but could not as easily apply those same emotions to themselves. They were defended and remote, and it was hard sometimes to warm towards them.

In the countertransference, sometimes it felt easy to have a slight sense of triumph over our respondents: when the great bankers, who normally come alive when faced with a complex puzzle, said the interviews with us were "stretching and tough" and "exhausting" because they were unable to answer some of our questions, or to look into themselves to find an answer; others seemed to have a straightforward "bat back" response devoid of thought—"it's about who people are".

We found it difficult at times to record all their words. Their monotone and rapid flow of words made listening and full exploration difficult. We tried, but the volume and speed with which their thoughts were verbalised made it difficult. We were presented with contradictions, for example,

- It is not easy to self-diagnose, but we are the best people to work out what went wrong and what to do about it.
- We are the right people to resolve problems, but outsiders are better at seeing issues.
- We have the brains to sort this out, if only we could get ourselves to sit in the same room together.
- Actually, we are powerless to change this, because bankers are all "self interested and conflicted".
- I can't fault the interventions and co-operation at a global level, but it has been politically motivated.

Interdependence

Interdependence of financial institutions is an issue thought about deeply since the financial crisis. Events had forced our respondents to change their perceptions of themselves and the world they moved in. Their role relationships with government, regulators, investors, customers, and society have forcibly come under scrutiny. They are troubled by the behaviour of the more powerful players in the financial industry and the impact this has on their organisations. Most are thoughtful people, aware of the need to act in socially responsible ways and of the role financial services plays in the "eco-system". But they are ignorant of the dynamics needed to achieve symbiosis—co-operative, mutually beneficial relationships between people and groups—that should, they believe, form part of their thinking and their values. They realise that unrestrained growth compromises the interconnectedness of financial systems where everything is inter-linked.

As a result of the crisis, and reinforced by our interviews, some respondents are open to considering the weaknesses in financial systems. They are open to the idea that their organisations might have been responsible for inflicting hurt and damage. Bankers and regula-tors alike agreed on establishing relationships with customers, rather than seeing them as units of transactions, encouraging them to spend responsibly within means, using money as a vehicle for developing and maintaining a standard of living, not offering unrealistic fantasies of unlimited wealth.

In others, another type of reaction is noticeable. Anger and disap-pointment are tempered by cultural norms of pragmatism and deal-ing in facts. Respondents who understand well the nature of relation-ships across society and globally are realistic in their evaluations of what had happened. They were stunned by the events and wish they had better ways of understanding their predicaments. In spite of their desire to know more, their limited understanding of structures and dynamics of interconnected systems of the financial industry are not as helpful as they would have liked to think. Equally, they find it hard to believe that the strength and power of the financial industry could derail the economy, but their commitment to the "eco-system" is strong, as are their values and beliefs in being helpful in developing people and business to achieve what they want. It seems that these respondents are unconsciously frightened of their own aggression and the strength of their industry to do harm. Fear of this aggression is expressed by projecting it on to other parts of the financial system, such as government, whom they describe as the real spoilers, who over-regulate and chase intelligent and motivated people away. Banks, they insisted, are nothing more than "intermediaries" between capital and commerce.

Senior people in all branches of the financial services say they value the principles of interdependence and are committed to the social values of funding infrastructure and building new communities (Hudson, 2009, p. 3). Public and private funding must work together, they say, but they do not readily know how. All agree that bankers and regulators and politicians must work together and break out of their closed mindsets, but few could articulate a way to make this truly happen. They would have to overcome the difficulties of listening to others, just as we struggled to listen to them. Even government organisations that are meant to represent and manage competing interests in society have become very technical and exclude other views. Regulators and civil servants describe how their prejudice against "greedy" bankers has changed with increased acquaintance and that they realise that bankers could be a force for good. Through talking in-depth with bankers, some of our own stereotypical views of bankers' narrow focus, high intelligence, and greed altered, and generalisations and bias surrendered. Our respondents said that contempt easily pervades their system where "experts look down on others who do not understand economics or financial products the way they do". Stakeholders interacting with one another in financial services see things primarily from their own group's perspective alone. This makes change difficult, as people become more dissociated from social reality and social obligation.

Conclusion

On the whole, our research demonstrates that bankers, regulators, shareholders, politicians, and civil servants have a good grasp of the issues that led to good and bad behaviour in the financial crisis. They clearly differentiate the fraudulent behaviour of individuals, which should not go unpunished, but they are unable to comprehend how the invisible forces of culture drove a particular type of behaviour that underpinned the crisis. Behaviours that are driven by culture present a paradox to them; on the one hand, they recognise and associate competition, rivalry, and pace of business transaction as positive forces very much at the root of their successes. On the other hand, they realise that these cultural norms might have played a far greater role in the crisis than they are able to understand. It is hard for the finance masters to believe that there are forces that impact on them over which they have little or no knowledge or control. Consequently, our respondents feel they should not be tainted with guilt about their involvement in the financial crisis, as the general culture of high risk and high leverage and high debt were the causes, in which everyone participated. Were they fraudulent or just found wanting? To what extent should they be held accountable for the powerful but impersonal forces that drive culture? Who should pay for the crisis? If you are part of the banking inner circle, you do not expect to have to pay for the crisis. Retail banking, blue collar workers, and public servants are paying, and being punished through loss of jobs and homes, for the crisis the investment bankers and leaders of the global finance system had created and who had managed to distance themselves from the problem.

Individual accountability *vs.* systemic accountability seems not to have been truly understood. Judgement was displaced, so guilt and anger are objictified and distanced and projected into "the market". Leaders in financial services talk about "The Market" in a similar way that clergy speak about God.

Our respondents overall wished to be fair, refusing to make generalisations or judge bankers or high earners simply because the bankers could not comprehend the large impersonal global and cultural forces playing on the system. As people living by rules, regulators and accountants are shocked by the descent into chaos. Those who were members of faiths were appalled at their unconscious collusion or self-justifying rationalisations leading to their participation in "sinful practices". All were "unnerved" and sought reassurance of a "society being robust" enough for things to right themselves again naturally. They could not face or deal with their helplessness to understand and put right wrongs they had wrought. They despaired of more regulation as the answer; the principles of self-regulation by people who were good, upright, and conscientious, they say, should be followed because, at all costs, their self-image must be maintained, they must not be found wanting. Guilt is a difficult emotion to acknowledge. It is easier to find fault and blame others.

Our respondents stress the importance of *collaboration and inter-dependence* as the most feasible way forward for government and society, but, on the whole, they seemed unable to consider that rivalry, fear, greed, competition, and conflict had played a significant role in the financial meltdown, and how ignorant they really are of human psychological and ecological systems and complex, large, and im-personal organisations. The balance between the positive forces of optimism, humanitarianism, and hope and the negative forces of competition, rivalry, envy, and greed had been distorted to such an extent that they had actually been redefined and glossed over as all positive in their own right. Little regard is given to how the forces of irrationality had inverted the meaning of language and had distorted and perverted reality.

The financial crisis has forced a paradigm shift in an understand-ing of interconnectedness and how it plays out between retail and investment banking, between governments globally, between govern-ment and the financial sector, between financial services and the media, and between the lender and the borrower. The illusion of sepa-rateness is no longer sustainable. Some of our respondents, the senior partners in accountancy firms, the regulatorsm and those bankers who acknowledged they were found wanting, were open to this as a concept. However, it is the wealthiest, the investment bankers, the ultimate judges of the economy, who have the furthest to go. Those who benefit the most and those who claim to know the most, have the most to unlearn and relearn.

REFERENCES

Abraham, F. (2011). New inter-organisational forms for UK local government partnership delivery. In: P. Lapointe, J. Pelletier, & F. Vaudreuil (Eds.), *Different Perspectives on Work Changes* (pp. 103–109). Quebec: Université Laval.

Adams, W., & Brock, J. W. (1986). *The Bigness Complex: Industry, Labour & Government in The American Economy*. New York: Pantheon Books.

Aram, E., Baxter, R., & Nutkevitch, A. (Eds.) (2009). *Adaptation and Innovation: Group Relations Conferences: Vol. II. Reviewing, Exploring Theory, Design, Role-Taking and Application*. London: Karnac.

Aram, E., Baxter, R., & Nutkevitch, A. (Eds.) (2012). *Tradition, Creativity and Succession in the Global Group Relations Network, Volume III*. London: Karnac.

Argyris, C. (1999). *On Organizational Learning* (2nd edn). Oxford: Blackwell.

Armstrong, D. G. (1992). Names, thoughts and lies: the relevance of Bion's later writing for understanding experience in groups. *Free Associations, 3 Pt II*(26): 261–282.

Armstrong, D. G. (1997). The institution in the mind; reflections on the relationship of psychoanalysis to work with institutions. *Free Associations, 7 Pt I*(41): 1–14.

Asaro, P. M. (2000). Transforming society by transforming technology: the science and politics of participatory design. *Accounting Management and Information Technology, 10*: 257–290.

Balint, E., & Norell, J. (Eds.) (1973). *Six Minutes for the Patient*. London: Tavistock.

Balint, M. (1957). *The Doctor, His Patient and The Illness* (2nd edn). London: Pitman Medical (1964, reprinted 1986). Edinburgh: Churchill Livingstone.

Balint, M., & Balint, E. (1961). *Psychotherapeutic Techniques in Medicine*. London: Tavistock.

Balint, M., Balint, E., Gosling, R., & Hildebrand, P. (1966). *A Study of Doctors*. London: Tavistock.

Balint, M., Joyce, D., Marinker, M., & Woodcock, J. (1970). *Treatment or Diagnosis: a Study of Repeat Prescriptions in General Practice*. London: Tavistock.

Bion, W. R. (1952). Group dynamics: a re-view. *International Journal of Psychoanalysis, 33*: 235–247; also in: Klein, M. (1955). *New Directions in Psychoanalysis*. London: Tavistock.

Bion, W. R. (1959). Attacks on linking. In: *Second Thoughts*. (pp. 93–109). London: Heinemann, 1967.

Bion, W. R. (1961). *Experiences in Groups and Other Papers*. London: Tavistock.

Bion, W. R. (1970). *Attention and Interpretation*. London: Tavistock.

Bion, W. R. (1985a). Container and contained. In: A. D. Coleman & M. H. Geller (Eds.), *Group Relations Reader 2* (pp. 127–133). Washington: A. K. Rice Institute.

Bion, W. R. (1985b). *All My Sins Remembered and the Other Side of Genius*. Abingdon: Fleetwood Press.

Bion, W. R. (1992). *Cogitations*. London: Karnac.

Blackler, F., & Kennedy, A. (2004). The design and evaluation of a leadership programme for experienced chief executives from the public sector. *Management Learning, 35*(2): 181–203.

Blount, A., Schoenbaum, M., Kathol, R., Rollman, B., Thomas, M., O'Donohue, W., & Peek, C. (2007). The economics of behavioural health services in medical settings: a summary of the evidence. *Professional Psychology: Research and Practice, 38*(3): 290–297.

BMA (1993). *Medical Ethics Today: Its Practice and Philosophy*. London: BMJ Publishing Group.

Bohm, D. (1994). *Thought As A System*. London: Routledge.

Bollas, C. (1989). *Forces of Destiny*. London: Free Association Books.

Bollas, C., & Sundelson, D. (1995). *The New Informants. Betrayal of Confidentiality in Psychotherapy and Psychoanalysis.* London: Karnac.

Bond, T. (1995). The nature and outcome of counselling. In: J. Keithley & G. Marsh (Eds.), *Counselling in Primary Health Care* (pp. 3–26). Oxford: Oxford University Press.

Boshyk, Y. (2002). *Action Learning Worldwide: Experiences of Leadership and Organizational Development.* London: Palgrave Macmillan.

Bridger, H., & Higgin, G. (1964). The psychodynamics of an inter-group experience. *Human Relations, 17:* 391–446. Also: *Tavistock Pamphlet No. 10.* Tavistock Institute of Human Relations, 1965.

Brook, A. (1967). An experiment in general practitioner-psychiatrist co-operation. *Journal of the College of General Practitioners, 13*(1): 127–131.

Brook, A., & Temperley, J. (1976). The contribution of a psychotherapist to general practice. *Journal of the Royal College of General Practitioners, 26:* 86–94.

Brunner, L. D., Nutkevitch, A., & Sher, M. (Eds.) (2006). *Group Relations Conferences: Reviewing and Exploring Theory, Design, Role-Taking, and Application.* London: Karnac.

Brunner, L. D., Perini, M., & Vera, E. (2009). Italian group relations conferences: between adaptation and innovation. In: E. Aram, R. Baxter, & A. Nutkevitch (Eds.), *Adaptation and Innovation* (pp. 73–88). London: Karnac.

Bunker, B., & Alban, B. (1997). *Large Group Interventions.* San Francisco, CA: Jossey Bass.

Burns, J. (1978). *Leadership.* New York: Harper & Row.

Cacioppe, R., & Edwards, M. (2005). Seeking the Holy Grail of organisational development: a synthesis of integral theory, spiral dynamics, corporate transformation and action inquiry. *Leadership & Organization Development Journal, 26*(2): 85–105.

Carr, W. (1996). Learning for leadership. *Leadership & Organization Development Journal, 17*(6): 46–52.

Carter, G. M. (1977). *The Politics of Inequality: South Africa Since 1948.* New York: Octagon.

Casement, P. (1985). *On Learning from the Patient.* London: Routledge.

Child, C. (2009). Intervening to support the development of partnership capacity and performance at strategic levels in local governance arenas. Unpublished thesis.

Clarke, S., & Hoggett, P. (Eds.) (2009). *Researching Beneath the Surface: Psycho-Social Research Methods in Practice.* London: Karnac.

Clements, D., Dault, M., & Priest, A. (2007). Effective teamwork in health-care: research and reality. *HealthcarePapers*, 7(Sp): 26–34.

Cohan, W. (2010). *House of Cards: How Wall Street's Gamblers Broke Capitalism*. London: Penguin.

Coleman, A. D., & Bexton, W. H. (Eds.) (1975). *Group Relations Reader I*. Washington: The A. K. Rice Institute.

Coleman, A. D., & Geller, M. H. (Eds.) (1985). *Group Relations Reader II*. Washington: The A. K. Rice Institute.

Cooper, C. (1988). The scientific status of the Defence Mechanism Test. *British Journal of Medical Psychology, 61*: 381–384.

Cummings, T., & Huse, E. (1989). *Organisation Development and Change*. St. Paul, MN: West.

Cummings, T., & Wolrey, C. (1996). *Organizational Development and Change*. Cincinnati: West Publishing.

Cunliffe, A. (2002). Reflexive dialogical practice in management learning. *Management Learning, 33*(1): 35–62.

Cytrynbaum, S. (1993). Learning about leaving: the lessons of institutional splitting. In: T. W. Hugg, N. M. Carson, & R. M. Lipgar (Eds.), *Changing Group Relations: The Next Twenty-Five Years in America* (pp. 31–43). Proceedings of the Ninth Scientific Meeting of the A. K. Rice Institute. Florida: A. K. Rice Institute.

Cytrynbaum, S., & Noumair, D. A. (Eds.) (2004). *Group Dynamics, Organizational Irrationality and Social Complexity: Group Relations Reader 3*. Florida: A. K. Rice Institute for the Study of Social Systems.

De Jager, W., & Sher, M. (2009). Knowing the price of everything and the value of nothing: the application of group relations to organisational development and change with a financial institution. In: E. Aram, R. Baxter, & A. Nutkevitch (Eds.), *Adaptation and Innovation* (pp. 145–162). London: Karnac.

Dopson, D., & Neumann, J. (1998). Uncertainty, contrariness and the double-bind: middle managers reactions to their changing contracts. *British Journal of Management, 9*: S53-S70 (Special Issue on 1997 BJM Conference).

Dunbar, R. (1993). Co-evolution of neocortex size, group size and language in humans. *Journal of Behavioural and Brain Sciences, 16*(4): 681–735.

Eijnatten, F. M. van (1993). The paradigm that changed the work place. In: *Historical Overview of 40 Years of Socio-Technical Systems*, with contributions by Hans van Beinum, Fred Emery and Ulbo de Sitter (316 pp). Assen/Stockholm: Van Gorcum/Arbetslivscentrum.

Ekehammar, B., Zuber, I., & Konstenius, M. L. (2005). An empirical look at the Defense Mechanism Test (DMT): reliability and construct validity. *Scandinavian Journal of Psychology*, 46(3): 285–296.

Elias, N. (1987). *Involvement and Detachment*. London: Basil Blackwell.

Emery, F. (1959). *Characteristics of Socio-Technical Systems*. London: Tavistock Institute Document, 527.

Emery, F. E., & Trist, E. L. (1960). Socio-technical systems. In: C. Churchman & M. Verhulst (Eds.), *Management Sciences, Models and Techniques* (pp. 283–297). Oxford: Pergamon.

Emery, F. E., & Trist, E. L. (1965). The causal texture of organizational environments. *Human Relations*, 18(1): 21–32. Reprinted in: E. Trist, F. Emery, & H. Murray (Eds.), *The Social Engagement of Social Science: A Tavistock Anthology. Vol III: The Socio-Ecological Perspective* (pp. 53–65). London: Free Association Books.

Emery, M. (Ed.) (1989). *Participative Design for Participative Democracy*. Australian National University, Canberra: Centre for Continuing Education.

Engeström, Y., Miettinen, R., & Punamaki. R. (Eds.) (1999). *Perspectives on Activity Theory*. Cambridge: Cambridge University Press.

Engeström, Y., Virkkunen, J., Helle, M., Pihlaja, J., & Poikela, R. (1996). Change laboratory as a tool for transforming work. *Lifelong Learning in Europe*, 1(2): 10–17.

Fairbairn, W. R. D. (1952). *An Object-Relations Theory of the Personality*. New York: Basic Books.

Financial Reporting Council (2010). *The UK Corporate Governance Code*.

Flyvbjerg, B., Bruzelius, N., & Rothengatter, W. (2003). *Megaprojects and Risk*. Cambridge: Cambridge University Press.

French, R., & Vince, R. (Eds.) (1999). *Group Relations, Management and Organisation*. Oxford: Oxford University Press.

Freud, S. (1911b). Formulations on the two principles of mental functioning. *S.E.*, 12: London: Hogarth.

Freud, S. (1916–1917). *Introductory Lectures on Psycho-analysis. S.E.*, 16. London: Hogarth Press.

Freud, S. (1921c). *Group Psychology and the Analysis of the Ego. S.E.*, 18: 67–143. London: Hogarth Press.

Freud, S. (1923b). *The Ego and the Id. S.E.*, 19: 3–66. London: Hogarth Press.

Gemmill, G., & Oakley, J. (1992). Leadership: an alienating social myth. *Human Relations*, 45(2): 113–129.

Gettler, L. (2005). *Organisations Behaving Badly: A Greek Tragedy of Corporate Pathology*. Queensland: Wiley.

Gherardi, S., & Nicolini, D. (2002). Learning in a constellation of interconnected practices: canon or dissonance? *Journal of Management Studies,* *39*(4): 419–436.

Gill, A., & Sanders, P. (2009). *Due Diligence: A Best Practice Guideline.* Institute of Chartered Accountants of England and Wales, Corporate Finance Faculty.

Ginat, Y. (1999). Changes in employment status following attendance at group relations conferences. Personal communication.

Ginzberg, E., & Votja, G. (1985). *Beyond Human Scale: The Large Corporation at Risk.* New York: Basic Books.

GMC (1993). *Professional Conduct and Discipline: Fitness to Practice.* London: GMC.

Goldberg, E. M., & Neill, J. E. (1972). *Social Work in General Practice.* London: Allen & Unwin.

Goldsmith, M. (2008). The madness of crowds, past and present: Charles Mackay's classic volume on speculative bubbles, published 167 years ago, sheds much light on the delusions of mass greed. *Bloomberg Business Week,* 16 December.

Gosling, J. (2004). Leadership development in management education. *Business Leadership Review, I:* I. www.Mbaworld.Com/Blr

Gosling, R. (1968). What is transference? In: J. D. Sutherland (Ed.), *The Psychoanalytic Approach* (pp. 1–10). London: Bailliere, Tindall and Cassell.

Gosling, R. (Ed.) (1973). *Support, Innovation and Autonomy: Tavistock Clinic Golden Jubilee Papers.* London: Tavistock.

Gosling, R. (1979). Another source of conservatism in groups. In: W. G. Lawrence (Ed.), *Exploring Individual and Organisational Boundaries: A Tavistock Open Systems Approach* (pp. 77–86). London: John Wiley & Sons [reprinted: Karnac, London, 1999].

Gosling, R. (1981). A study of very small groups. In: J. S. Grotstein (Ed.), *Do I Dare Disturb the Universe? A Memorial to Dr Wilfred Bion* (pp. 633–645). New York. Aronson. Also in: A. D. Colman & M. H. Geller (Eds.) (1985). *Group Relations Reader 2.* Washington: A. K. Rice Institute.

Gosling, R., Miller, D. M., Turquet, P. M., & Woodhouse, D. (1967). *The Use of Small Groups in Training.* Hitchin: Codicote Press.

Gould, L., Stapley, L., & Stein, M. (2001). *The Systems Psychodynamics of Organisations: Integrating the Group Relations Approach, Psychoanalytic and Open Systems Perspectives.* London: Karnac.

Gould, L., Stapley, L., & Stein, M. (2004). *Experiential Learning in Organizations: Applications of the Tavistock Group Relations Approach.* London: Karnac.

Greenspan, A. (1996). The challenge of central banking in a democratic society. Speech at the Annual Dinner and Francis Boyer Lecture of The American Enterprise Institute for Public Policy Research, Washington, DC, 5 December.

Grotstein, J. (1981). Bion the man, the psychoanalyst, and the mystic: a perspective on his life and work. In: J. S. Grotstein (Ed.), *Do I Dare Disturb the Universe? A Memorial to Wilfred R. Bion* (pp. 1–36). Beverly Hills, CA: Caesura Press.

Grotstein, J., & Rinsley, R. B. (1994). Fairbairn and the origins of object relations. *Journal of the American Psychoanalytic Association, 43*: 241–244.

Hale, R., Minne, C., & Zachary, A. (2000). Assessment and management of sexual offenders. In: M. G. Gelder, J. J. L. Ibor, & N. C. Andreasen (Eds.), *New Oxford Textbook of Psychiatry, Volume 2.* Oxford: Oxford University Press.

Hall, E. T. (1976). *Beyond Culture.* Anchor, Garden City, CA: Random Books.

Hare, P., & Babiak, R. (2006). *Snakes in Suits: When Psychopaths Go to Work.* New York: Regan Books.

Harré, R. (1984). Social elements as mind. *British Journal of Medical Psychology, 57*: 127–135.

Harrison, T., & Clarke, D. (1992). The Northfield experiments. *British Journal of Psychiatry, 160*: 698–708.

Heins, J. (1987). But the grass looked greener over there. *Forbes,* 27 April.

Higgins, G., & Jessop, N. (1965). Communications in the building industry. *Report of a Pilot Study, TIHR.* London: Tavistock.

Hill, J. M. M. (1977). *The Social and Psychological Impact of Unemployment. A Pilot Study.* Tavistock Institute of Human Relations, Doc. no. 2T 74.

Hills, D., & Child, C. (2000). *Leadership in Residential Care, Evaluating Qualification Training.* Chichester: John Wiley & Son.

Hinshelwood, R. D., & Skogstad, W. (2000). *Observing Organisations: Anxiety, Defence and Culture in Health Care.* Hove: Brunner-Routledge.

Hoggett, P. (1992). *Partisans in an Uncertain World: The Psychoanalysis of Engagement.* London: Free Association Books.

Holti, R. (1997). Consulting to organisational implications of technical change. In: J. E. Newmann, K. Kellner, & A. Dawson-Shepherd (Eds.), *Developing Organisational Consultancy* (pp. 213–227). London: Routledge.

Hornby, S. (1993). *Collaborative Care: Interprofessional, Interagency and Interpersonal.* Oxford: Blackwell Scientific Publications.

Hudson, L. J. (2009). *The Enabling State: Collaborating for Success.* www.fco. gov.uk/resources/en/pdf/pdf9/enabling-state-v3 published by the Foreign and Commonwealth Office.

Huffington, C., Armstrong, D., Halton, W., Hoyle, L., & Pooley, J. (2004). *Working Below the Surface: The Emotional Life of Organisations.* London: Karnac.

Hupkens, L. (2006). Applying group relations learning to the daily work of consultants and managers: theorists solve the problems they want to; practitioners solve the problems they have to. In: L. D. Brunner, A. Nutkevitch, & M. Sher (Eds.), *Group Relations Conferences* (pp. 138–150). London: Karnac.

Huys, R., Sels, L., Van Hootegem, G., Bundervoet, J., & Henderickx, J. (1999). Toward less division of labour? New production concepts in the automotive, chemical, clothing and machine tool industries. *Human Relations, 52*(1): 67–93. London: Sage.

Janis, I. L. (1972). *Victims of Groupthink.* Boston, MA: Houghton Mifflin.

Jaques, E. (1951). *The Changing Culture of a Factory: A Study of Authority and Participation in an Industrial Setting.* London: Tavistock Publications.

Jaques, E. (1955). Social systems as a defence against persecutory and depressive anxiety. In: M. Klein, P. Heimann, & R. E. Money-Cyrl (Eds.), *New Directions in Psychoanalysis* (pp. 478–498). London: Tavistock Publications.

Jaques, E. (1976). *A General Theory of Bureaucracy.* London: Heinemann Educational.

Jaques, E. (1989). *Requisite Organisation. The CEO's Guide to Creative Structure and Leadership.* Arlington, VA: Cason Hall.

Jaques, E. (1997). *Requisite Organization: Total System for Effective Managerial Organization and Managerial Leadership for the 21st Century.* London: Gower.

Jenkins, G. C. (2002). Promoting and measuring behavioural health services in family medical practices in the United Kingdom. *Families, Systems, & Health, 20*(4): 399–415.

Jenkins, G. C., Barkham, M., Mellor-Clark, J., Rain, L., & Fitzgerald, P. (2010). *A Guide to Counselling in Primary Care.* London: Sage.

Jensen, M. (1998). Self-interest, altruism, incentives and agency theory. In: *Foundations of Organisational Strategy* (pp. 39–50). Cambridge, MA: Harvard University Press.

Joffe, W. (Ed.) (1968). *What is Psychoanalysis?* The Institute of Psycho-analysis. London: Baillière, Tindall & Cassell.

Johnson, R. A. (1976). Psychotherapy in general practice. *Journal of the Royal College of General Practitioners, 26*(165): 261–262.

Kelley, H. H., & Thibaut, J. W. (1978). *Interpersonal Relations: A Theory of Interdependence.* New York: Wiley Interscience.

Kernberg, O. F. (1992). *Aggression in Personality Disorders and Perversions.* New Haven, CT: Yale University Press.

Khaleelee, O. (2007). The use of the defence mechanism test to aid under-standing of the personality of senior executives and the implications for their careers, conference paper, 15 June 2007: *Current Developments in the Use of Projective Techniques Across the Life Span.*

Kissinger, H. (1979). *The White House Years: Memoirs covering November 1968–January 1973.* Boston: Little Brown.

Klauber, T. (2004). A child psychotherapist's commentary on Hans Asperger's 1944 paper, "'Autistic psychopathy' in childhood". In: M. Rhode & T. Klauber (Eds.), *The Many Faces of Asperger's Syndrome* (pp. 54–69). London: Karnac.

Klein, M. (1946). Notes on some schizoid mechanisms. In: *Envy and Gratitude and Other Works 1946–1963* (pp. 1–24). London: Hogarth Press and the Institute of Psycho-Analysis [reprinted 1975].

Klein, M. (1957). *Envy and Gratitude.* London: Tavistock. Reprinted in: *The Writings of Melanie Klein, 3* (pp. 176–235). London: Hogarth Press, 1975.

Klein, M. (1959). Our adult and its roots in infancy. In: *Envy and Gratitude and Other Works (1946–1963)* (pp. 247–263). London: Hogarth Press.

Klein, M. (1975). A note on depression in the schizophrenic: In: *Envy and Gratitude and Other Works* (pp. 264–267). London: Hogarth Press.

Klein, S. (Ed.) (1969). *Sexuality and Aggression in Maturation.* The Institute of Psychoanalysis. Baillière, London: Tindall & Cassell.

Kragh, U. (1955). *The Actual–Genetic Model of Perception–Personality.* Lund: Gleerup.

Krug, J. (2008). The big exit: executive churn in the wake of mergers & acquisitions. *Journal of Business Strategy, 29*(4): 15–21.

Lacan, J. (1977). *Ecrits.* London: Tavistock.

Lahav, Y. (2009). Exploring Jewish identity, belonging and leadership through the lens of group relations: reflections and challenges. In: E. Aram, R. Baxter, & A. Nutkevitch (Eds.), *Adaptation and Innovation* (pp. 163–178). London: Karnac.

Lanchester, J. (2010). *Whoops! Why Everyone Owes Everyone and No One Can Pay.* London: Allen Lane.

Lasky, G. B., & Riva, M. T. (2006). Confidentiality and privileged communication in psychotherapy. *International Journal of Group Psychotherapy*, 56: 455–476.

Law, J., & Singleton, V. (2003). Allegory and its others. In: D. Nicolini, S. Gherardi, & D. Yanow (Eds.), *Knowing in Organizations: A Practice-Based Approach* (pp. 225–254). Armonk, NY: ME Sharpe.

Lawrence, W. G. (1977). Management development: ideals, images and realities. *Journal of European Industrial Training*, 1(2): 21–25 [also in: A. D. Coleman & M. H. Geller (Eds.), *Group Relations Reader 2*. Washington, DC: A. K. Rice Institute, 1985].

Lawrence, W. G. (Ed.) (1979). *Exploring Individual and Organisational Boundaries*. Chichester: Wiley [reprinted by Karnac, 1999].

Lawrence, W. G. (1982). *Some Psychic and Political Dimensions of Work Experience*. London: Tavistock Institute, Occasional Paper.

Lawrence, W. G. (1986). A psychoanalytic perspective for understanding organisational life. In: G. Chattopadhyay, Z. Gangee, L. Hunt, & W. G. Lawrence (Eds.), *When the Twain Meet* (pp. 20–37). Allahabad: A. H. Wheeler.

Lawrence, W. G. (1993). Signals of transcendence in large groups as systems. *Group*, 17(4): 254–266.

Lawrence, W. G. (1997). Centering of the Sphinx for the psychoanalytic study of organizations. Lecture given at the ISPSO conference in Philadelphia, USA, 27 June.

Lawrence, W. G. (2000). *Tongued with Fire, Groups in Experience*. London: Karnac.

Lawrence, W. G., & Miller, E. J. (1976). Epilogue. In: E. J. Miller (Ed.), *Task and Organisation* (pp. 361–366). Chichester: John Wiley.

Lawrence, W. G., Bain, A., & Gould, L. J. (1996). The fifth basic assumption. *Free Associations*, 6(37): 28–55.

Levine, D. (2005). The corrupt organisation. *Human Relations*, 58(6): 723–740.

Lewin, K. (1943). Defining the "field at a given time". *Psychological Review*, 50: 292–310. Reprinted in: *Resolving Social Conflicts & Field Theory in Social Science*. Washington, DC: American Psychological Association, 1997.

Lewin, K. (1946). Action research and minority problems. *Journal of Social Issues*, 2: 34–46.

Lewin, K. (1947). Frontiers in group dynamics: concept, method and reality in social sciences; social equilibria and social change. *Human Relations*, 1: 5–41.

Lewin, K. (1950). *Field Theory in Social Science*. New York: Harper.

Litvin, I., & Bonwitt, G. (2006). Sexual abuse: application and adaptation of basic group relations concepts, technique and culture to a specific social issue. In: L. D. Brunner, A. Nutkevitch, & M. Sher (Eds.), *Group Relations Conferences* (pp. 47–60). London: Karnac.

Long, S. (2008). *The Perverse Organisation and its Deadly Sins*. London: Karnac.

Mackay, C. (1841). *Extraordinary Popular Delusions and the Madness of Crowds*. New York: Barnes & Noble.

Main, T. (1978). Some medical defences against involvement with patients. *Journal of the Balint Society, 6*: 3–11.

Maris, P. (1984). *Loss and Change*. New York: Routledge & Kegan Paul.

Marsick, V. J., & O'Neil, J. (1999). The many faces of action learning. *Management Learning. 30*(2): 159–176.

Mayo, E. (1933). *The Human Problems of an Industrial Civilization*. New York: Macmillan; London: Routledge & Kegan Paul.

McLaughlin, H., & Thorpe, R. (1993). Action learning – a paradigm in emergence. *British Journal of Management, 4*(1): 19–27.

Mellor-Clark, J., Simms-Ellis, R., & Burton, M. (2001). National survey of counsellors working in primary care: evidence for growing professionalism? Occasional Paper 79. London: Royal College of General Practitioners.

Menzies, I. E. P. (1959). A case study in the functioning of social systems as a defence against anxiety: a report on a study of the nursing service of a general hospital. *Human Relations, 13*: 95–121. Reprinted as Tavistock Pamphlet No. 3, Tavistock Institute (1961) and in Menzies-Lyth, I. E. P. (1988). *Containing Anxiety in Institutions* (pp. 43–85). London: Free Association Books.

Menzies Lyth, I. E. P. (1970). Psychosocial aspects of eating. *J. Psychosom. Res., 14*: 223–227. Reprinted in Menzies Lyth, I. (1989). *The Dynamics of the Social* (pp. 61–67). London: Free Association Books.

Menzies Lyth, I. E. P. (1988). *Containing Anxiety In Institutions: Selected Essays*, Volume 1. London: Free Association Books.

Menzies Lyth, I. E. P. (1989). *The Dynamics of the Social. Selected Essays*, Volume 2. London: Free Association Books.

Menzies Lyth, I. E. P. (1990). A psychoanalytical perspective on social institutions. In: E. Trist & H. Murray (Eds.), *The Social Engagement of Social Science*, Volume I (pp. 404–464). London: Free Association Books.

Milgram, S. (1974). *Obedience to Authority; An Experimental View*. New York: Harper Collins.

Miller, E. (1990a). Experiential learning in groups I: the development of the Leicester Model. In: E. Trist, & H. Murray (Eds.), *The Social Engagement of Social Science, Volume 1. The Socio-Psychological Perspective* (pp. 165–185). London. Free Association Books.

Miller, E. (1990b). Experiential learning in groups II: recent developments in dissemination and application. In: E. Trist & H. Murray (Eds.), *The Social Engagement of Social Science, Volume 1. The Socio-Psychological Perspective* (pp. 186–198). London. Free Association Books.

Miller, E. J. (1959). Technology, territory and time: the internal differentiation of complex production systems. *Human Relations, 12*: 243–272.

Miller, E. J. (1976). The open system approach to organisational analysis, with special reference to the work of A. K. Rice. In: G. Hofstede & M. Samikassem (Eds.), *European Contributions to Organisation Theory* (pp. 43–61). ASSEN/Amsterdam : Von Gorchum.

Miller, E. J. (1983). Work and creativity. *Occasional Paper No. 6*. Tavistock Institute of Human Relations.

Miller, E. J. (1993a). *From Dependency to Autonomy; Studies in Organisation & Change*. London: Free Associations Books.

Miller, E. J. (1993b). The human dynamic. In: R. Stacey (Ed.), *Strategic Thinking and the Management of Change: International Perspectives on Organisational Dynamics* (pp. 98–116). London: Kogan Page.

Miller, E. J. (1995). Integrated rural development: a Mexican experiment. From the Archives: *Occasional Paper No. 1*. London: The Tavistock Institute.

Miller, E. J. (1997). Effecting organisational change in large systems: a collaborative consultancy approach. In: J. Neumann, K. Kellner, & A. Dawson-Shepherd (Eds.), *Developing Organisational Consultancy* (pp. 187–212). London: Routledge.

Miller, E. J., & Rice, A. K. (1967). *Systems of Organisation: Task and Sentient Systems and their Boundary Control*. London: Tavistock Publications.

Miller, P., & Rose, N. (2008). *Governing the Present: Administering Economic, Social and Personal Life*. London: Wiley.

Moon, J. (2000). *Reflection in Learning and Professional Development. Theory and Practice*. London: Kogan Page.

Morgan, G., & Ramirez, R. (1983). Action learning: a holographic metaphor for guiding social change. *Human Relations, 37*(1): 1–28.

Moylan, D. (1990). Unpublished communication.

Mumford, E. (1997). Assisting work restructuring in complex and volatile situations. In: J. Neumann, K. Kellner, & A. Dawson-Shepherd (Eds.), *Developing Organisational Consultancy* (pp. 228–249). London: Routledge.

Murray, B. K. (1982). *Wits, the Early Years: A History of the University of the Witwatersrand, Johannesburg, and its Precursors, 1896–1939.* Johannesburg: Witwatersrand University Press.

Neumann, J. E., Miller, E. J., & Holti, R. W. (1999). Three contemporary challenges for OD practitioners. *Leadership and Organizational Development Journal,* 20(4): 216–221.

Nicolini, D., Gherardi, S., & Yanow, D. (Eds.) (2003). *Knowing in Organization. A Practice Based Approach.* Armonk, NY: ME Sharpe.

Nutkevitch, A., & Triest, J. (2009). "Doth my father yet live?": psychoanalysis and group relations conferences revisited. In: E. Aram, R. Baxter, & A. Nutkevitch (Eds.), *Adaptation and Innovation* (pp. 51–68). London: Karnac.

Obholzer, A. (2001). The leader, the unconscious and the management of the organisation. In: L. Gould, L. Stapley, & M. Stein (Eds.), *The Systems Psychodynamics of Organizations* (pp. 197–216). New York: Karnac.

Obholzer, O., & Roberts, V. (Eds.) (1994). *The Unconscious at Work: Individual and Organisational Stress in the Human Services.* London: Routledge.

O'Neil, J. (1997). Set advising: more than just process consultancy? In: M. Pedler (Ed.), *Action Learning in Practice* (3rd edn) (pp. 243–256). Aldershot: Gower.

O'Shaughnessy, E. (1995). Minus K. Presented at the Panel "Bion's Contribution to Psychoanalytic Theory and Technique" at the 39th International Psychoanalytic Conference in San Francisco, CA, Monday 31 July.

Owen, H. (1992). *Open Space Technology. A User's Guide.* Potomac, MD: Abbott.

Owen, H. (1995). *Tales from Open Space.* Potomac, MD: Abbott.

Pattison, S., Manning, S., & Malby, B. (1999). I want to tell you a story. *Health Service Journal,* 25 February.

Pedler, M. (Ed.) (1997a). *Action Learning in Practice* (3rd edn). Aldershot: Gower.

Pedler, M. (1997b). What do we mean by action learning? A story and three interpretations. In: M. Pedler (Ed.), *Action Learning in Practice* (3rd edn) (pp. 61–76). Aldershot: Gower.

Pettigrew, A., Felie, E., & McKee, L. (1992). *Shaping Strategic Change.* London: Sage.

Pickering, A. (2001). Practice and posthumanism: social theory and a history of agency. In: T. Schatzki, K. K. Cetina, & E. von Savigny (Eds.), *The Practice Turn in Contemporary Theory* (pp. 163–174). London: Routledge.

Pritchard, P., Pritchard, P. M., & Pritchard, H. (1992). *Developing Teamwork in Primary Health Care: A Practical Workbook*. Oxford: Oxford Medical Publications.

Raelin, J. (2001). Public reflection at the basis for learning. *Management Learning*, 32(1): 11–30.

Raelin, J. (2002). I don't have time to think! Versus the art of reflective practice. *Reflections*, 4(1): 66–74.

Ratoff, L., Rose, A., & Smith, C. (1974). Social workers and general practitioners – some problems of working together. *Journal of the Royal College of General Practitioners*, 24: 750–760; *Social Work Today*, 5: 497–500.

Revans, R. (1980). *Action Learning: New Techniques for Management*. London: Blond and Briggs.

Revans, R. (1997). Action learning: its origin and nature. In: M. Pedler (Ed.), *Action Learning in Practice* (3rd edn) (pp. 3–14). Aldershot: Gower.

Reynolds, M. (1998). Reflection and critical reflection in management learning, *Management Learning*, 29(2): 183–200.

Reynolds, M. (1999). Critical reflection and management education: rehabilitating less hierarchical approaches. *Journal of Management Education*, 23(5): 537–553.

Rice, A. K. (1958). *Productivity and Social Organisation: The Ahmadabad Experiment*. London: Tavistock [reprinted New York: Garland, 1987].

Rice, A. K. (1963). *The Enterprise and its Environment*. London: Tavistock.

Rice, A. K. (1965). *Learning for Leadership: Interpersonal and Intergroup Relations*. London: Tavistock [reprinted London: Karnac, 1999].

Rice, A. K. (1969). Individual, group and inter-group processes. *Human Relations*, 22: 565–584.

Rodman, F. R. (2003). *Winnicott: Life and Work*. Cambridge: Perseus.

Roethlisberger, F. M. & Dickson, W. (1939). *Management and the Worker*. Cambridge, MA: Harvard University Press.

Rose, N. (1998). *Inventing Our Selves: Psychology, Power and Personhood*. Cambridge: Cambridge University Press.

Rosenfeld, H. (1987). *Impasse and Interpretation*. London: Routledge.

Rowley, T. J., & Moldoveanu, M. (2003). When will stakeholder groups act? An interest- and identity-based model of stakeholder group motivation. *Academy of Management Review*, 28(2): 204–219.

Royal College of Psychiatrists, Council Report CR85 (2000). *Good Psychiatric Practice: Confidentiality*. Hertfordshire: Sacombe Press.

Rustin, M. (2001). *Reason and Unreason. Psychoanalysis, Science and Politics*. Middletown, CT: Wesleyan University Press.

Rustin, M. (2008). Taming the forces of globalisation: two tasks now loom before us – re-regulating the markets and safeguarding the environment. *Guardian*, Wednesday 29 October.

Scharff, D., & Birtles, E. F. (Eds.) (1994). *From Instinct to Self: Selected Papers of W. R. D. Fairbairn*. New York: Jason Aronson.

Schulz, K. (2010). *Being Wrong: Adventures in the Margin of Error*. New York: HarperCollins.

Scoggins, M., Litton, R., & Palmer, S. (1998). Confidentiality and the law. *Counselling Psychology Review, 13*: 141.

Shapiro, E. (Ed.) (1997). *The Inner World in the Outer World: Psychoanalytic Perspectives*. New Haven, CT: Yale University Press.

Shapiro, E., & Carr, A. W. (1991). *Lost in Familiar Places*. New Haven, CT: Yale University Press.

Shear, M. (1996). *Wits: A University in the Apartheid Era*. Johannesburg: Witwatersrand University Press.

Sher, M. (2010). Moving psychotherapy into community settings: Alexis Brook's life's work. *Psychoanalytic Psychotherapy, 23*(4): 303.

Shiller, R. (2005). *Irrational Exuberance*. Princeton, NJ: Princeton University Press.

Siebert, K., & Daudelin, M. (1999). *The Role of Reflection in Managerial Learning: Theory, Research and Practice*. London: Quorum.

Slovenko, R. (1998). *Psychotherapy and Confidentiality: Testimonial Privileged Communication, Breach of Confidentiality and Reporting Duties*. Springfield, IL: Charles C. Thomas.

Smith, P. A. (2001). Action learning and reflective practice in project environments that are related to reflection. *Management Learning, 33*(1): 63–78.

Sofer, C. (1961). *The Organisation From Within: A Comparative Study of Social Institutions Based on a Socio-Therapeutic Approach*. London: Tavistock Publications.

Solvik, P. (2003). Mapping the market for the Leicester Conference. Unpublished Report.

Sorenson, G., & Goethals, G. (2001). Leadership theories overview. In: *Encyclopaedia of Leadership* (pp. 867–874). Boston, MA: Berkshire.

Steiner, J. (1985). Turning a blind eye: the cover-up for Oedipus. *International Review of Psycho-analysis, 12*: 161–173.

Steiner, J. (1993). *Psychic Retreats: Pathological Organisations in Psychotic, Neurotic and Borderline Patients*. London: The Melanie Klein Trust.

Steiner, J. (Ed.) (2006). *Rosenfeld in Retrospect: Essays on his Clinical Influence*. London: The Melanie Klein Trust.

Stern, E. (2005). Evaluation research methods. *Editor and introductory essay for a 4 volume collection in "Benchmark Series in Social Research Methods.* London: Sage.

Supreme Court of the United States (1996). *Jaffee, Special Administrator for Allen, Deceased v. Redmond et al.* Certiorari to the United States Court of Appeals for the Seventh Circuit, No 95–266. Argued February, 1996. Decided June 13, 1996.

Sutherland, J. (Ed.) (1968). *The Psychoanalytic Approach.* The Institute of Psychoanalysis. London: Baillière, Tindall & Cassell.

Tarnas, R. (1991). *The Passion of the Western Mind.* Reading: Pimlico.

Tavistock Institute of Human Relations (2010). *Articles of Association.* Adopted by Special Resolution dated 22 July 2010.

Tett, G. (2009). *Fool's Gold: How Unrestrained Greed Corrupted a Dream, Shattered Global Markets and Unleashed a Catastrophe.* London: Little, Brown.

The British Psychological Society (1993). Ethical principles for conducting research with human participants. *The Psychologist,* 6(1): 33–35.

The Master of the Rolls (1996). Confidentiality – an inter-disciplinary issue. The Inaugural Spring Lecture.

Thomas, K. J., Carr, L., Westlake, B., & Williams, A. (1991). Use of non-orthodox and conventional health care in Great Britain. *British Medical Journal,* 302: 207–210.

Trist, E. (1981). The evolution of socio-technical systems: a conceptual framework and an action research programme. In: A. van de Ven & W. Joy (Eds.), *Perspectives on Organisational Design and Behaviour* (pp. 7–67). Ontario Ministry of Labour, Ontario: Wiley Interscience.

Trist, E. (1990). Culture as a psycho-social process. In: E. Trist & H. Murray (Eds.), *The Social Engagement of Social Science: A Tavistock Anthology, Volume 1. The Socio-Psychological Perspective* (pp. 539–545). London: Free Association Books.

Trist, E., & Bamforth, K. (1951). Some social and psychological consequences of the longwall method of coal-getting. *Human Relations,* 4: 3–38.

Trist, E., & Murray, H. (Eds.) (1990). *The Social Engagement of Social Science: A Tavistock Anthology, Volume 1: The Socio-psychological Perspective.* Philadelphia, PA: University of Pennsylvania Press.

Trist, E., & Murray, H. (Eds.) (1993a). *The Social Engagement of Social Science: A Tavistock Anthology, Volume II. The Socio-technical Perspective.* Philadelphia, PA: University of Pennsylvania Press.

Trist, E., & Murray, H. (Eds.) (1993b). *The Social Engagement of Social Science: A Tavistock Anthology, Volume III. The Socio-ecological Perspective*. Philadelphia, PA: University of Pennsylvania Press.

Trist, E., Higgin, G., Murray, H., & Pollock, A. (1963). *Organisational Choice: Capabilities of Groups at the Coalface Under Changing Technologies*. London: Tavistock Publications.

Tuckett, D. (2011). *Minding the Markets: An Emotional Finance View of Financial Instability*. London: Palgrave.

Tuckett, D., & Taffler, R. (2008). Phantastic objects and the financial market's sense of reality: a psychoanalytic contribution to the understanding of stock market instability. *International Journal of Psychoanalysis, 89*: 389–412.

Turquet, P. (1975). Threats to identity in the large group. In: L. Kreeger (Ed.), *The Large Group: Dynamics and Therapy* (pp. 87–144). London: Constable [reprinted London: Karnac, 1994].

Turquet, P. (1985). Leadership: the individual and the group. In: A. Colman & M. Geller (Eds.), *Group Relations Reader 2* (pp. 71–88). Washington: A. K. Rice Institute.

Turquet, P., & Boreham, J. (1976). An interdisciplinary programme of training in adult psychotherapy for experienced professional workers in the health and social services. Internal unpublished document No. LT 2495. Adult Department, Tavistock Clinic.

Vince, R. (2002a). Organising politics of imagined stability. A psychodynamic understanding of change at Hyder plc. *Human Relations, 55*(10): 1189–1208.

Vince, R. (2002b). The leadership development. *Management Learning, 32*(1): 31–48.

Vince, R., & Martin, L. (1993). Inside action learning: the politics and the psychology of the action learning model. *Management Education and Development, 24*(3): 205–215.

Viswanath, R. (2009). Identity, leadership and authority: experiences in application of group relations concepts for Dalit empowerment in India. In: E. Aram, R. Baxter, & A. Nutkevitch (Eds.), *Adaptation and Innovation* (pp. 179–196). London: Karnac.

Von Bertalanffy, L. (1950a). The theory of open systems in physics and biology. *Science, 3*: 23–29.

Von Bertalanffy, L. (1950b). An outline of general system theory. *British Journal of the Philosophy of Science, 1*: 134–165.

Von Bertalanffy, L. (1951). General system theory – a new approach to unity of science (Symposium). *Human Biology, 23*: 303–361.

Walker, D. (2009a). *A Review of Corporate Governance in UK Banks and Other Financial Institutions. Final Recommendations*. London: HM Treasury.

Walker, D. (2009b). Commemoration of benefactors. Sermon by The Lady Margaret's Preacher, 1 November 2009. Great St Mary's Church, Cambridge.

Wall, A. (1999). Courtin' the middle. *Health Service Journal*, 4 February.

Wasdell, D. (1997). Tavistock review. Self and society. Personal communication.

Weisbord, R. G. (1967). The dilemma of South African Jewry. *Journal of Modern African Studies, 5*: 233–241.

Western, S. (2008). *Leadership: A Critical Text*. London: Sage.

Westley, W. A. (1979). Problems and solutions in the quality of working life. *Human Relations, 32*(2): 113–123.

Winnicott, D. M. (1950). Some thoughts on the meaning of the word "democracy". *Human Relations, 3*(2): 171–185. Reprinted in: E. Trist & H. Murray (Eds.), *The Engagement of Social Science*. London: Free Association Books, 1990.

Winnicott, D. M. (1980). *Human Nature*. New York: Schocken Books.

Winnicott, D. W. (1958). The capacity to be alone. *International Journal of Psychoanalysis, 39*: 416–420.

Winnicott, D. W. (1965). *Maturational Processes and the Facilitating Environment: Studies in the Theory of Emotional Development*. London: Hogarth.

www.grouprelations.com/index.php?mode=03375a710f31006b5176527a

BIBLIOGRAPHY

Mannie Sher publications 1976–2012

Books

Brunner, L., Nutkevitch, A., & Sher, M. (Eds.) (2006). *Group Relations Conferences: Reviewing and Exploring Theory, Design, Role-Taking and Application*, Volume I. London: Karnac.

Wiener, J., & Sher, M. (1998). *Counselling and Psychotherapy in Primary Health Care*. London: Macmillan.

Book chapters

Childerstone, S., Gorli, M., Nicolini, D., & Sher, M. (2004). In search of the "structure that reflects": promoting organisational reflection practices in a UK health authority. In: R. Vince & M. Reynolds (Eds.), *Organising Reflection*. London: Ashgate.

Gill, A., & Sher, M. (2009). Annex 4: psychology and board performance. In: D. Walker (Ed.), *A Review of Corporate Governance in UK Banks and Other Financial Industry Entities*. London: HM Treasury.

Gill, A., & Sher, M. (2012). Inside the minds of the money minders: deciphering reflections on money, behaviour and leadership in the financial crisis of 2008. In: S. Long & B. Sievers (Eds.), *Beneath the Surface of the Financial Industry: Towards a Socio-Analysis of Money, Finance and Capital*. London: Taylor & Francis.

Jager, de W., & Sher, M. (2009). "Knowing the price of everything and the value of nothing". The application of group relations to an organisational development transformational change programme in a national financial institution. In: E. Aram, R. Baxter, & A. Nutkevitch (Eds.), *Adaptation and Innovation: Theory, Design, Role-Taking in Group Relations Conferences and their Applications*, Volume II. London: Karnac.

Sher, M. (1977). Short-term contracts in general medical practice. In: J. Hutten, *Short-term Contracts in Social Work*. London: Routledge & Kegan Paul.

Sher, M. (2003). From groups to group relations: Bion's contribution to the Tavistock– "Leicester" conferences. In: R. M. Lipgar & M. Pines (Eds.), *Building on Bion: Branches. Contemporary Developments and Applications of Bion's Contributions to Theory and Practice*. London: Jessica Kingsley.

Sher, M. (2003). Ethical issues for psychotherapists working in organisa-
tions. In: H. Solomon & M. Twyman (Eds.), *Ethics in Contemporary
Psychotherapy Practice*. London: Free Associations Books.
Sher, M. (2004). Leadership. In: *Encyclopaedia of Leadership*. Boston, MA:
Berkshire.
Sher, M. (2004). Systems theory and groups. In: *Encyclopaedia of Leadership*.
Boston, MA: Berkshire.

Journal articles

Aram, E., & Sher, M. (2010). Isabel Menzies Lyth: traditions and innova-
tions. *British Journal of Psychotherapy, 26*(2).
Archer, C., & Sher, M. (2012). The Leicester Conference. *Therapy Today*,
April.
Childerstone, S., Nicolini, D., & Sher, M. (2003). Can organisations learn
from experience? Intervening to improve cross-boundary management in health and social care. *Health Management*, October.
Graham, H., & Sher, M. (1976). Social work and general medical practice:
personal accounts of a three-year attachment. *British Journal of Social
Work, 6*(2). Also: *Journal of Royal College of GPs, 26*(163).
Laughlin, R., & Sher, M. (2010). Developing leadership in a social care
enterprise: managing organisational and individual boundaries and
anxiety: a systemic approach to leadership development. *Organisational and Social Dynamics, 10*(1).
Nutkevitch, A., & Sher, M. (2004). Group relations conferences: reviewing
and exploring theory, design, role-taking and application. *Organisational and Social Dynamics, 4*(1).
Rabson, J., & Sher, M. (1963). The effects of success and failure tasks on
primary and secondary functioning individuals. *Journal of Undergraduate Studies in Perception*, June.
Sher, M. (1976). Identifying the dilemmas of the social worker in a multi-
cultural environment: the psychiatric hospital. *Social Work Today, 8*(12).
Sher, M. (1983). Psychodynamic work with clients in the latter half of life.
Journal of Social Work Practice, 1(1).
Sher, M. (1992). Dynamic teamwork in general medical practice: expectations, values and effectiveness. *Proceedings of the Conference: Counselling
in Primary Care: British Association of Social Psychiatry*, November.
Sher, M. (1992). Courtin' the middle: challenges to health service
managers. *Social Work Today*, February.
Sher, M. (1996). A psycho-social exploration of the Jewish community's
sensitivity to criticism. *European Judaism, 29*(1).

Sher, M. (1997). A psychoanalytic perspective of leadership and follower-ship in Jewish institutional life. *European Judaism*, November.

Sher, M. (1997). Redundancy: what it does to people. *Journal of the British Association of Psychotherapists*, November. Also in Spanish: Despidos: Lo que producen en las personas. In: *Psiquiatrica y Salud Mental*, 25(1–2).

Sher, M. (1997). Hopes, fears and reality in a merger of two charities. *Journal of the British Association of Psychotherapists*, 32(2): Part 1.

Sher, M. (2007). Birth of an institution: early correspondence leading to the establishment of OFEK and Tavistock group relations in Israel. *KAV OFEK*, 8.

Sher, M. (2009). Splits, extrusion and integration: the impact of "potential space" for group relations and sponsoring institutions. *Organisational and Social Dynamics*, 9(1).

Sher, M. (2010). Moving psychotherapy into community settings: Alexis Brook's life's work. *Psychoanalytic Psychotherapy*, 23(4): 303.

Sher, M. (2010). Corruption: aberration or an inevitable part of the human condition? Insights from a "Tavistock" approach. *Organisational & Social Dynamics*, 10(1): 40–55.

Sher, M., & Crewe, J. (1982). The changing role of social work managers in health care settings. *Social Work Today*, 13(48).

Tonak, D., & Sher, M. (1979). Sharing clinical responsibility. *Probation Journal*, 26(4).

INDEX

Abraham, F., xxvii, 215
abuse, 41, 43–44, 76, 189, 209
  of authority, 187
Adams, W., 155, 215
aggression, xxxix, 7, 55, 102, 160, 199–200,
  206, 212 see also: behaviour
Alban, B., 134, 217
anger, xxi, xxxix, 3, 5–8, 10, 14, 18, 37, 100,
  104, 108, 180, 188, 200, 211, 213
anxiety, xii–xiv, xvii, xxi–xxii, xxvii,
  xxxiii–xxxiv, xxxviii, 3–4, 8, 12, 14–15,
  27, 31, 44, 61, 64, 67, 69, 83, 86, 91,
  95–96, 99–101, 104, 107–108, 116,
  125–126, 134–135, 137, 145–146,
  148–149, 153–154, 158–163, 165,
  172–173, 180–181, 192, 197, 207
  acute, 180
  institutional, 96
  persecutory, xxxv
  primitive, 91
  psychotic, 164
  separation, 155
  systemic, 190
  unconscious, xiii, xxxi
Aram, E., xxix, 215
Argyris, C., xxxii, 215
Armstrong, D. G., xvi, xxv, 110, 215, 222
Asaro, P. M., xliii, 216

Babiak, R., xxxv, 221
Bain, A., xxx, 224
Balint, E., xxiv, 13, 216
Balint, M., xxiv, 216
Bamforth, K., xv, 230
Barker, M., xiv, 64, 182
Barkham, M., xxiii, 222
Baxter, R., xxix, 215
behaviour(al), xii, xvii, xxx, xxxiii–xxxviii,
  xliii, xlv–xlvi, 16, 101, 105, 112–118,
  137, 164, 169, 171–172, 183–189, 196,
  199, 201, 204, 206, 209, 211, 213
  active, 35
  aggressive, 160
  assumption, 165
  bad, 199, 201, 212
  change, xxxiv

corrupt, 175
criminal, xxxvi
critical, 139
dynamic, xxxiv, xxxvii, 205
fraudulent, xxxviii, 212
good, 185, 201, 212
group, 63, 92–93, 112, 116, 118, 175
herd-type, 171
human, xiii, xxxv, xliv, 11, 196
influences, xxxviii
leadership, 186, 199
limitations, 187
maturity, 184
neurotic, 112
of employees, xli
paranoid–schizoid, 172
problems, 30
professional, 22
rational, 173
repertoire, 185
selfish, 209
sense, 154
social, xv, 169
systemic, 184
Bexton, W. H., xxvii, 130, 218
Bion, W. R., xvi, xxix–xxx, 63–64, 92–94,
  96, 99, 101–102, 104, 107, 109–115,
  117, 145, 170, 173, 184, 216
Birtles, E. F., xviii, 229
Blackler, F., 126, 144, 216
Blount, A., xxi, 216
Bohm, D., xxxv, 216
Bollas, C., xxxvi, 52, 197, 216–217
Bond, T., 23, 217
Bonwitt, G., xxvi, 225
Boreham, J., xx, 231
Boshyk, Y., 129, 217
Bridger, H., xxv–xxvi, 64, 217
British Association of Counselling (BAC),
  23, 36
British Association of Psychotherapists
  (BAP), xviii, xxiv
British Medical Association (BMA), 22, 24,
  216
British Psychological Society, The, 52, 230
Brock, J. W., 155, 215

Brook, A., xxi, 4–5, 217
Brunner, L. D., xxvi, xxix, 217
Bruzelius, N., xliii, 219
Bundervoet, J., xl, 222
Bunker, B., 134, 217
Burns, J., 188, 217
Burton, M., xxi, 18, 225

Cacioppe, R., xv, 217
Carr, A. W., xx, 229
Carr, L., 23, 230
Carr, W., 192, 217
Carter, G. M., xvi, 217
Casement, P., xxii, 217
Catholic University of Leuven, xl
Child, C., xxvii, 217, 221
Clarke, D., xxvi, 221
Clarke, S., xl, xliv, 217
Clements, D., xxii, 218
clinical material
    Chapter Two
        coping with anger, 37
        dynamics of practice meetings, 30–32
        Miss D, 9
        Miss K, 6–7
        Mrs N, 7–8
Cohan, W., xxxv, 218
Coleman, A. D., xxvii, 130, 218
conscious(ness), xxxv–xxxvi, xxxviii, 72,
        82, 10, 115, 118, 175, 177, 206 see also:
        unconscious(ness)
    dynamics, xxx, 174
    elements, 85
    expression, 197
    industrialised, xli
    manifestation, 175
    pre-, 197
    process, 76
    relationships, 196
    wishes, 117
Cooper, C., xxxii, 218
corruption, xxxv–xxxvi, 87, 169–182
countertransference, xiv, xix, xxx–xxxi,
        62–63, 196, 210 see also: transference
    of denial, 205
    phenomena, 63
    sadistic, 43–44
Cummings, T., xxxi, 127, 218
Cunliffe, A., 130, 137, 218
Cytrynbaum, S., xxvii, 65, 71, 218

Dartington, T., xxvi, 68
Daudelin, M., 123, 229

Dault, M., xxii, 218
De Jager, W., xxvi, 218
delusion, 164, 171, 177 see also: self
    heroic, 117
    psychotic, 178
    semi-, 173
depression, xxxiv, 4, 6–9, 12, 55, 99–100,
        110, 115, 164, 181
    acute, 55
    aspects, 7
    position, 93, 172, 177–178, 180–181
    social, xxxiv, 164
Dickson, W., xli, 228
Dopson, D., 126, 218
Dunbar, R., 190, 218

Edwards, M., xv, 217
Eijnatten, F. M. van, xl, 218
Ekehammar, B., xxxii, 219
Elias, N., xli, 219
Emery, F. E., xv, xl, 219
Emery, M., xix, 219
Engeström, Y., 145, 219

Fairbairn, W. R. D., xviii, 219
fantasy, xiv, 28, 74, 76–77, 97, 106, 128,
        148–149, 151, 163, 165, 176, 178, 181,
        196, 202 see also: Oedipal,
        unconscious
    omnipotent, xxxiii, 153
    sadistic, 52
    unrealistic, 211
Felie, E., 128, 227
Financial Reporting Council, xxxvii, 219
Fitzgerald, P., xxiii, 222
Flyvbjerg, B., xliii, 219
Follett, M. P., 63
free association, xxiv, xxxviii, 45–46, 196
French, R., 149, 219
Freud, S., 63, 92–93, 109, 170, 172, 184, 219

Geller, M. H., xxvii, 130, 218
Gemmill, G., 184, 219
General Medical Council (GMC), 22–23,
        220
Gettler, L., 174, 219
Gherardi, S., 137, 144, 220, 227
Gill, A., 186, 220
Ginat, Y., 67, 220
Ginzberg, E., 155–156, 220
Goethals, G., 188, 229
Goldberg, E. M., 18, 220

Goldsmith, M., xxxv, 203, 220
Gosling, J., xl, 220
Gosling, R., xiv, xvii–xviii, xxiv–xxv, xxix, 64, 94, 216, 220
Gould, L., xxv–xxvi, xxx, 66, 220–221, 224
Greenspan, A., xxxv, 206, 221
Grotstein, J., xviii, 170, 221
guilt, xiii, xxvi, xxxviii–xxxix, 7–8, 16–17, 79, 84, 114–115, 138, 163, 171–173, 180–181, 197, 202, 208, 213–214

Hale, R., 55, 221
Hall, E. T., 191, 221
Halton, W., xvi, 222
Hare, P., xxxv, 221
Harré, R., 175, 221
Harrison, T., xxvi, 221
Heins, J., 156, 221
Helle, M., 145, 219
Henderickx, J., xl, 222
Higgin, G., xv, xxv–xxvi, 217, 231
Hildebrand, P., xxiv, 216
Hill, J. M. M., xxx, 221
Hills, D., xxvii, 221
Hinshelwood, R. D., xvi, 221
Hippocrates, 24
Hoggett, P., xl, xliv, 174, 217, 221
Holti, R. W., xxxi, 221, 227
Hornby, S., xviii, 222
Hoyle, L., xvi, 222
Hudson, L. J., 212, 222
Huffington, C., xvi, 222
Hupkens, L., xxvi, 222
Huse, E., xxxi, 218
Huys, R., xl, 222

instinct, xiii, 184
  death, 116
  gut, xlvi
  life, xxxvii
  primitive, xiii
Institute of Psychoanalysis, xvii
International Code of Medical Ethics, 24
International Society for the Psychoanalytic Study of Organisations (ISPSO), xv, 69
intervention, xx, xxii, xlii–xliii, 6, 15, 31, 41, 55, 94, 107, 116, 128–130, 133–134, 139–140, 147, 179, 210
Israel Association for Group and Organisational Processes (OFEK), xv, xxviii, 62, 68, 79–80, 87–88

Jackson, D. C., xli
Janis, I. L., xxxiv, xliv, 191, 222
Jaques, E., xxvii, xxxix–xl, 191–192, 222
Jenkins, G. C., xxiii–xxiv, 222
Jensen, M., xxxvi, 222
Joffe, W., xvii, 223
Johnson, R. A., xxi, 223
Joyce, D., xxiv, 216

Kathol, R., xxi, 216
Kelley, H. H., xviii, 223
Kennedy, A., 126, 144, 216
Kernberg, O. F., 177, 223
Khaleelee, O., xxxii, 223
Kissinger, H., 178, 223
Klauber, T., xxxvi, 223
Klein, M., xiii, xviii–xxx, 63, 93, 163, 170, 177–178, 192, 223
Klein, S., xvii, 223
Konstenius, M. L., xxxii, 219
Kragh, U., xxxii, 223
Krug, J., xxxiii, 223

Lacan, J., 175, 223
Lahav, Y., xxvi, 223
Lanchester, J., xxxv, 206, 223
Lasky, G. B., xxiv, 224
Law, J., 149, 224
Lawrence, W. G., xiv, xxv, xxx, xxxvi, xlii–xliii, 62, 64, 92, 97, 115, 173, 184, 224
le Bon, G., 63
Levine, D., 175, 224
Lewin, K., xii, xvi, 63, 129, 224–225
life, xxii, xxix, xli, 7, 15, 31, 76, 111, 145, 197–198
  adult, xviii
  -blood, 199
  changes, 67
  communal, xv
  crippled, 10
  -cycle, 155
  early, xiv, 44
  emotional, 93
  -giving, 84
  group, 93, 187
  healthy, 21
  instinct, xxxvii
  later, 170
  mental, 118
  organisational, 109, 174, 197
  psychic, xiii

real, xxxiii, 129, 150
social, xli
stage, 4
style, xxiii, 25
support system, 178
threatening, 31
working, 137
Litton, R., 46, 229
Litvin, I., xxvi, 225
London School of Economics (LSE), xvii
Long, S., xxxv, 174–176, 191, 205, 225

Mackay, C., xxxv, 225
Main, T., xxiv, 225
Malby, B., 126, 227
Manning, S., 126, 227
Marinker, M., xxiv, 216
Maris, P., xxxvi, 225
Marsick, V. J., 129–130, 225
Martin, L., 144, 231
Master of the Rolls, The, 52, 230
Mayo, E., xli, 63, 225
McDougall, W., 63
McKee, L., 128, 227
McLaughlin, H., 132, 225
Mellor-Clark, J., xxi, xxiii, 18, 222, 225
Mental Health Act, 46, 55
Menzies Lyth, I. E. P., xiv, xxvii, 64, 125,
    160, 174, 225
Miettinen, R., 145, 219
Milgram, S., xxxv, 225
Miller, D. M., xviii, 220
Miller, E. J., xiv, xviii–xix, xxv, xxix–xxxi,
    xxxvi, 64, 66, 86, 94, 162, 173, 184,
    187, 196, 224, 226–227
Miller, P., xlii, 226
Minne, C., 55, 221
Moldoveanu, M., xv, 228
Moon, J., 123, 226
Morgan, G., 132, 144, 226
mother, xviii, xxii, 6–8, 17, 30, 84, 98,
    175–178, 201
Moylan, D., 164, 226
Mumford, E., xxxii, 226
Murray, B. K., xvii, 227
Murray, H., xv, 230–231

narcissism, xxxv, xxxix, 114, 174–175, 178,
    207
characteristics, 175
culture, 109
destructive, xxxvi

healthy, 177
issues, 87
primary, 177–178
Neill, J. E., 18, 220
Neumann, J. E., xxxi, 126, 218, 227
Nicolini, D., 137, 144, 220, 227
Norell, J., 13, 216
Noumair, D. A., xxvii, 218
Nutkevitch, A., xxvi, xxviii, xxix, 68, 79,
    88, 215, 217, 227

Oakley, J., 184, 219
Obholzer, A., 187, 227
Obholzer, O., xxiii, 173, 227
object, xxvi, xxxv, xli, 86, 175 see also:
    phantasy
    combined, 164
    feeding, 176
    internal, 169–170, 181
    of reflection, 138
    part, 77
    relations, 63, 77
    satisfying, 176–177
objective/objectivity, xv, xl, 39, 70, 133,
    136, 139, 157, 162, 170, 186
    behavioural, 185
    practical, 154
    professional, 33
O'Donohue, W., xxi, 216
Oedipal
    conflict, xxx, 177
    dynamics, 97
    fantasies, 96
    situation, 92, 96
Oedipus, 97
O'Neill, J., 129–130, 139, 225, 227
O'Shaughnessy, E., 170, 227
Owen, H., 134, 227

Palmer, S., 46, 229
paranoid, 107 see also: behaviour
    feelings, 135
    mechanisms, 180
    –schizoid position, 93, 172, 180–181
    state, 180–181
parent(s), xviii, 6–8, 30, 55, 87, 116, 170,
    181
    -hood, 4
    primitive, 35
Pattison, S., 126, 227
Pedler, M., 132, 144, 148, 227
Peek, C., xxi, 216

Perini, M., xxvi, 217
Pettigrew, A., 128, 227
phantasy, xxxv, 62 *see also*: unconscious
    group, 62
    infantile, 176–177
    objects, 172
    seductive, 172
    world, 172
Pickering, A., xli, 227
Pihlaja, J., 145, 219
Poikela, R., 145, 219
Pollock, A., xv, 231
Pooley, J., xvi, 222
Priest, A., xxii, 218
Pritchard, H., xxii, 228
Pritchard, P. M., xxii, 228
projection, xix, xxii, xxvi, xxx, xxxix, 62,
    95, 116, 149, 157, 159, 161, 172, 176,
    191–192, 202, 205, 212–213
    hostile, xiv
    psychic, xiii
projective
    identification, xix, xxx, 63, 93, 116
    mechanisms, 72, 125
    processes, 96
Punamaki, R., 145, 219

Raelin, J., 123–124, 228
Rain, L., xxiii, 222
Ramirez, R., 132, 144, 226
Ratoff, L., 11, 18, 228
repression, xvii, 171–172, 181, 196
Revans, R., 129, 228
Reynolds, M., xxxii, 123–124, 143–144,
    228
Rice, A. K., xxv, xxix–xxx, 64, 92, 110–111,
    162, 187, 226, 228
    Institute, xv, 62
Rinsley, R. B., xviii, 221
Riva, M. T., xxiv, 224
Roberts, V., xxiii, 173, 227
Rodman, F. R., xvii, 228
Roethlisberger, F. M., xli, 228
Rollman, B., xxi, 216
Rose, A., 11, 18, 228
Rose, N., xlii, 226, 228
Rosenfeld, H., xxxvi, 228
Rothengatter, W., xliii, 219
Rowley, T. J., xv, 228
Royal College of Psychiatrists, Council
    Report CR85, 46, 228
Rustin, M., xxxi, xxxv, 228–229

Sanders, P., 186, 220
Scharff, D., xviii, 229
Schoenbaum, M., xxi, 216
Schulz, K., xxxvi, 229
Scoggins, M., 46, 229
self, xxxv, 92, 110
    -actualisation, 92
    -aggrandisement, 202
    -assured, 209
    -authorising, xxvii, xxix, 88
    -confidence, 159, 185
    -contained, 72
    -criticism, 107
    -deception, xxxvi, 112, 175
    -delusion, xxxvi, 202
    -destructive, 55
    -determination, 23–24
    -diagnosis, 210
    -discovery, 92
    -doubt, 16
    -empowerment, 141
    -esteem, xxii
    -evident, 41, 112
    -examination, 92
    -fulfilling, 192
    -image, 214
    -inflicted, 110
    -interest, xxxvi, 157, 172, 188, 210
    -justifying, xxxix, 213
    -knowledge, 23
    -managing, 73
    -organised, 134
    -perpetuating, 128
    -pitying, 145
    -preservation, xxxvi, 116
    -regulation, 203, 213
    -respect, 111
    -serving, 181
    -sustaining, 124, 199
    -worth, 161
Sels, L., xl, 222
sexual, 41
    a-, 105
    characteristics, 6–7
    exploitation, xxiv
    mores, 114
    relationship, 7
sexuality, 103, 105
    feminine, 105
Shapiro, E., xx, 229
Shear, M., xvii, 229
Sher, M., xxi, xxvi, xxix, xlv, 79, 89, 97,
    217–218, 229

Shiller, R., xxxv, 206, 229
Siebert, K., 123, 229
Simms-Ellis, R., xxi, 18, 225
Singleton, V., 149, 224
Skogstad, W., xvi, 221
Slovenko, R., xxiv, 229
Smith, C., 11, 18, 228
Smith, P. A., 123, 229
Sofer, C., xli, 229
Solvik, P., 65–66, 229
Sorenson, G., 188, 229
splitting, xxiii, xxx, xxxiv, xl, xliv, 18, 34–35, 53, 63, 71–72, 77, 96–97, 110, 118, 163–165, 191–192, 205
Stapley, L., xxv–xxvi, 66, 220–221
Stein, M., xxv–xxvi, 66, 220–221
Steiner, J., xxxvi–xxxvii, 174, 229
Stern, E., xxxi, 230
Sundelson, D., 52, 217
Supreme Court of the United States, 52, 230
Sutherland, J., xvii, 230

Taffler, R., xliv, 171–172, 206, 231
Tarnas, R., xxvii, 196, 230
Tavistock Institute, xi–xii, xv–xvi, xix, xxvi, xxviii–xxix, xxxi–xxxii, xxxvii, xlv, 61, 63–69, 77, 79–80, 86–87, 89, 91–93, 98, 100–101, 107–108, 110, 127, 129
Temperley, J., xxi, 4–5, 217
Tett, G., xxxvii, 230
Thibaut, J. W., xviii, 223
Thomas, K. J., 23, 230
Thomas, M., xxi, 216
Thorpe, R., 132, 225
transference, xiv, xvii, xix, xxiii, xxx, 52, 62–63, 106, 196 see also: countertransference
    dynamic, 196
    feelings, 77, 107
    group, 109
    negative, 102–103
    parental, 35
    process, 140
    relationship, xxv
    split, 35
Triest, J., xxvi, 227
Trist, E. L., xv, xxxi, xl, 219, 230–231
Tuckett, D., xliv, 171–172, 206, 231
Turquet, P. M., xiv, xviii, xx, xxv, 64, 190, 220, 231

unconscious(ness), xxxii, xxxviii, 14, 16, 73, 82, 86, 95, 97, 102, 115, 118, 171, 177, 190, 196, 212 see also: anxiety, conscious(ness)
    collusion, 209, 213
    degeneration, xxxv
    dynamics, xiv, xxiii, xxx, xxxvii, 63, 85, 115, 164, 174–175, 206
    elements, 85
    envy, 192
    factors, 156
    fantasy, xx–xxi, xxxi, 209
    feelings, xiv
    group, xxx, xlv, 108, 116
    impulses, 172
    internal disintegration, xxxvi
    phantasies, 117, 172
    players, 204
    primary task, xxxvi
    process, xii–xv, xviii, xxvii, 67, 76, 115
    relationships, 196
    representations, 115
    social structure, 175
    wishes, 97

Van Hootegem, G., xl, 222
Vera, E., xxvi, 217
Vince, R., 124, 144–145, 149, 219, 231
Virkkunen, J., 145, 219
Viswanath, R., xxvi, 231
Von Bertalanffy, L., xvi, 231
Votja, G., 155–156, 220

Walker, D., xxxiv, xxxvii, xxxix, 232
    Review, xxxiv, xlv–xlvi
Wall, A., 126, 232
Wasdell, D., xxvi, 232
Weisbord, R. G., xvii, 232
Western, S., 184, 232
Westlake, B., 23, 230
Westley, W. A., xv, 232
Williams, A., 23, 230
Winnicott, D. M., xiv, xvii, xxxv, 145, 148, 177, 232
Wolrey, C., 127, 218
Woodcock, J., xxiv, 216
Woodhouse, D., xviii, 220
Woolf, R., xxxii
World Medical Association, 55
www.grouprelations.com, xxvii, 232

Yanow, D., 144, 227

Zachary, A., 55, 221
Zuber, I., xxxii, 219